Disrupting Data in Qualitative Inquiry

POST-
anthropocentric
INQUIRY

Gaile S. Cannella
General Editor

Vol. 1

The Post-Anthropocentric Inquiry series is part of the Peter Lang Education list.
Every title is peer reviewed and meets
the highest quality standards for content and production.

PETER LANG
New York • Bern • Frankfurt • Berlin
Brussels • Vienna • Oxford • Warsaw

Disrupting Data in Qualitative Inquiry

Entanglements with the Post-Critical and Post-Anthropocentric

Edited by Mirka Koro-Ljungberg,
Teija Löytönen, and Marek Tesar

PETER LANG
New York • Bern • Frankfurt • Berlin
Brussels • Vienna • Oxford • Warsaw

Library of Congress Cataloging-in-Publication Data

Names: Koro-Ljungberg, Mirka, editor. | Löytönen, Teija, editor. | Tesar, Marek, editor.
Title: Disrupting data in qualitative inquiry: entanglements with the post-critical and
post-anthropocentric / edited by Mirka Koro-Ljungberg, Teija Löytönen and Marek Tesar.
Description: New York: Peter Lang, 2017.
Series: Post-anthropocentric inquiry; vol. 1
ISSN 2381-5914 (print) | ISSN 2381-5922 (online)
Includes bibliographical references.
Identifiers: LCCN 2017006394 | ISBN 978-1-4331-3338-1 (hardcover: alk. paper)
ISBN 978-1-4331-3337-4 (paperback: alk. paper) | ISBN 978-1-4331-4234-5 (ebook pdf)
ISBN 978-1-4331-4234-5 (epub) | ISBN 978-1-4331-4236-9 (mobi)
Subjects: LCSH: Qualitative research. | Social sciences—Research—Methodology.
Classification: LCC H62 .D57 2017 | DDC 001.4/2—dc23
LC record available at https://lccn.loc.gov/2017006394
DOI 10.3726/b11070

Bibliographic information published by **Die Deutsche Nationalbibliothek.**
Die Deutsche Nationalbibliothek lists this publication in the "Deutsche
Nationalbibliografie"; detailed bibliographic data are available
on the Internet at http://dnb.d-nb.de/.

The paper in this book meets the guidelines for permanence and durability
of the Committee on Production Guidelines for Book Longevity
of the Council of Library Resources.

This book is inspired by all qualitative researchers, friends and colleagues, whose work challenges and disrupts the machinery of mass production and technologies of exploitation of data in both research and practice.

Table OF Contents

Illustrations

Contributors

Annette Arlander, DA, is an artist, researcher and a pedagogue, one of the pioneers of Finnish performance art and a trailblazer of artistic research. She was professor of performance art and theory 2001–2013 at Theatre Academy Helsinki and is at present visiting researcher at University of the Arts Helsinki. For research interests, artworks and publications see https://annettearlander.com.

Sonja Arndt is a lecturer in early childhood education and global studies in education at the University of Waikato. Her research deals with formations and conceptualizations of the self and the Other in the human and more-than-human realm, and uses philosophy as a method and as its conceptual-analytical framework.

Bidisha Banerjee is Assistant Professor in the Department of Literature and Cultural Studies and Director of the Centre for Popular Culture in the Humanities at The Education University of Hong Kong. Her research interests include South Asian diasporic fiction and film, visual culture and urban studies, particularly the Hong Kong cityscape. Her current book project attempts to study the narrated image in South Asian diasporic literature which functions as a photographic metaphor to enhance the themes of the literary text.

Angelo Benozzo is senior lecturer in Work and Organizational Psychology and Qualitative Research Methods and researcher at the University of Valle d'Aosta, Italy. His current research interests include professional identity and sexual identity in the workplace and beyond.

Mindy Blaise is a Professor of Early Childhood Education at Victoria University, Melbourne, Australia. She is a founding member and principal researcher of the Common Worlds Research Collective (commonworlds.net). Her feminist and postfoundational research sets out to interfere with the dominant developmental discourse that pervades early childhood education. She is currently conducting a multispecies, multisensory, and affect-focused ethnography of children's relations with the more-than-human.

Sarah Bridges-Rhoads is an assistant professor of literacy in the Department of Early Childhood and Elementary Education at Georgia State University. Her research experiments with critical, poststructural, and posthuman theories as well as writing, ethics, and responsibility in qualitative research and teacher preparation.

Elizabeth DeFreitas's research focuses on philosophical investigations of mathematics, science and technology, pursuing the implications and applications of this work across the social sciences and humanities. She has published over 50 chapters and articles on a range of topics. Her recent work examines the material practices and bio-political dimensions of STEM activity, both recreational and expert. She also writes extensively on social science research methodology, exploring alternative ways of engaging with digital and quantitative data, and developing experimental and speculative research methods.

Norman K. Denzin is Professor of Communications, University of Illinois, Urbana-Champaign. His most recent book is *Indians in Color: Native Art, Identity, and Performance in the New West* (Left Coast, 2015).

Iris Duhn is a Senior Lecturer in early childhood education at Monash University in Australia. She has a longstanding interest in education for sustainability and the politics of childhood. Her academic background draws on feminist theories, governmentality studies and the sociology of childhood to explore how to share planetary liveliness in all its forms with respect and care. Her current research interests focus on contingent multispecies and vibrant matter alliances of all sorts.

Mirka Koro-Ljungberg is a Professor of qualitative research at the Arizona State University. Her scholarship operates in the intersection of methodology, philosophy, and socio-cultural critique and her work aims to contribute to methodological knowledge, experimentation, and theoretical development across various traditions associated with qualitative research. She has peer reviewed publications in various qualitative and educational journals and she is the author of *Reconceptualizing qualitative research: Methodologies without methodology* (2016) published by SAGE.

Teija Löytönen (Doctor of Arts, Theatre Academy Helsinki; Ed. M., University of Helsinki) currently works as a Senior Specialist for Art and Creative Practices at Aalto University, Finland. Prior to her current position she was a full-time scholar for over ten years funded by the Academy of Finland. Her particular research interests include higher arts education, arts and creativity in academia as well as (disciplinary) differentiation in professional and academic development. Her special interest is in collaborative research endeavors and in "new" modes of (post) qualitative research. She has published in several national and international refereed journals and edited volumes as well as presented her research in various international networks. The editorial work was supported by the Academy of Finland (project number 253589).

Maggie MacLure is Professor of Education in the Education and Social Research Institute at Manchester Metropolitan University. Her research interests include the development of theory and methodology in qualitative research; discourse analysis; early childhood education; classroom ethnography and child language development. She is the founder and director of the Summer Institute in Qualitative Research. http://www.esri.mmu.ac.uk/resstaff/profile.php?name=Maggie&surname=MacLure

Karen Malone is Professor of Sustainability, Director, Centre for Educational Research, HDR Director and Leader sustainability research group at Western Sydney University. She researches on children/human geographies, child-animals relations, environmental education, sustainability learning, human, nature and animals rights, and theorising using posthumanism and new materialism in the Anthropocene. She has attracted over 1.6 million dollars in grants and published 6 books, 28 book chapters and 48 refereed journal articles. Recent books include a sole-authored publication *Children in the Anthropocene* and a co-edited book *Reimaging Sustainability in Precarious Times*. She is Editor-in-Chief of the new *International Research Handbook on ChildhoodNature*.

Dr. Casey Y. Myers is an Assistant Professor of Early Childhood Education and the Coordinator of Studio and Research Arts at the Child Development Center, an early years laboratory school at Kent State University. Her research and teaching interests revolve around the everyday materialities of young children's school lives.

Susan Naomi Nordstrom is an Assistant Professor of Educational Research specializing in qualitative research methodology at The University of Memphis. She received her PhD from The University of Georgia. Her research agenda includes poststructural and post-humanist theories about human and nonhuman relations, ontology, and qualitative research methodology.

Ann Merete Otterstad is a Docent/Professor in early childhood pedagogy and cultural diversity at the Institute of Early Childhood Education, Oslo and Akershus University College of Applied Sciences, Norway. E-mail: Ann.Otterstad@hioa.no. She works with discursive and new-material theories. Affective and diffractive methodologies, focusing on politics of methods entwined with 'becoming another researcher' as well as unpacking constructions of lifelong learning, quality, and equity in official policy documents.

Pauliina Rautio is an Adjunct Professor and a research fellow at the Faculty of Education, University of Oulu, Finland. She uses posthumanist theoretical and methodological approaches in studying education and childhoods beyond humanism and notions of development. Of special interest to her are child–animal relations. And especially close to her heart you'll find human–bird cohabituation.

Anne Beate Reinertsen is Professor in Education at Queen Maud University College Early Childhood Education, Trondheim, Norway. E-mail: Anne.B.Reinertsen@dmmh.no. She works with discursive and new-material theories. Affective and diffractive methodologies focusing on nature/culture entanglement and sustainability, immanent assessment practices, body as profession, poeticalizing, transpersonal leadership and educational justice.

Leena Rouhiainen is a dancer and somatic practitioner who has worked with phenomenologically oriented dance research and artistic researcher for nearly two decades. She currently works as Professor in Artistic Research at the Theatre Academy of the University of the Arts Helsinki and she can be reached at leena.rouhiainen@uniarts.fi.

Margaret Somerville is Professor of Education, Western Sydney University. Drawing on a long history of collaborative research with Australian Aboriginal communities about their relationship to place, she is interested in developing creative and alternative approaches to research towards planetary wellbeing. Her most recent research explores posthuman and new materialist frameworks that honor our ethical responsibility to develop philosophical positions and languages that name new modes of thought and action for the time of the Anthropocene.

Marek Tesar is a Senior Lecturer in childhood studies and early childhood education at the Faculty of Education at the University of Auckland. His focus is on the philosophy, sociology, and history of childhood and his research is concerned with the construction of childhoods and notions of the place/space of childhoods, and theorizing qualitative inquiry. Marek's work has received numerous national and international awards and he has published and disseminated his work in many books and journals.

Jasmine B. Ulmer (Ph.D., University of Florida) is an Assistant Professor of Education Evaluation and Research at Wayne State University. In addition to critical qualitative inquiry, her research interests include visual, spatial, and writing methodologies. Her work has appeared in journals such as *Qualitative Inquiry, Cultural Studies <=> Critical Methodologies*, and *Educational Philosophy and Theory*.

Jessica Van Cleave is an associate professor of education specializing in qualitative research and secondary English teacher preparation in the Department of Education at Mars Hill University. Her research explores the intersection of poststructural theory, qualitative methodology, and educational policy.

Anna Vladimirova is a PhD Researcher in Education at the University of Oulu, Finland. Her main interests are in the outdoor education (particularly forest pedagogy), posthumanism and photomicrography. She is currently writing a systematic review of the human-nonhuman entanglement conceptualisations in the scientific literature.

Foreword

MAGGIE MACLURE

The field of qualitative inquiry has undergone seismic upheavals in recent years. Theories such as poststructuralism, posthumanism and the 'new materialisms' have unsettled the foundations of conventional qualitative methodology, challenging its assumption of the centrality of human subjects and their entitlement to interrogate the world and mine it for meaning. It is becoming customary to rethink the status of agency, consciousness and causality, and to envisage distributed forms of relationality and responsibility among human and nonhuman entities. Strangely, though, the status of 'data' in this reconfigured field of qualitative inquiry has received much less attention. Interviews and fieldnotes are still the staple forms, and the relation of researchers to 'their' data is still largely taken for granted.

This collection opens up an expanded view of qualitative data, one that engages its materiality and its sensory qualities—data as snow, water, landscape, affect—without denying that data also have linguistic, symbolic, imaginary and narrative force. It invites interrogation of the very possibility of data, at least where this is conceived of as separate and subservient to human rationality. It unfolds hidden complexities within conventional methods of data 'collection' such as video recording or image capture, and proposes a whole range of alternative and embodied ways of encountering data.

This book does not aspire to provide a consensual view, or even an overview, of contemporary issues around data in qualitative inquiry; nor does it offer a menu of methods for engaging with data. Each of the contributions has its distinct 'take' on the question of data. Taken as a whole, however, the collection reflects a commitment to experimentation and speculative thought that is characteristic of research within the material or posthuman 'turn'. It is dedicated to the art of asking better questions rather than providing definitive answers, and as a result, it takes data well beyond the circumscribed role that it has typically occupied in methods textbooks. It is interesting to note, for instance, how the problematizing of data seems to lead, in many chapters, towards experimental writing and art practice, as ways of attending to that which lies beyond the limits of language and rationality. It could be said that the collection mobilises data as a resource for thought about some of the key ontological issues that are running though qualitative inquiry. In so doing, it introduces readers to many of the philosophers and writers whose work is shaping the direction of qualitative methodology—Barad, Deleuze, Bergson, Spinoza, Bennett.

This is a provocative book. Its proliferating questions about data are liable to work or worm their way through the architecture of conventional qualitative inquiry, eating holes in its foundational concepts and practices. This is simultaneously exhilarating and disconcerting. But in a good way.

Manchester Metropolitan University
August 2016

Introduction

Multiplicities of Data Encounters

MIRKA KORO-LJUNGBERG, TEIJA LÖYTÖNEN,
AND MAREK TESAR

play on linguistic structure + written information, data.

This book is a part of a larger global conceptual and ontological movement within qualitative inquiries and traditions to move away from persisting post-positivist epistemological ruins, and humanistic, human centred, and neo-positivist practices of research and scholarship. In this book the authors give their theoretical and practically oriented attention to 'data'. More specifically, we (the editors) hope that the book will expand qualitative researchers' notions of data and that it will exemplify scholars' diverse encounters and interactions with data. Rather than collecting or even producing data, we focus on data encounters and diverse ways in which scholars and data (in their multiple forms) can come together, interact, intra-act, and. Different ways to encounter data are endless and as such are likely to reflect a variety of ontological and epistemological stances.

Data are both possible and impossible in some ways. For example, data are possible since scholars need them, funders hail them, journals ask for their sources, and IRBs call for data procedures. Data have a place in research systems, discourses, and practices. Data in some ways materialize research, and they generate inter and intra-actions. Data produce. Data also make many of our scholarly practices possible. At the same time these possibilities of data are impossible; impossible to be known ahead of time, predictable, repeatable, neutral, or always readily identifiable. Data could be seen especially impossible in post-qualitative and post-human frameworks, which question the very fundamental concepts often associated with data such as a knowing individual, stable knowledge, documentation, and representation. Yet the impossibilities of data could keep scholars in motion, critical, and careful. Alternatively, the impossibilities might slow scholars down in productive ways or close down and terminate inquiry. Sometimes data take time, seem distant and inaccessible, and they might not function as expected, thus again appearing to be impossible.

At the same time, because of their putative simplicity, primitiveness, or intuitiveness, data have also been considered to possess a kind of innocence or authenticity, as-yet-uncontaminated by the interventions and the interest of human acts of selection, interpretation and analysis. Data are not ethically neutral, but can function as advocating, supporting or dirty, powerful and dangerous entities or practices. Data have been assigned and dedicated to serve policy, indigenous communities, participants, children, adults, learners, and teachers. Data are, moreover, associated with a range of discourses and master narratives, many of which we highlight in this book. For instance, the term data has been argued to carry an odour of scientificity, lending a spurious scientific rigor to the critical and cultural projects of qualitative research, alongside such concepts as validity and triangulation. Data have also been recruited into neoliberal discourses of accountability, as input to the assurances of 'evidence-based' policy and practice. And importantly, data have served researchers, turning research into a legitimized business, a rigorous enterprise, and a fundable set of propositions. Data have become part of the economics of everyday life. This book critically reviews the production and 'machinations of data' within various canons of qualitative research.

To work against existing machinations of data, we desire to make data a *(methodological) project* (data broadly conceptualized and practiced) to encourage readers to pay close attention to data and their numerous variations and manifestations. We encourage readers to think data beyond anthropocentrism toward different human and nonhuman forces creating, generating, and reproducing knowing, affect, and sensory experiences. Data produce and can be produced in relational fields composed of forces underlying a number of different experiential and materials connections (see also Coole & Frost, 2010; Hultman & Lenz Taguchi, 2010) rather than privileging human (data) superiority over animals, plants, and other forms of organic life. Ecological data, more-than-human data, eco-data, and multispecies symbiotic assemblages (see Ivanova, 2016) highlight some potentialities and encounters discussed in this edited book and elsewhere, as potentialities to disturb human (data) dominance and human species' (data) colonization of other species. Furthermore, the expansion of bio, eco and technological spheres create continuously shifting challenges to think data differently. Additionally, it is important to place data in relation to ecosystems and within the context of biopolitics and global political economies that extend beyond anthropocentrism and the isolation of human species (data). What kinds of data-forms or life-forms shape inquiry and qualitative research? What are the ethical consequences of our decisions related to ecological sustainability?

Throughout the text, the authors promote actions and activities that view data as something to be continuously changing, interrogated, and critically examined.

In addition, the authors create materials, texts, insights, and exampl age and remake 'old/known/familiar/visible data' (e.g., interviews artefacts, images), live 'new/unknown/emerging/invisible data' (e.g. breath, remains, spectral data), or illustrate completely unexpected interactions with unimaginable and unthinkable 'data' (e.g., data holes, anarchives, data mattering, befriended data). In other words, data and descriptions of data encounters are rethought as a conceptual, theoretical, philosophical, ethical, material, performative, practical, ontological, and spatial projects and.

Multiplicity of data provides both challenges and novel insights. It is possible that this book does not provide answers to the 'data question' that many scholars may have come to expect. In this volume data might not necessarily be 'readily available' but data's diverse functions must first be invented (see Deleuze & Guattari, 1994). Ideas proposed in this book might not be immediately transformable or uncritically usable but they may serve as provocateurs, seeds, and fluid formations of ideas to be played with. In some ways this book simulates a fluid methodological space (see Koro-Ljungberg, 2016; Koro-Ljungberg, Carlson, Tesar, & Anderson, 2015; Mol, 2002) where data, theories, methods and research approaches melt, transform, circumvent, infiltrate, appear, and disappear. There is no "need for police action to safeguard the stability of [data] elements and their linkages—for there is no network structure to be protected" (Mol & Law, 1994, p. 662). Change, divergence, and difference might stimulate data and methodological practices that are inseparable, coincidental but also disjunct (see also Massumi, 2002). Data may be actualized through movement from one set of data to another, through foldings, redoubling and reductions, data pasts projecting ahead to the data future. Fluid, dissolving, and multiple data could be a reprocess—actualized by being differentiated and differentiating themselves.

Data's methodological (im)possibilities and their role in post-qualitative and artistic inquiry is also an onto-epistemological question; a question of truths, knowledges, presences, absences, technologies, appearances, and power. As such it is important to consider what data might do to us, to other data: without colonizing or taming the other and unfamiliar in data. In addition, we question the very ontology of data, and wonder if data are tainted by a persistent humanism lodged deep inside qualitative research, even of a post-structural or post-humanist orientation, perpetually reinstating the autonomous human subject behind its own back, and relegating data once more to a subordinate role. Data as a creation of humanist 'man' or privileged human species calls for questioning and troubling. Dialectics of data/non-data, alive or dead data, truth or false data, valid or invalid data seem insufficient. Instead, the monistic life of data enables various possibilities beyond anthropocentrism and it supports more complex relationships between data, human, and non-human others including animals, plants, and various forms of technology. Or is there still some unforeseen future potential in the notion or 'doings' of data as problem or on-going experiment? In some ways, this edited collection examines the landscape of a post-data-turn in qualitative inquiry, of research with data without data, or immanent data becomings.

Instead of providing simple definitional answers or unified representational signifiers of what are data, what counts as data, or how data operate we hope that chapters in this edited volume will leave the readers with the open prospect of productive unsettlement, discomfort, and uncertainty. If data are seen as a concept or enactment of diverse connections then some forms of data are *necessarily* ontologically fictional and *vitally* illusive, and vibrant in their performances. At the same time, some chapters illustrate how data provoke, call for action, change, or transformation, and for becoming something unanticipated and other. It is also our intention to guide students and researchers to reconsider or revision their actions, plans, and future direction regarding data. We suggest that data may manifest itself as an event in which data, theories, writing, thinking, artistic processes and practices, as well as inquiries, researchers, participants, past, future, present, and body-mind-materia are entangled, or connected, where data might perform their own subjectivities.

In addition, it is interesting to pay closer attention to data's 'pull' or gravitational forces. These forces might stem and initially originate from research traditions and normative scholarly discourses. However, these gravitational forces also have the potential to guide scholars beyond the 'expected' and pre-described toward more open-ended experimentations with, alongside, and in conjunction with data. For example, data might have multiple presences some of which can be absent or still becoming. Data might not only function as a noun but also a verb, adjective, proposition, pause, hole, and it can even function as a question mark or maybe as a gendered pronoun, among other things. In some ways data have potential everywhere but without scholars and participants' interactions, directionality, and intentionality data might remain, at least momentarily, mute, invisible, and inaccessible. Furthermore, scholars' desire to pin down data and their potential can considerably limit data's capability to surprise and provoke. In many ways data's double move (simultaneous and fluid notions of creation and elimination, past and present, for and against) can generate continuously changing and unforeseen possibilities to inform our thinking as scholars and qualitative researchers.

Data's double move might also indicate that data are both decided and undecided. By this connection we refer to the "presence" of data. Data are here, with us, in some ways knowable and expressing, simulating, possible, repeating diverse forms knowledge. However, at the same time data's absence haunts scholars, and absent-presence (e.g., Derrida, 1997) reproduces data again and again in their different forms, at different sense times (e.g., Deleuze, 2001, 2003). Data's epistemological agency shapes us, data themselves, and our surroundings. Scholars might sense data and knowledge, they might see something surprising or disturbing, or sounds or colors in the classroom, for example, might produce various effects, events, and flows.

Intra-active data might also guide qualitative researchers to think and talk in certain ways in relation to the objects, material, and forces around them. At the same time data's epistemological agency might be in flux enough not to be recognizable. In many contexts data are here and there, everywhere and nowhere, coming and going.

However, we are not ready to propose that qualitative researchers can do without data. The linguistic problematics and discursive inaccuracies associated with the label data do not stop data. Data continue. Data might turn into bits, pieces, micro seconds, millimetres, fragments, partial utterances, diverse forces, ecological initiatives, ethical responses or stuttering, and so on. Alternatively, data might stay undecided, uncertain, or fearful and beyond the control of scholars. For some scholars, this undecidedness and uncertainty could be troublesome and for some it might be a resource and endless source of rethought, deconstruction, and conceptual/theoretical inspiration.

This book also discusses some of the ways in which the very notion of data has been challenged as a result of the major upheavals that have shaken qualitative inquiry over the last 30 years, in the wake of the various "turns" that have convulsed the humanities and social sciences: post-structuralist, postmodernist, deconstructive, Deleuzian, performative, posthumanist, affective, artistic, material feminist and so on. In contemporary qualitative research (or 'post qualitative'), data have become much more than containable and controllable objects of research, acquiring a kind of agency. Furthermore, the current 'post-truth' intellectual and political contexts of many Western countries questions again the ontological connections established through data. Fake-data, post-truth data, fabricated subjects and knowers, obvious intentional inaccuracies of knowledge, change the way readers, users of social media, and ultimately us, the scholars, view and respect data. Post-truth data are here to stay but how should scholars react to that?

A part of our effort to work against containable and controllable objectifications of data we also need to pay attention to text-writing. 'Data-ideas' expressed in these chapters are not thematised, grouped, or categorized. Chapters are arranged in random order. By doing this we desire to communicate wonder, randomness, surprise, relatedness of unthought thought and more, in relation to data. Furthermore, some chapters perform ideas and notions of being, writing with data, tainted and dirty data, and challenge traditional ways of writing about and with data. The artistic and performative aspect of these chapters thus allow a transformation of the reader-subject-text—to challenge not only what data are, but what data do—to data and to the subject alike. Data in post-human and post-qualitative contexts calls for critique, challenges, and continuously changing ways to innovate and recreate data. Data's limits are similar to our limits as thinkers, researchers, and humans. Data are (within, through, by, over, alongside, a part of) us: scholars, researchers, teachers, mothers, fathers, friends, bodies, minds, particles, and different yet interacting and intra-acting bodies and materia. We work with data in various ways, 'data'r'us'.

Rather than providing a separate chapter written by us (the editors) about our recent interactions and puzzlements with data, we have written irruptions that aim to disturb the flow and linearity of this text as a whole. Our irruptions focus on different ways data could function as a hole, absence, or a type of perforation in the host (host functioning as the texts written by others). Our irruptions also offer a sort of escape from sometimes theoretically very dense chapters, providing readers a snack between the meals, an intermission in the opera, an alternative plateau to stretch one's thoughts, or other types of fluid in-between spaces. Furthermore, Dataholes prompt scholars to move beyond the expected and normative, data that are or have, toward data that are not, have not, and potentially create or perform (more) less.

In the lieu of thematizing the randomly placed chapters, which in many ways are beyond shared themes and as such resist linearity and structural organization, we will offer some data potentialities and possible lines of reading. Each following line offers diverse linguistic, material, textual, and collective traces but also some invisible connections between the chapters to produce different and potentially unexpected (data) affects in readers.

Possibilities with breath: Possibilities with data-breath-data- form a line between the chapters of Duhn, Somerville, Rautio and Vladimirova, Rouhiainen, Nordstrom, Van Cleave and Bridges-Rhoads, Arlander, and beyond. These chapters draw attention to breath and its' various functions and formations as data. Data-breath-data- potentially functions as immaterial material, (im)possible exchange, and potentially inexpressible language. Data-breath-data- might serve as a substance-matter-embodiment that can be spaced, bypassed, lived, shared, and heard but not ignored. It is also possible that data-breath-data- generates various affects and diverse assemblages in itself and others. Authors making connections to data-breath-data- encourage readers to hum and sing their breaths, to see what might happen under breath or within spaces between the breaths. Breathing becomes our world as we breathe the world molecules and inhale past, present, and future data-breath-data- of ourselves and others.

Possibilities with performance: Performance could be considered as one platform to reconceptualize and re-enact data. In this book the performative data lines are illustrated in the chapters by Duhn, Rouhiainen, Denzin, Benozzo and Koro-Ljungberg, Banerjee and Blaise, Ulmer, Arlander and beyond. Data-performance or performance-data conceptualizations and practices take into account the vibrancy of data, diverse ways for data to stay open to potentialities, resonances, and theoretical practices and bodily orchestrations. Data-performance or performance-data could be recognized through its different modes including the jester, serious, and plastic modes. In addition, data could be formed through or within plastic performances of political and ethical entanglements or through diverse processes of un-formation. Data-performance or performance-data have potential to become a part of co-performance with machines and technology and as such illustrating human-machine intra-actions. Ethnographical, rhetorical, and continuously moving and shifting performances of data can co-produce cultural interpretations and technological interventions. As such data are likely to resist conclusions and summaries. Some data-performance or performance-data might be staged or completely imaginary or fictional. Who knows? Or data-performance or performance-data might also enable the writing of spacetimemattering generating multiplied data-performances in particular timespaces.

Possibilities with textuality and writing: Data might express, articulate, provoke, and challenge through their textuality, materiality, and subjectivity. However, data's textuality, literary or epistemological functions are not always clearly definable. For example, Rautio and Vladimirova, Somerville, Rouhiainen, Denzin, Arndt, Van Cleave and Bridges-Rhoads, Nordstrom, Reinertsen and Otterstad and others are puzzled by the shifting relationship between data and experimental forms of writing. When scholars engage in experimental forms of writing what happens to data and how data might function? How might collective subjects write, authorless texts be written, multiple texts multiply themselves, or how could excess overflow writing become data? Is it possible that writing data create and regenerate other forms of data, data-events are expressed in or though writing, and sensory resonances become accessible through diverse but also absent linguistic compositions and expressions? Breathing blends with writing and poetic writing writes itself. The writing of water can function as data and short instrumental refrains constitute knowers/writers. Or something else might happen.

Possibilities with matter: Many authors across the book acknowledge the close relationship between data and matter. Data are not objectified to represent a 'worldly thing' but they can be seen as agents in continuously changing relationality and interchange between subjects and matters. The material turn enables scholars to approach data as vibrant, lively, and vital (see Bennett, 2010). From this perspective, materiality promotes liveliness of data and data's spontaneity and ecology. Data matter could carry interactive and generative forces on their own (outside the human) enabling tendencies and trajectories. Data could be used as a human or nonhuman actant and source of action. In this line of thinking not-quite human, more than human, or multi-species data have unexpected potential. The agency of assemblages (Bennett, 2010) creates data within human-non-human and intra-active working groups. Human-non-human working groups, data ecologies and data monism are illustrated, for example, in the chapters of Ulmer, Duhn, Rautio and Vladimirova, Myers, Malone, Arndt, Somerville, DeFreitas, Banerjee and Blaise, Benozzo and Koro-Ljungberg, Reinertsen and Otterstad, Arlander and others.

Possibilities with process: Drawing from Whitehead's, Griffin's, and Sherburne's (1978) process philosophy or philosophy of organisms one might generate data similar to the creation of a subject. Similar to data, the subject emerges from the world and there is no visible distinction between the subject and object. Subjects and data are immanent to their own production. Decisions and thought/thinking might occur immanent to the process especially when subjects are not individual but collective. Multiple data futures are likely to hang together and this becoming includes and encompasses differences, contradictions, and dissonance. Sometimes speculative propositions about data or of data call for simultaneous expert and non-expert awareness and creativity. In addition, process philosophy also carries with itself a sense of tragedy since the increased amount of newness or creativity (in/of data) is balanced out by the same amount of loss/perpetual perishing (of data). Data generation is followed by other data generation, endlessly and singular, data is always many. Singular plural data alternate rhythmically. DeFreitas, Myers, Somerville, Arlander, Malone, and others form process lines of thinking in this book.

Note: It is also important to keep in mind that more traces and alternative possibilities are of course possible. Possibilities with philosophy. Possibilities with technology. Possibilities with aporias. Possibilities with absences. Possibilities with form. Just to name a few.

Finally, similar to Deleuze and Guattari's *A Thousand Plateaus* (1987) this edited collection can be read in any order. Knowledge or data are not arranged in piece-meal-style but readers need to create their own, unique, situational readings and relations to the text. It is our hope that the diverse perspectives and the differing order in which chapters can be read generate a possibility for something else to occur and emerge in the readers. We encourage readers to create their own data experiences allowing something different and emerging to become. This type of free-associating and readers' responsibility could also function as one type of resistance to normative scholarly practices and linear textual representation of research ideas. In some ways, this kind of responsibility also promotes methodologies without methodologies (see e.g., Koro-Ljungberg, 2016) and scholarly work after or against fixed and expected method (Law, 2004, 2006). Each differing reading of the book might promote unlike research-creations bringing together scholarship and artistic forms of inquiry, each time differently and in unanticipated ways (Manning, 2016). For Manning (2016), research-creations "open the field of experience to the more-than of objects and subjects preformed" (p. 12). Research-creations are pragmatically speculative practices and immanent activities, always producing an immanent critique bringing thinking to making and making to thinking. Research-creations study the world and us within it in ways, which do not focus on the form or outcome but on processes (see also Whitehead et al. 1978). Furthermore, "the differential, the active hyphen that brings making to thinking and thinking to making, ensures that research-creation remain an ecology of practices" (Manning, 2016, p. 13). Research-creations are concerned with artful and artistic practices where some data things, doings, processes, encounters, and interactions are expressed but others are left unspoken and un-expressed.

In Auckland↔Helsinki↔Tempe, December 2016

REFERENCES

Bennett, J. (2010). *Vibrant matter: A political ecology of things*. Durham, NC: Duke University Press.

Coole, D., & Frost, S. (2010). Introducing the new materialisms. In D. Coole & S. Frost (Eds.), *New materialisms: ontology, agency, and politics* (pp. 1–43). Durham, NC: Duke University Press.

Deleuze, G. (2001). *Cinema 1: The movement-image* (H. Tomlinson & B. Habberjam, Trans.). Minneapolis, MN: University of Minnesota Press.

Deleuze, G. (2003). *Cinema 2: The time-image* (H. Tomlinson & R. Galeta, Trans.). Minneapolis, MN: University of Minnesota Press.

Deleuze, G., & Guattari, F. (1987). *A Thousand plateaus: Capitalism and schizophrenia*. (B. Massumi, Trans. Original work published 1980 ed.). Minneapolis, MN: University of Minnesota Press.

Deleuze, G., & Guattari, F. (1994). *What is philosophy?* (H. Tomlinson & G. Burchell, Trans.). New York, NY: Columbia University Press.

Derrida, J. (1997). *Of grammatology*. (G. Spivak, Trans.). Baltimore, MD: The Johns Hopkins University Press.

Hultman, K., & Lenz Taguchi, H. (2010). Challenging anthropocentric analysis of visual data: a relational materialist methodological approach to educational research. *International Journal of Qualitative Studies in Education, 23*(5), 525–542.

Ivanova, N. (2016) Non-anthropocentric Poetics: The creative signature of mycobacteria. *Technoetic Arts. A Journal of Speculative Research, 14*(3), 225–233.

Koro-Ljungberg, M. (2016). *Reconceptualizing qualitative research: Methodologies without methodology*. Los Angeles, CA: Sage.

Koro-Ljungberg, M., Carlson, D., Tesar, M., & Anderson, K. (2015). Methodology *brut*: philosophy, ecstatic thinking, and some other (unfinished) things. *Qualitative Inquiry, 21*(7), 612–619. doi: 10.1177/1077800414555070

Law, J. (2004). *After method*. London: Routledge.

Law, J. (2006). *Making a mess with method*. Retrieved from http://www.heterogeneities.net/publications/Law2006MakingaMesswithMethod.pdf

Manning, E. (2016). *The minor gesture*. Durham, NC: Duke University Press.

Massumi, B. (2002). *Parables for the virtual*. Durham, NC: Duke University Press.

Mol, A. (2002). *The body multiple: ontology in medical practice*. Durham, NC: Duke University Press.

Mol, A., & Law, J. (1994). Regions, networks and fluids: Anaemia and social topology. *Social Studies of Science, 24*(4), 641–671.

Whitehead, A. N., Griffin, D. R., & Sherburne, D. W. (1978). *Process and reality: An essay in cosmology*. New York, NY: Free Press.

CHAPTER ONE

Performing Data

IRIS DUHN

ABSTRACT

The chapter introduces different data performance modes (jester-like, serious, plastic) to explore perceptions of data. Exploration involves the following of shadow trails, of being curious with data, and of not trusting what the researching I/eye would like to believe. The data performance mode generates fleeting intensities that make thinking/thought/text move out of line to tangle with modernist data-zombies and post-qualitative data-liveliness and whatever lives between the two. In a performative mode, the shadow trails appear in brackets and/or are italicised to indicate moments of out-of-line entanglements where data foci blur vision. These entanglements bring to the fore the awareness that data-zombies linger on, and that data performance as search for potentialities criss-crosses data liveliness and data stasis. Data collection is this sense is about imagining possibilities and creating conditions for possibilities to materialise in a sharing of the world in all its liveliness, where differences are valued. It raises questions about intentionality or agency and ethics and politics, about what is perceived (and what lies outside of human perception), by whom and why, about underlying assumptions regarding the liveliness of data as matter and form.

Keywords: plasticity, performance, perception

DATA LAUGHS

Data are troublesome. Data is troublesome? Is data always more than one? Or is it better understood as a powerfully singular THING, king-like in its omnipresence and its power to affect change (Dreher, Nunnenkamp, & Thiele, 2008)? Does data have to have a presence, be discernible, describable, bounded, or can data be almost non-perceptible, re-configured in the moment, fleeting and a-flutter? What about data as something that hovers as potential in all encounters? How does data make its presence, omni or other, felt? Does it? Or does data need the expert I/eye to come to matter? Or is 'data' about the perception of an encounter where a self meets difference of some sort, and everyone and everything changes, to various degrees, in the process?

The more I think about 'data', the more troubled I become. Maybe thinking is not the best approach to a creative encounter with data. Perhaps playfulness as a quality (Lieberman, 2014) that brings light-heartedness and even humour to the endeavour will encourage imagination and curiosity in data encounters (Haraway, 2015). Maybe 'data' is jester-like, tempting me to go here, there and somewhere else, following a shadow trail, with the data-jester performing as a not particularly trustworthy guide?

DATA IS SERIOUS

In every application for funding the data collection method and its design play a major role. Consistently haunted by post-positivist spectres, research bodies react with nervous shakes to 'post-qualitative' or to experimental research design and there will be (most likely) no funding (Stengers & Despret, 2014). I have come to treat data as something of an necessary irritant that provokes ongoing engagement in many ways. The more capable I am of describing what I am going to do about data as evidence, when, with whom, for what purpose, the more likely I am to get funding in a culture of auditing and accountability (Bansel, Davies, Gannon, & Linnell, 2008). As long as I promise to collect something and as long as I can give solid reasons for the collection and make grand statements about the benefits of data gathering and analysis, I am in the clear and possibly on the road to a successful grant application. The promise of data as solid certainty is the key. A clearly articulated promise of data as foundation for serious evidence raises the chances of research (funding) success and thus of prestige and authority as a truthful knowledge-producer (Bratich, 2004). Data is serious indeed.

PLASTIC DATA

Yet data is not what it used to be, perhaps data is indeed dead (Denzin, 2013) and lingers zombie-like in the remnants of the modernist research imagination (and its practices). Interestingly enough, due to their immense loadbearing capacity, their ability to create ever-lasting forms and their initial malleability, concrete and steel are the foundations of modernist world-making (Denzin, 2013). And yet, concrete is not as solid and ever-lasting as it appears. Indeed, concrete is 'plastic', in Malabou's (2009, 2013) sense, in that concrete can give shape, receive shape and it can mutate (be destroyed, shattered). Like the modernist dream of utopian, sanitised, controlled and uniform cities built of concrete and steel, the modernist dream of clean, objective, pure data that reveals the concrete truth about reality and enables the making of better futures, is an illusion (Koro-Ljungberg, 2013). If concrete's nature is plastic (Ulmer, 2015), then maybe data's nature is plastic too.

Data as plastic, then, as less solid, certain and ever-lasting as hoped for (by some). Data as a plastic, as not one, then, as there are distinctly different perspectives on the nature of data in postindustrial neoliberal postconsumer times and places. However, the desire for data as proof and as the raison d'être for research remains in a climate where 'truth' is increasingly contested, political and multiple (Beck, 2004). What can data do now? What is the purpose of having it when scientific truths have lost their shine as harbingers of enlightenment (Van Loon, 2000)? As researchers and thinkers, what is our role in a world with/out data or with data that is plastic? How to move towards an imaginary of data as that which gives form, receives form, destroys form? Data as plastic can be malleable, solid, shattered. It can be explosive (Malabou, 2009). Plasticity means that something is stretchable and willing to give, willing to take, willing to bring together, and also willing to tear apart (Ulmer, 2015).

Data as a plastic, then, as there are distinctly different perspectives on the nature of data in postindustrial neoliberal postconsumer times and places (St. Pierre, 2013a). However, the desire for data as proof and as the raison d'être for research remains in a climate where 'truth' is increasingly contested, political, multiple and possibly even malleable (Beck, 2004). What can data do? What is the purpose of having it when scientific truths have lost their shine as harbingers of enlightenment (Van Loon, 2000)? As researchers and thinkers, what is our role in a world with/out data? How to move towards an imaginary of data as that which is not known, as that which is not always visible, tangible, senseable? Research as a search for the im/possibilities of data as that which is to come. Data as performance and as openness towards potentiality and search for connections, data collection as curating, as creating conditions for a coming together of all sorts (McKenzie, 2009). It is no longer obvious where, or when, data ends or begins.

CHOOSING A PERFORMANCE MODE

After the introduction of different data performance modes (jester-like, serious, plastic), this chapter engages with data as jester, which means moving on, following shadow trails, being curious and not trusting what the I/eye would like to believe. The jester-like data performance mode generates fleeting intensities that make thinking/thought/text move out of line (Cixous & Sellers, 2014), to tangle with modernist data-zombies and post-qualitative data-liveliness and whatever lies between (Koro-Ljungberg, 2013; MacLure, 2013b; St. Pierre, 2013a). In a performative mode, the shadow trails appear in brackets and/or are italicised to indicate moments of out-of-line entanglements where data-jesting blurs vision. The entanglements bring to the fore, for me at least, the awareness that data-zombies linger on, and that data performance as search for potentialities criss-crosses data liveliness and data stasis. [*Note to self: the challenge is to avoid black and white. Life and death/stasis should not be opposites as one can't be without the other. They make each other.*]

THE THING WITH DATA

A re-imagined conversation about planning for data.

So, in this new project I want to really play with data and I've been thinking that I'd like the kids to tell stories, over time, I really like Haraway's 'Children of the Compost' idea where a group of storytellers speculate on generational multispecies entanglements. Not sure yet how this would work, especially over a period of time. And who would keep the story alive when I'm not there? Would it work?

Interesting idea. How would you capture the data? What is your data? What happens if you're not there when the story develops?

Maybe one of the children could be the story keeper? They could tell it to an adult who writes it down, or they could speak it into some recording device? Or draw it? Or is it enough that it has been said, without recording it?

Thoughts on data that informed the conversation: Data is something that can be collected, gathered, manipulated, made sense of, something that can be perceived and shaped, in some form or other. [*A story would fit this description, if it is recorded in some way. But I like the idea of a story that lives on breath, a story that lives through the telling, not the recording. Performing data as breathing into the void of possibilities? Immaterial materialisation with breath and sound.*]

Data is something that has its own life and can escape, unless captured. In fact, data-as-story-in-the-making, in the conversation above, is illusive and unpredictable but somehow 'there' if caught in the right moment. It needs a 'catcher', someone who hunts it. Or someone who nurtures it? Cares for it? Someone who welcomes it and politely invites it into the encounter, or space (Despret, 2015a; Irigaray, 2008)? [*What if data is that which lives in the moments between breaths? Data as that which is unformed in every breath, contend to be birthed into meaning and matter through the exchange of air? Data as pure possibilities in every moment and in every breath, in the research encounter? Whom do I invite into breathing with the*] *world? What would such an exchange feel like? What would it do? And also, in curative mode: inviting something/someone politely in may open the door to vampires. What do ethical, reciprocal, caring collaborations look like in a fiercely competitive knowledge culture?* Irigaray's (2008) notion of the coming together of self and other through the passing of a threshold is helpful to my imagining of this process of creating encounters. *Data as potential and as that which lives unformed in the air between self and other allows for exchange between two worlds before they materialise. I breathe in molecules that already contain worlds within worlds. Between us we begin to create a shared spaced when we become aware of this exchange, when we change the air into vibrations, words, language, sounds].*

Perhaps data requires someone, like a conductor, to orchestrate its appearance and performance? The liveliness of data [*before it ends up quiet, tamed or seemingly dead*] requires a firm hand that disciplines and guides, and a clear eye on the end goal [*a cognito to master the mess*]. Good data is data that is rich and passive and ripe for interpretation and mastery. It drips like honey from the hive when it is taken from those who made it, and sweetens the analyst's life as it is consumed. It brings the light of knowledge to the shadows of ignorance and assumptions when it burns like a candle [*what about the beings whose hard labour produced the goods? They often receive sugar water in return. The honeycomb structure is pure hexagon ingenuity—does burning a candle do justice to the brilliance of the bees' labour and incredible intelligence? Is there something here about the ethics of reciprocity in the process of data harvesting? What is to be exchanged here, who invites whom, and for what?*]

And: data is like precious butterflies (or bees!), and like those pinned butterflies under glass in museum collections, data-as-evidence also needs to be pinned down somehow to study it in its complete stillness. Vague and shadowy data becomes true and firm data when it can be put under a microscope (or into a software program) to be gazed at, when it is static and preserved for eternity. When it has given up its own vitality. [*Data as sacrifice at the altar of knowledge? Or does data have a life of its own even in stillness, an agency and presence that makes the researcher dance to data tunes, even when it is considered dead matter (Holmes & Jones, 2013)? Does data, as king-like thing, make me do things that I would not have done otherwise? Is data re-forming me, without my knowledge? Am I being data-ed? The concern over privacy issues, mega-data and new forms of surveillance spring to mind. Zombie-like 'dead' data reforms with a vengeance! Data as explosive.*]

Maybe my trouble with data is about form and re-form. What is the purpose of re-search, and what is the relationship between re-search, new search and data? Is research possible without a focus on something? Isn't the focus on something creating its own 'data'? As soon as I hone in on a focus [*I have something in mind, now I will look for it in real life to prove that it's not just in my head*] I am in an entanglement that changes me in the process. Even hard data, the supposedly dead kind, re-forms me. For example …

... if I look at the butterfly or species display in a museum collection I am in awe and shock. Awed by the intricacy of patterns and beauty of the collection, shocked by the mass deaths that are on display.

One million creatures in glass jars, systematically ordered. The evidence of serious data gathering and effective methods of analysis. And then there is the art of displaying data as findings. One million dead animals in jars, two million eyes. Staring back at us. Forever. [*Dead matter? Is it possible to walk through this chamber of horrors and not be affected? Spectres of German history appear, death and science are intimately cut together. Ghosts are present here. What if I walk in with my scientist's gaze, able to distance myself from the data collection that has gone on here and only see the end result? With a cool, steady eye on species, sub-species, categorisations, measurements? Here is hard evidence of my top spot in the evolutionary hierarchy. Even with a scientist's gaze, I am still affected by the display but the self that governs this encounter feels solidly anchored in its birth right to exceptionalism, rather than becoming more porous to difference and entanglements. My heart weeps but my mind does not notice. What if I walk in with an open heart and mind? Human cruelty and show-man-ship make me gag. I love/hate this display because I tentatively touch the boundaries of all-too-human inhumanity (Barad, 2012)*].

Following the data-jester: the process of imagining something into possible form. How to create conditions for data to appear, how to 'see' or perceive it, be touched by it, once the conditions have been created? [*How to imagine with the other? How to resist the latent desire to pin something/someone down? What are conditions are necessary for either possibility to materialise? What would the butterfly in the jar have wanted? To live! To flutter with joy and escape the pin! This connects me to the butterfly. Is there an opening for shared imagination, cautious avoidance of the pin, and changed perception of what's possible?*]

And isn't the search for data also about the desire to make something visible/tangible that wasn't visible before, and once materialised to keep form from changing into something else? The desire to bring into matter, then fixing matter as form, formaldehye-ing matter, mummifying it so that it sticks around? Is that what drives the ongoing obsession with data-as-thing? Data as evidence of the human ability to generate and preserve dead matter.

THE PERCEPTION OF DATA

Everything that can be perceived has form and boundaries, everything that is sense-able that is. Data is, at its most basic (or perhaps at its most complex?), about the entanglement of perception and experiencing the self as an entity that is able to sense the world. In other words, a bounded self with an interior life that experiences the external world, with data as the in-between. The eye/I perceives colour, shape, depth and sends this information to the brain which then interprets and makes sense. There is no 'real reality' out there that is the same for all of us. Each brain makes its own reality [*Much of what is seen is learned. Blind people who regain vision often have difficulties with depth perception and can't always make sense of the world around them visually. Brain research tells us that the brain architecture of those who are blind for a long period differs to those who are not blind, with stronger capacity to perceive smell or touch. And animals 'see' the world different again, of course*]. What I perceive depends on what I have learned to perceive. Learning can be un-learned or opened up or modified. Learning is plastic, the brain is plastic (in the lively, malleable sense, not the 'plastic-is-dead' sense) (Malabou & Butler, 2011).

Data and form in this relationship are about noticing phenomena 'out there' in the real world, and making sense of them 'in here', in my mind. This is an understanding about the relationship between the researcher and data which assumes an object (perceptible in some form) and a subject (with interior life, able to interpret and generate knowledge about the object). In a way it is about the consumption of 'what is out there' through internalising it, making it one's own. The researcher as data-gobbler. Data has to die and become digested, to make the researcher live (see the image of 'the boy who loved data', Koro-Ljungberg, 2013, p. 276). And data is about knowledge-as-language and as meaning-making, and about knowledge-as-power. Data is about politics and ethics, always (McKenzie, 2009).

DATA AND MEANING MAKING

A lot has been written about post-qualitative data to raise questions about the relationship between reality, agency, and experience particularly to question the ability of language to represent reality in the process of knowledge production and meaning making (MacLure, 2013a; St. Pierre, 2013a, 2013b; Youngblood Jackson, 2013). Data as 'brute' and as something that represents what is out there as fixed and stable reality has been the focus of critical analysis for some time, from post-structural feminist thought (Weedon, 1987) to Derridean entanglements (Barad, 2010; Kirby, 2012) and Foucauldian genealogies (Ashenden, 2002), to post-phe-nomenology and the affective turn in ethnography (Thrift, 2008). More recently, and following on from poststructural concerns with language and its materialities, questions regarding the nature of language have pinpointed an anthropocentric assumption behind language as an essentially human system (Kirby, 2014; Kohn, 2013; Marder, 2013). Raw data becomes polished data when it is captured in language and put through the meaning making machine. It seems the entire world is constantly generating meaning (Hird, 2010). Birds do it. Bees do it. Plants do it. Microbes do it. They all make meaning through perception and create their world accordingly (Marder, 2013; Despret, 2015b). Data performance is everywhere, and everyone and everything performs.

But perhaps language, as the process of making sense of the (human) self in its relation to the world, is re-formed in its encounter with data? By focusing on something and expressing this focus in language I may be touched and changed in the process, if I am porous enough to enable a flow between self/the world. The story I create and the meanings I make are shaped by what I encounter. Language then is the medium of exchange between inner/outer. Or perhaps language is a membrane that holds the self together? The membrane is porous and specific to the individual self, however, perhaps the membrane that facilitates the exchange between inner/outer, self and world is plastic, in the Malabou-sense of plasticity. This would mean that what is exchanged via the membrane can change. Data may be the trigger that modifies the membrane. [*Having witnessed hostility towards a homeless person on the street changes my perception of poverty. Now that I become porous I notice homelessness everywhere. With a few bad turns homelessness is something that could happen to me. The barriers that protect me from such shocking insight are normally high. Perception-as-undoing: Will I not walk away but perceive the homeless person as a possible version of my less-lucky self? And then what?*]

Maybe gracefulness and hospitality are conditions that allow for otherness and difference to enter and to unfold within, and around, the self. Becoming porous with the world, yet not so porous that the membrane dissolves. What worlds do we want to create together and what is it that we perceive, together, apart? How can we make, and share world/s of 'impossible differences' (Deutscher, 2002)? [*This is so difficult to begin to imagine. The language of trees? How do trees perceive their worlds? How does rain as 'data' feel to trees? (Kohn, 2013). The language of trees is complex and different and completely foreign to me. But so are the languages of many human minorities (Viruru, 2001). What membranes are needed to perceive radical differences that matter? To bring form to radical differences? How to perceive making and un-making as plastic performances of political, ethical entanglements?*]

PERFORMANCE CONCLUDES

My shadow trails have led me towards entangling myself with the idea that data performance is about the process of un-formation. Data is less about object/subject and interior/exterior relationships and more about the convoluted and complex encounters that take place when form is given to a collective experience that is perceived as somehow noteworthy. Noticing something noteworthy, which in the end is what gives form to 'data', depends on (1) decision-making processes (What is noteworthy? On what basis? In what context? For whom? What/who is to be excluded? Why?), and (2) on governance of the process (Who can make decisions? What can make decisions? Who decides what's to be in-or excluded? Who makes boundaries?). It matters what matters, it matter what stories are told, by whom, where and how (Haraway, 2015). It matters who listens, whose sounds make the story, whose breath carries the sounds and the silence. Breath as exchange between and betwixt membranes, across species and across voids.

Data performance shortcut: When I cup my hands over my ears, I am immediately immersed in the pulsing, rushing aliveness of my own body. I sense my self from the outside which is haunted by its interior, always. The aliveness of my body, the intense and ongoing encounters of multitudes within that are 'me' as a living body. Immediate change of perception.

The sounds of the invisible interior are a reminder that what I think I see and know as reality is only the version of reality that my mind creates in this moment. Without this short moment of listening to internal body sounds, my sense of body would be what I see: fingers tapping on the keyboard, eyes taking in the immediate surroundings, perhaps a fleeting sense of my back as it touches the chair. So what is data? Is it that which my mind focuses on in any given frame? Who, or what, determines the frame? What is a frame anyway? What my eye sees? What my fingers seem to touch [*nothing ever touches, all that is felt is electromagnetic repulsion—so much for the solidity of data. There is more mystery in every blink of the eye than my mind can fathom (Barad, 2012).*]

Seeking encounters with data as a researcher may be the sensing of the self in its relation to the world, and giving shape to this encounter with as much awareness of what may be possible. Data collection is this sense is about imagining possibilities and creating conditions for possibilities to materialise in a sharing of the world in all its liveliness, where differences are valued. It raises questions about intentionality, ethics and politics, about what is perceived (and what lies outside of human perception), by whom and why, about underlying assumptions regarding the liveliness of data as matter and form. And it also raises questions about that which is not easily accessible through (human) perception and, at least in empirical research, does not count as data. Just because I/eye can't see it, it doesn't mean it's not there.

REFERENCES

Ashenden, S. (2002). Policing perversion: The contemporary governance of paedophilia. *Cultural Values, 6*(1&2), 197–222.

Bansel, P., Davies, B., Gannon, S., & Linnell, S. (2008). Technologies of audit at work on the writing subject: A discursive analysis. *Studies in Higher Education, 33*(6), 673–683.

Barad, K. (2010). Quantum entanglements and hauntological relations of inheritance: Dis/continuities, spacetime enfoldings, and justice-to-come. *Derrida Today, 3*(2), 240–268.

Barad, K. (2012). On touching—The inhuman that therefore I am. *Differences: A Journal of Feminist Cultural Studies, 23*(3), 206–223.

Beck, U. (2004). The truth of others: A cosmopolitan approach. *Common Knowledge, 10*(3), 430–449.

Bratich, J. Z. (2004). Regime-of-Truth change. *Cultural Studies ↔ Critical Methodologies, 4*(2), 237–241.

Cixous, H., & Sellers, S. (2014). *White ink: Interviews on sex, text and politics.* Stocksfield: Acumen.

Denzin, N. K. (2013). "The Death of Data?". *Cultural Studies ↔ Critical Methodologies, 13*(4), 353–356.

Despret, V. (2015a). The enigma of the raven. *Angelaki, 20*(2), 57–72.

Despret, V. (2015b). We are not so stupid. … animals neither. *Angelaki, 20*(2), 153–161.

Deutscher, P. (2002). *A politics of impossible difference: The later work of Luce Irigaray.* Ithaca, NY: Cornell University Press.

Dreher, A., Nunnenkamp, P., & Thiele, R. (2008). Does aid for education educate children? Evidence from Panel Data. *The World Bank Economic Review, 22*(2), 291–314.

Haraway, D. (2015). A curious practice. *Angelaki, 20*(2), 5–14.

Hird, M. J. (2010). Indifferent globality gaia, symbiosis and 'other worldliness'. *Theory, Culture & Society, 27*(2–3), 54–72.

Holmes, R., & Jones, L. (2013). Flesh, wax, horse skin and hair: The many intensities of data. *Cultural Studies ↔ Critical Methodologies, 13*(4), 357–372.

Irigaray, L. (2008). *Sharing the world.* London: Continuum.

Kirby, V. (2012). Initial conditions. *Differences: A Journal of Feminist Cultural Studies, 23*(3), 197–205.

Kirby, V. (2014). Human exceptionalism on the line. *SubStance, 43*(2), 50–67.

Kohn, E. (2013). *How forests think. Toward an anthropology beyond human.* Berkeley and London: University of California Press.

Koro-Ljungberg, M. (2013). "Data" as vital illusion. *Cultural Studies ↔ Critical Methodologies, 13*(4), 274–278.

Lieberman, J. N. (2014). *Playfulness: Its relationship to imagination and creativity.* New York, NY: Academic Press.

MacLure, M. (2013a). Researching without representation? Language and materiality in post-qualitative methodology. *International Journal of Qualitative Studies in Education, 26*(6), 658–667.

MacLure, M. (2013b). The wonder of data. *Cultural Studies ↔ Critical Methodologies, 13*(4), 228–232.

Malabou, C. (2009). *What should we do with our brain?* New York, NY: Fordham University Press.

Malabou, C. (2013). Living room. Über Gastlichkeit, Plastizität und Form. *Springerin, 19*(2), 33–37.

Malabou, C., & Butler, J. (2011). You be my body for me: Body, shape, and plasticity in Hegel's phenomenology of spirit. In S. Houlgate & M. Baur (Eds.), *A companion to Hegel* (pp. 611–640). Oxford: Wiley-Blackwell.

Marder, M. (2013). *Plant-thinking: A philosophy of vegetal life.* New York, NY: Columbia University Press.

McKenzie, M. (2009). Scholarship as intervention: Critique, collaboration and the research imagination. *Environmental Education Research, 15*(2), 217–226.

St. Pierre, E. A. (2013a). The appearance of data. *Cultural Studies ↔ Critical Methodologies, 13*(4), 223–227.

St. Pierre, E. A. (2013b). The posts continue: Becoming. *International Journal of Qualitative Studies in Education, 26*(6), 646–657.

Stengers, I., & Despret, V. (2014). *Women who make a fuss. The unfaithful daughters of Virginia Woolf.* Minneapolis, MN: Univocal Publishing.

Thrift, N. (2008). *Non-representational theory: Space, politics, affect.* London and New York, NY: Routledge.

Ulmer, J. (2015). Plasticity: A new materialist approach to policy and methodology. *Educational Philosophy and Theory, 47*(10), 1096–1109.

Van Loon, J. (2000). Virtual risks in an age of cybernetic reproduction. In B. Adam, U. Beck, & J. Van Loon (Eds.), *The risk society and beyond: Critical issues for social theory* (pp. 165–182). London: Sage Publications.

Viruru, R. (2001). Colonised through language: The case of early childhood education. *Contemporary Issues in Early Childhood, 2*(1), 31–47.

Weedon, C. (1987). *Feminist practice and poststructural theory.* Oxford: Basil Blackwell.

Youngblood Jackson, A. (2013). Posthumanist data analysis of mangling. *International Journal of Qualitative Studies in Education, 26*(6), 714–748.

CHAPTER TWO

Befriending Snow

On Data as an Ontologically Significant Research Companion

PAULIINA RAUTIO AND ANNA VLADIMIROVA

ABSTRACT

In this chapter data is personified and befriended as an ontologically significant nonhuman other. Data are/is suggested to be someone we work with, a companion, a colleague. The particular data to be befriended is snow: a long-term companion in both authors' everyday lives and in our research. As an ontologically significant other snow is alluringly paradoxical: both hard and soft, cold and warm, wet and dry, solid and liquid, moving yet still. The kind of being we can become in our encounters with snow is in itself new knowledge—of a possible way of being and knowing otherwise. In the chapter, we suggest that if data is considered a personified companion, more emotions and complexities have access to research practices.

Keywords: snow, friendship, befriending, love, interdependency

The 'I' befriending snow in this chapter is a fusion of two human individuals and two post-anthropocentric approaches to working with snow as an ontologically significant research companion, namely posthumanism at large and what is termed posthuman animism in particular (Rudy, 2013).

INTRODUCTION

Subscribing to an ontological approach according to which our existence does not precede our encounters with other beings or things is at the core of posthumanist thinking. To carry this ontology through to how we conceive data in our research would mean nothing less than understanding that we gain our existence in encounters with our data: the things and beings we orchestrate and then perform as data always play also us.

In this chapter data is personified and befriended as an ontologically significant nonhuman other. Data are/is someone we work with, a companion, a colleague. Someone who is interested in us and manages to get our attention. Someone with whom we come into being as of certain kind: someone who is, in this sense, life-giving. As such, data does not represent as if an outside reality, he is not a courier or a mediator, rather a companion with whom we gain new possibilities of being. In this chapter befriending data is conceptualised as a practice of 'becoming other': data will help us to not only analytically dissect our research themes but to enact otherwise, to already be and do otherwise, thus constructing horizons of hope (Braidotti, 2013).

The particular data to be befriended is snow. A long-term companion in both of our everyday lives and in our research. As an ontologically significant other snow is alluringly paradoxical: both hard and soft, cold and warm, wet and dry, solid and liquid, moving yet still. The kind of being we can become in our encounters with snow is in itself new knowledge—of a possible way of being and knowing otherwise.

More than hybrid, snow is also multifarious. It allows humans to experience his diverse hypostases through engagement, which is often beyond human initiative. From this and a linguistic point of view, snow appears like an obstacle to people, because it can *fall, cover, drift, block,* or *bury.* Hiding from a heavy snowfall, people have to shovel its consequences afterwards. Snow is freezing, snow is dangerous. Nevertheless, people do acknowledge amidsts this 'confrontation' that snow can be *sociable, supportive, playful, emerging, informative.* Many love snow for his flawless purity and elegance and for the "it's so much fun" quality, but hardly any would decide to actually talk to snow or his beautiful wasp—like snowflakes, and befriend or know them on a deeper ontological level.

Winter as any other season envelops us in various audible, visual, tactile, gustatory and olfactory experiences. Not only envelops, but percolates and simultaneously gives birth to another type of meaningful experience, which I will address as relational knowledge. From the perspective of the contemporary animist philosophy, this knowledge is a product of onto—epistemological encounters of human and nonhuman persons determined by the factor of immediacy. As Naveh and Bird—David (in Harvey, 2014) put it: "Animism … is about a world full of immediate relational beings" (p. 27). Befriending snow (or 'using snow as data') is working a horizon of hope in which skills of becoming less human and more a being among others (Pedersen, 2010, p. 243) are integral to the relational ontology of being human.

It is important to understand that rather than *humanised*, snow has been *personified* in this paper. This is to say that by treating snow as a 'nonhuman person' we seek to keep open the possibility of snow—just like any other person—to continually change and evolve, also ontologically; and to uphold specific relationships to specific individuals in specific situations. To humanise or anthropomorphise snow would be to totalize its ontological friendship violently. To personify snow, as a research companion, is to purposefully break down the illusion of an inert object, unable to think and speak to us. It is also to ease the way we express ourselves as researchers for the rest of the human audience to comprehend our reasoning.

BECOMING COMPANIONS

My meeting with snow happened as soon as I was born into deep January winter, it bearing all the Siberian coldness and harshness as well as virginity and natural grandeur and beauty of the snowy surroundings. We lived in a big remote village where snow is not a bypasser, as in modern cities, but a ruler. He 'wheels and deals', while people contemplate his orders, sometimes acting as rebels in an attempt to explain that they also possess specific rights. My name and address were written on the flip side of a sheep hide, in bold black marker. The hide was dyed bright yellow with black highlights. I would lay on it in a sledge and my mother would pull me. I would get snow on my face. The year was 1978 and I was one-year-old. Since then I have avoided, manipulated, ploughed, sculpted, hated, loved, talked to, listened to, been inspired by, missed, anticipated, gone over, around and under, been covered, surrounded, amazed and fed up with snow.

Until recently I thought that most of my research interests have included snow. I now realise they have never been *my* research interests, my unadulterated decisions, rather interests I have developed with snow. With someone who I grew up with, got fed up with but nevertheless got attached to. As a researcher, I have been on the lookout for stories, experiences, phenomena and ideas that appear simple on the surface but entail galaxies worth of complexities when time unfolds. Things that matter intensely for those involved, but don't necessarily mean much to an onlooker (e.g., Rautio, 2013; Rautio & Jokinen, 2015).

Working backwards and outwards from being a scholar reveals a researcher who is conditioned and trained into thinking she 'designs' her research, 'collects' or even 'produces' data alone or with fellow researchers. Who is it really that I have done my thinking with? Who have been my allies and co-designers? The following two quotes are by participants in a study I conducted in a small, desolate village in the Lapland of Finland—a village dubbed as "dying" for decades now (Rautio, 2010).

Snow reflected the sun so that I was nearly blinded driving my car. Trees and bushes were white with snow. Coming back in the evening everything was blue. The moon shone bright and the trees and shrubs cast shadows onto blue snow. The next day everything was grey. It was cloudy. And in the evening it snowed so hard I could not see the road. No tracks in the snow, I thought to myself. And right then a rusty coloured fox ran across the road, leaving tracks on the snow.

As the temperatures drop a little I plough the yard from snow, in the dark evening, in the light from the lampposts. It's been days since it snowed. The yard is filled with tracks; of people and of cars. In the middle of the yard I find a lace pattern, courtesy of night time visitors. Criss crossing imprints of mountain hare paws look like black holes in the white snow, making the combination appear lacelike.

As a decently trained qualitative inquirer I took these passages to convey the meanings and experiences of the participating human individuals. I had made it explicit that I was studying everyday life environments and human environment relations. Yet I failed to see, for a long time, the nonhuman partner who designed, affected, infected, directed my research and worked alongside me and the participating people. The invisible friend I had reduced into a thematic category in what I thought my proper data. Snow.

Snow has made much of my research possible both literally and as an existential thinking aid. In my post-doctoral research spring snow carried the weight of the child participants but not me, enabling the children to control their distance to the adult/researcher as they pleased. Running fast on top of snow they gained literal distance from me, making my recorded data of our urban environment explorations abound with passages of inaudible talk and instead my audible heavy breathing, resulting in discussions of the nature of data, of the potential of post-qualitative research of childhoods (Rautio, 2014), and the political implications of studying what matters to children and how (Rautio et al., *forthcoming*). Accommodating clusters of children, mittens, stones, light, pushing, climbing, shouting, snowpiles have contributed to ways in which I have been able to reconceptualise childhood and 'mattering' beyond developmental frameworks (Rautio, 2013; Rautio & Jokinen, 2015).

Most of all, and most recently, snow has aided me in questioning the anthropocentrism of my research practices. The anthropocentrism embedded in the very idea of who and what can be identified as taking part in research—contributing 'data'. For the purpose of retraining myself, and perhaps the like-minded reader, I have begun to re-track my research weaving in snow as the friend and the ally he always was.

In his blog about design and research of end user experiences Jussi Ahola (2013) talks about desire paths made visible by snow. Aerial images of parks and yards after snowfall, with clearly discernible walking paths as tracks in snow, are easy to find online (search "desire paths in snow").

Sometimes the problem is that you cannot easily see where these desire paths run. You might not have the luxury of a snowfall covering the official paths; the ground is covered with concrete revealing nothing about people's behaviour. In these cases, it is only through careful observation and rigorous data collection that these desire paths can be uncovered. (Ahola, 2013)

I am beginning to think that working with snow has indeed been a luxury; that snow has revealed tracks—ways of being and thinking—which would have remained invisible otherwise. That snow has been a methodological luxury the absence of which would have had to be substituted by 'careful observation and rigorous data collection'.

GETTING ATTACHED

The windscreen at the rear of my car has a small wiper. Whenever temperatures remain in the awkward in between grades of undulating thaw and frost, the wiper accumulates layers of ice and stops doing its job. I was driving home from work one day and wanted to wipe the window clean from patches of melting snow. The wiper moved back and forth as it should but because of the ice it didn't even touch the screen and all of the slushy snow remained intact. I looked at the window from the rearview mirror, the wiper going dutifully back and forth but not touching the windscreen, the snow remaining completely still and blocking my view. I heard myself saying out loud to the wiper: "Dude, it's like you live in a completely different reality".

Feeling compassionate towards a nonhuman being, even towards an inanimate material or organic being—redefining, through daily practices (talking, petting, regarding, acting) what 'being' encompasses—is simultaneously a prerequisite and a product of befriending data, a practice of becoming other. As an everyday life practice it is not magical or transcendental, rather a set of concrete deliberative acts which seem to take on a life of their own. Talking out loud to inanimate things, naming things, observing movement, intensities, intentions and processes in the surrounding nonhuman world—in a word anthropomorphising—is a habit we can either cultivate or repress. So called 'western' academics, heirs of Enlightenment, we have however been trained to foreground reason (as have many colonised others) (Pedersen, 2010; Snaza et al., 2014) and so de-/retraining ourselves is an intentional endeavour.

The relevant skill of a researcher, in producing data, is then the skill of getting attached, of being able to befriend others through mutual curiosity and affect. The 'unit of analysis' is the interdependency between the elements studied (Pickering, 2005)—e.g., snow and human—rather than either of the beings prior to their attachment. Andrew Pickering (2005) posits posthumanism in the interface of natural sciences and social sciences between which there is a neat labor division: natural sciences focus on things, social sciences on people/

meanings. Pickering argues that this dualism produces two sets of units of analysis, either objects or subjects but not both—save their interaction perhaps. What is left out is the interdependence between objects and subjects. A unit of analysis which is not about objects/things/matter *or* people/meanings but the heterogeneous assemblage comprising both, the "dance of human and nonhuman agency" (Pickering, 1995).

The study of interdependencies between our researcher-human selves and the other humans, nonhuman beings and things, events, ideas and materials cannot but change us. A new politics becomes possible; one that emerges from realising the limits of humanist versions of democracy—the political implications of the very category of 'human'—and the possibility of "political forms that are not narrowly restricted to humans" (Snaza et al., 2014, p. 49) and their possessed interests.

In the wake of growing up, my encounters with snow became more frequent and longstanding. I was learning to listen and hear as only human will and ability to listen can enable access to a wisdom of other-than-human world (Barrett in Harvey, 2014). Once my grandfather and I were coming back from a party. It was a dark wintery evening with a navy blue star-spangled sky, huge moon and lots of snow piles around, winking at me with their glints. Stillness of the moment was only interrupted by us crunching across the white sea of snow. And then I had asked my grandfather to stop and stay for while in this instant of time. We stopped and I was listening and breathing, and looking at the glimmer. Back then, what did I think about? What kind of thoughts bothered me? That immediate event was so powerful and stuck in my memory as a moment of absolute tranquility, harmony, estimated not in minutes, degrees or kilocycles per second, but in a quality of knowledge I was receiving from snow and stars.

By applying a special vocabulary, I was decolonising myself and my relations with a nonhuman person represented by snow (Barrett in Harvey, 2014). I do not think I was realising at the time that snow possessed consciousness and communicated to me something, including that feeling of peace. Instead, I was on my way to defining snow as a sentient being and my life as an attempt to live in a world as if "the world is a community of living persons, all of different species" (Harvey, 2014, p. 5).

LOVE

We are professionally socialised into not showing affection, let alone feelings or expressions of love in our research practices (Laura, 2013). Love can very well be the object of research but lo and behold if we as researchers should feel it or capitalise on it in research. Helena Pedersen (2010) has done extensive ethnographies in veterinary schools, exploring how the governance of emotions and move from attachment to detachment is equalled with becoming a professional. And how pedagogies of detachment are internalised by the veterinary students as they take on and explore their new profession.

The fact that I have been trained to avoid love and attachment in my research, as well as the cultural models I've learnt for who/what are appropriate subjects and objects of affection, have inhibited me from realising the ways in which an inanimate element such as snow work as ontological friends. Befriending snow as data and a research ally is reschooling yourself to be able to get attached and to work with affects in research. Getting attached to cold and wet snow ("Ewww!"), to falling snow ("Aww!"), to icy hard snow ("Ouch!") or to snow melting inside your boots making your socks damp and feet miserable ("Seriously?") is work: conscious, serious, affective and far from objective work. Treating snow as a person requires you to pay respect and attention to it in its various forms and ways to engage with you. Falling snow makes for data that covers and highlights, melting snow makes for data that immerses, flushes away and washes off, freezing snow makes for serendipitously forming data, snowflakes are near mathematical perfection and make for data which is simultaneously unique (at the micro level each flake is different) and engulfingly universal (at the macro level vast blankets of white snow can even cause snow blindness).

Being in love with snow is nothing less, but an ability *to give* among the rest. Philosophical underpinnings of new/contemporary animism never limit their definition of animism to some concrete practices as those vary from one human—nonhuman community to another. However, an ability to respect, give, and give with respect is attributed to the entire animist philosophy depending, though, on the level of relational personhood and degree of localness (Naveh & Bird-David in Harvey, 2014). Naveh and Bird-David define this giving as an 'offering' during which humans can give back energies in acknowledgement of friendship, companionship and engagement for the purpose of being and doing otherwise.

Crystal Laura (2013) paints a scene of future qualitative inquiry where love would be added to the compendium of most utilised approaches. For her, love-based scholarship has real consequences for all involved, researcher included, and not just for imagined 'others' out there. Acknowledging snow—or any other non-human element—as a research ally makes possible interruptions to anthropocentric and solidified research practices that Maggie MacLure (2010, p. 730) suggests we seek. By welcoming serendipity, unpredictability and a tolerable amount of mess contributed by nonhuman research allies we can get as if beyond our human selves, if never entirely. We can let these interruptions highlight the otherwise invisible interdependencies between elements comprising seemingly simple events (Pickering, 2005; Rautio et al., *forthcoming*).

LONG TERM (RESEARCH) COMPANIONSHIP

Being accustomed to working with snow as an ontological partner is relating to his peculiar ontology with a sympathetic interest. Generating and cultivating a taste and a sense of affection towards how snow is. Essentially impermanent and transient, yet a multimodal materialisation of the neverending hydrological cycle of life, snow offers a thinking partner particularly suited to studying of mattering—of seemingly trivial things that matter intensely to all involved, yet often without clear reasons or meanings (e.g., Rautio, 2013; Rautio & Jokinen, 2015).

Snow has a role in developing a particular aesthetic sensitivity—a keen and refined interest—towards the impermanent and the evanescent. Phenomena such as rain, snow, dew and wind eloquently express transience and impermanence, making us become aware that humans and nature exist ultimately by the same principle (Saito, 2005, p. 171). Yuriko Saito describes a Japanese tea ceremony as a unique, one-time only event, due to it being constituted by various transient and serendipitous factors. Snow is one of the most central of the serendipitous participants in the ceremony. Sometimes snowfall would be an entire cause for impromptu tea ceremonies as it lended singularity and poignancy to the event (Saito, 2005, p. 171). Saito translates and quotes a twelfth century poem by Empress Guno Daibu Toshinari:

Thinking that

Perhaps today you might come and visit,

I gaze at the garden—

Trackless snow. (p. 167)

The appeal of snow here is due to its power to heighten the felt loneliness, to its ability to make material the presence or absence of the other. The sense of melancholy becomes an object of aesthetic contemplation through the contribution of snow (Saito, 2005, p. 167). This is the sense in which snow functions as an ontological research partner: thinking with it, being of a certain kind in relation to it, yields access to being, thinking and feeling in certain ways. With snow children's relations to the more-than-human world, to name a particular example, are explored beyond the developmental framework of the autonomous individual child agent. Responding to the calls for de-individualisation made within recent early childhood advances; in the words of Taylor, Blaise, and Giugni (2013, p. 81):

For us, the notion of the autonomous individual child perpetuated by child development theory is not only an illusion, it is also a grossly inadequate conceptual framework for responding to the challenges of growing up in an increasingly complex, mixed-up, boundary blurring, heterogeneous, interdependent and ethically confronting world.

Weather, snow in particular, is something we humans still have not figured out how to control and manipulate, yet we work with it endlessly—perhaps because of its own serendipitous agency. The unpredictable participation and friendship of snow is most often appreciated within arts proper. Andy Goldsworthy's snowball pieces are a delicate exploration of the ontological similarities various human and nonhuman elements share of physical existence in time: "Each snowball is an expression of the time it was made" (Goldsworthy, 2015). However, in research, even qualitative research, serendipitous agency of nonhuman research partners is only beginning to be taken seriously (see Banerjee & Blaise, 2013, on research with air).

Before writing about snow, I actually went outside and asked him what I shall write about. It took couple of seconds preceding the emerging scent of the Gulf of Siam waters off the coast of which I used to live. Immediately I thought that I lived near different bodies of water but somehow only South China Sea reached me then. I felt myself as if I were a big organic sponge that absorbs the sea scents, sounds and the albedo of the fresh snow. It was quite explicitly that snow has an ability to move people through time and space, emerge them in the immediate but deep and compelling moment of truth happening in the present. Articulating in animist terms, that moment can be interpreted as me being focused on our joint selves with snow and our mutual influence of each other. "This epistemology generates knowledge which inheres in, grows from and supports social engagement" (Naveh & Bird-David in Harvey, 2014, p. 31). Simultaneously, this sociomaterial assemblage is to further develop, move, flow, change, being explored and each time give birth to a unique splash of relational knowledge of immediate being.

It is often considered that befriending nonhumans is nothing more than a stand-in for human relations. Likewise, we can get emotionally attached to inanimate things such as one's car and it is nothing unusual. Calling a car a friend, however, instantly raises the question of whether this is so in lack of 'real' friends, that is: humans. In this paper, we have argued that to befriend a nonhuman is not only possible and life-enriching on a daily basis but also worthwhile in research. Befriending anything or anyone is treating them as a person: striving for kinship, sensorial distribution and exchange of information with them.

If data is considered a companion, a personified companion even, we argue that more emotions, affects and complexity is added to research practices. Imagine how we are with other persons whom we consider our friends. We rarely (want to) view persons as mechanistic, one-sided, straightforward, predictable or independent of history. We can argue with friends, disagree with them, deceive them, praise them, stroke and cuddle with them. Leave them. Come back. Think about them while gone. Then think about what friends do to us. They make us see ourselves through their eyes. They comfort, annoy, remind, keep us on our toes but also relax us. We want to spend time together because of the productive differences between who we are. Is this not something a post-qualitative scholar would want her relationship with data to be like?

Furthermore, there are things in the world which cannot become data if we consider data as a research companion, a friend. Rather than problematic this breaks down the illusion that anyone could study anything. The limits that companionship and friendship—our ability to get attached—set to what can count as data are crucially indicative of the themes and foci of studies that we are at ease with and those we wish to avoid—or those that avoid us. It is of political worth to be able to tap into the blind spots in not only one's own scholarship but collectively as well. Are there topics and modes of data that researchers in certain disciplines find hard to befriend? If so, why?

REFERENCES

Ahola, J. (2013, December 2). Desire paths. Retrieved from https://medium.com/@jussiahola/desire-paths-2b6b5b0f0e92#.sliowucou

Banerjee, B., & Blaise, M. (2013). There's something in the air: Becoming-with research practices. *Cultural Studies <=> Critical Methodologies, 13*(4), 240–245.

Braidotti, R. (2013). *The Posthuman.* Cambridge: Polity Press.

Goldsworthy, A. (2015). *Ephemeral works: 2004–2014.* New York, NY: Harry N. Abrams.

Harvey, G. (Ed.) (2014). *The handbook of contemporary animism.* Routledge Ltd—M.U.A.

Laura, C. T. (2013). Intimate inquiry: Love as "data" in qualitative research. *Cultural Studies <=> Critical Methodologies, 13*(4), 289–292.

MacLure, M. (2010). The offence of theory. *Journal of Education Policy, 25*(2), 277–286.

Pedersen, H. (2010). Is 'the posthuman' educable? On the convergence of educational philosophy, animal studies and posthumanist theory. *Discourse: Studies in the cultural politics of education, 31*(2), 237–250.

Pickering, A. (1995). *The mangle of practice: Time, agency, and science.* Chicago: University of Chicago Press.

Pickering, A. (2005). Asian eels and global warming: A posthumanist perspective on society and the environment. *Ethics & The Environment, 10*(2), 29–43.

Rautio, P. (2010). *Writing about everyday beauty in a northern village. An argument for diversity of habitable places* [Doctoral dissertation]. Oulu: Acta Universitatis Ouluensis (E 109).

Rautio, P. (2013). Children who carry stones in their pockets: On autotelic material practices in everyday life. *Children's Geographies, 11*(4), 394–408.

Rautio, P. (2014). Mingling and imitating in producing spaces for knowing and being: Insights from a Finnish study of child–matter intra-action. *Childhood, 21*(4), 461–474.

Rautio, P., & Jokinen, P. (2015). Children and snow piles: Children's relations to the more-than-human world beyond developmental views. In J. Horton & B. Evans (Eds.), *Play, recreation, health and well being,* Vol. 9 of T. Skelton (Ed.), *Geographies of children and young people.* Singapore: Springer Singapore.

Rautio, P., Hohti, R., Leinonen, R-L., & Tammi, T. (forthcoming). Shitgulls and Shops are Nature—Urban child-nature reconfigurations. *Environmental Education Research.*

Rudy, C. (2013). If we could talk to the animals. On changing the (post) human subject. In M. De Mello (Ed.), *Speaking for Animals: Animal autobiographical writing*. London: Routledge.

Saito, Y. (2005). "The Aesthetics of Weather". In A. Light & J. M. Smith (Eds.), *The aesthetics of everyday life* (pp. 156–76). New York, NY: Columbia University Press.

Snaza, N., Applebaum, P., Bayne, S., Carlson, D., Morris, M., Rotas, N., ... Weaver, J. (2014). Toward a posthumanist education. *Journal of Curriculum Theorizing, 30*(2), 39–55.

Taylor, A., Blaise, M., & Giugni, M. (2013). Haraway's 'bag lady story-telling': Relocating childhood and learning within a 'post-human landscape'. *Discourse: Studies in the Cultural Politics of Education, 34*(1), 48–62.

CHAPTER THREE

(Becoming-with) Water as Data

MARGARET SOMERVILLE

ABSTRACT

I begin with water. What if I considered water as data and human subjects as only coming into being in relation to water? How does water produce the human and what does a reading of data as water produce? In considering the possibilities of water as data, I become aware that my research activities have generated a large body of work oriented towards water as onto-epistemological force. Adapting the method of anarchiving, I extract moments of water becoming data from four previous research project publications which moving between contemporary Australian Aboriginal and Western new materialist frameworks. The segments extracted from these books form the archive. The anarchive, or new creation, is produced with the addition of a complementary piece of water data from recent writing, resulting in a conversation between Then and Now. The chapter is structured in the form of these four anarchives, each with brief analytical notes. It concludes with a consideration of the ontological, epistemological and methodological implications of becoming-with water as data.

Keywords: Water, onto-epistemological force, anarchiving method

INTRODUCTION

Beginning with water.

Rain brings small girl to ponds and water soon alive with wriggle of tadpoles. Peer into brown dank smelling water for stirring of mud as small black bodies wriggle at edge of spiky reeds. Tadpole pool is a whole world. Glutinous eggs stick in clumps to reeds and grass, tiny black spot in each one turns into baby tadpole. Excited anticipation over days of looking. Front legs then back legs, black fishy body turns stripy brown and green. Frog jumps out of its watery world.

The small girl started her life suspended in a watery world. She once had remnant gills, genetic traces of her amphibian ancestry. How did water continue to shape her world and how did it shape the small girl's growing into the air dwelling creature she became? In some senses she continues to inhabit water, having spent all her academic life studying watery topics. Not intentionally, almost by accident. What if she considered water as data and human subjects as only coming into being in relation to water? How does water produce the human and what does a reading of water as data produce?

This chapter considers how we become-with bodies of water as data by drawing on this lifetime of research with water. Adapting the method of anarchiving used by artists (Springgay, 2014), I extract moments of water-becoming-data from four previous research project publications: *Place, pedagogy, change* (2007), *Singing the Coast* (2010), *Water in a dry land* (2013), and *Children, place and sustainability* (2015). The segments extracted from these previous research projects (*Then*) did not necessarily focus on water as data but water stories are present. These extracted segments form the archive. The anarchive, or new creation (*Now*), is produced with the addition of a complementary piece of water data from recent writing where the water itself shapes the response. This water sounds, feels, smells, moves, floods, offers habitat, has power, gathers up all in its force. It may have been recorded in the form of embodied sensory response, memory, affect, curiosity, small videos, or still photographs. Ultimately, however, in a written chapter, there is a necessary movement from sensory water to writing. How this takes place and what it means to consider becoming-with water as data in research is the focus of the chapter.

The paper is structured in the form of four anarchives, each followed by a summary of the implications of re-thinking data from the perspective of water and its ontological and epistemological implications.

Anarchive 1# Becoming-frog (2007 in Place, pedagogy, change, 2011)

Anarchive 2# Crying-songs to remember (Singing the coast, 2010)

Anarchive 3# A literature review of water (Water in a Dry Land, 2013)

Anarchive 4# Emergent literacies (Children, place sustainability, 2015)

ANARCHIVE 1#
THEN: BECOMING-FROG (2007)

Wetlands as Bodies of Water

It's just on dusk, mid Autumn a half full moon and cool wind blows over Wetlands, freeway humming in front and Hazelwood Power Station behind. Partly natural, partly artificial, original river is somewhere nearby. Here in the wetlands frog chorus begins. Frogs' skin is permeable membrane between inside and out, frogs are a good measure of a watery place. Last month, because of drought, snakes hide in giant open cracks, no Community Frog Watch. Tonight, after recent rains, make our way through frog calls along softening cracked edges of water, under a rising moon. Kids record frog calls, whistling tree frog, common froglet, and on the ground read telltale signs of fox, wallaby and kangaroo.

Becomings

There are two key Deleuzean inspired ideas that I want to take up in this analysis— 'becomings' and 'assemblages'. Becomings focuses on the body-in-process, a dynamic conception of the body that includes "the transformations and becomings it undergoes, and the machinic connections it forms with other bodies, what it can link with" (Grosz, 1994, p. 165). It is a body that is itself dynamically constituted as part of other bodies, human and non-human, animate and inanimate. I find this particularly useful when thinking of the human body's relationship with landscapes, weather, rocks and mountains, as well as other non-human animate beings.

Subject and object are a series of flows, energies, movements, strata, segments, organs, intensities—fragments capable of being linked together or severed in potentially infinite ways other than those which congeal them into identities. Production consists of those processes which create linkages between fragments, fragments of bodies and fragments of objects. Assemblages or machines are heterogeneous, disparate, discontinuous alignments or linkages brought together in conjunctions (Grosz, 1994, p. 167).

Website

I navigate this populated and complex site along pathways of desire. I listen to the calls of many different frogs and match their calls with a photo and common and scientific names. My greatest excitement, however, is when I find the photos and audio-recordings that I witnessed on that night when we visited and watched the children playfully using their Pentax Optio digital cameras and taking photos and audio recordings of the place. The photos are here now: Dragon fly, Yabby hole,

Kangaroo prints, Kangaroo scats, Brown tree frog, and Common froglet. Yes, we were here. Then there is the sound of Kylie's recording:

Quarter to seven pm
29th of March 2007
Morwell River Wetlands
A half moon
getting bigger
it's pretty dark,
about to record
some frogs.

And then the sound of frogs.

ANARCHIVE 1#
NOW: THE EYE OF THE FISH (MARCH–APRIL 2016)

Clambering awkward narrow
shady
escape hot sun
find
tiny flat space
perched
bags clothes shoes watch glasses
body launch into
cool silky water
lightness
swim like a fish
up and down around and over
rocky ledge big logs
in watery titree coloured world.
Sally cannot enter
Return looking for fish
sit immersed
rocks water logs sand silty edge of pool
white feet lost in dark sludge
still
tiny fish come to inhabit
new white object
dart in and out
movement only at first
lit golden in late light of day
sunlight almost gone
last rays of sun
penetrate

boulders and rocks
long time peers into sandy bottom
finally launches twists and turns
body onto back
feet held tightly upwards
toes braced
cruises upside down beetle
talking between breaths
tiny girl once caught a Fish
Fish's eye looked into mine
threw rod line hook fish back into lake
can never enter
fish's watery worlds
for fear of
eye of the Fish.
then
different shapes colours sizes speed style
flickering in and out
of being
as light fades and darkness
shrouds
deep watery gorge.
Searching but find only
surprise of water
in swirling water's flow
leaf litter rocks pebbles
could be tiny fish
all is flickering movement in

deep into watery gorge
flickering golden patterns of moving
ripples

water's play of light and shadow
transfixed by water
as if water's eye itself looks into mine.

The data that informed Anarchive #1 *Then* continues my interest in the merging of frog and child identity. Water is essential for the shared life of frog and child in these stories and becoming-frog is understood through water-frog-child assemblage where: 'Subject and object are a series of flows, energies, movements, strata, segments, organs, intensities'. Water intensities evoke our other-than-human entangled becomings. In conversation I have counterposed Anarchive 1 *Now*, a recent piece of water-as-data, written in response to walking methodology fieldwork. Unexpectedly it was the watery world of swimming and fish that took over the experience. Sally's 'eye of the fish' continued to haunt me, until I returned and a search for the elusive fish became a search in and of water. Water claims its space and is present as an onto-epistemological force that produces data as much as it produces the humans who inhabit this story.

ANARCHIVE 2#
THEN: CRYING-SONGS TO REMEMBER (SOMERVILLE & PERKINS, 2010)

Massacre

Dawn light hazy walk through moist she-oaks with dewdrop needles in shadow of sand dunes. On top of dune single golden flower catches first rays of sun. Walk with slight shiver from river to little beach, quieter and protected in curve of headland. At river's mouth red rock shocks my senses, lit blood red in pink light of dawn. Float in shallow waves and contemplate the stories of this place. 'Blood Rock', they once called it.

M'grandmother was tellin' me
about the time
her mother was lookin' after a baby
between Blackadder Creek and Cassons Creek,
she said these policemen
come along on horses
all the men were there
and the women
they were washin' an' that sort of thing
and she said
they shot the men there.
Then they chased them

down through to Red Rock
the men was swimmin' across the river
and up here where they started
and down there
the water was red
just red
with the blood
where they shot 'em.
She grabbed the baby
and the women hid
in the rushes on the creek banks.
She told me that was the worst thing
she ever seen
they just came along
and started shootin'. (Tony Perkins in Singing the Coast, 2010)

… the quiet landscape has only two very gentle sounds, shallow running river over smooth river rocks … less than a gurgle … something like the resonance of your own circulatory system.[1]

I tell the story with the desire to make language, time and place stutter through it and I turn to the senses to try and keep us there within that moment where a body thought agonises. I hope that such stories change our worlds.[2]

ANARCHIVE #2
NOW: DAPHNE'S CRYING SONGS TO REMEMBER (2016)

It's a special story, because I had tears. Very rarely I have tears. Yeah.

Well they rang, the elders and they went Daph we need you, gotta come out to Pilliga where they're protesting. I said I got no money, no petrol and they went oh we know someone might be coming out. So they ring Michael and organise it and next minute Michael rings to pick me up and turn up at home and took me half an hour to get ready. We went to three sites to see with our own eyes the destruction and devastation and poisoning the land, poisoning the water. That's why I went to see with me own eyes. So anyway we get out to Pilliga and when we got back from the gate, at the gate where the fence was, big fence, it's all fenced off and one of the waste water dams busted and it ran through the Pilliga Forest like a river and nothing grows there no more and me, and [the elders] we just felt like crying. We had tears crying for the land and mother earth. It's really hard to explain. It's just really upsetting to see, it really hurts and like elders always say they cut mother earth they're cutting us.

Yeah well two weeks before I did the background [looking at Daphne's painting] at the workshop in Tamworth and then I went protesting overnight and then I'm looking at what I did in Tamworth and I went oh that's where that poison, the dam had busted and spilt with all this poison and nothing grows there no more. Three of us were crying. Well they're a serpent, one serpent with two heads. The story goes like, and in this picture it representing the underground water but they split, one was good and one was bad. They split from the head and they went their own ways. That's Clarity. She'd been sitting in a tree camping out in the tree. That's big foot. Yowie. So that's him there, that's his country. This tree itself, like the actual tree. I think when we were kid they used to call it Bunya tree. It's name. The law is we're not allowed to be there especially after dark. Even with Mum and Dad we never stayed in the Pilliga at dark time. We travelled through day time but not night time. We used pull up at Pilliga bore and have a swim. I just can't get over that nothing grows there, and that's bigger than that when you're actual there at that place, it's shocking. Three of us, we had tears and we wanted to cry and biggest mob was there and yeah, we just felt like having a good ole cry (Interview, Daphne Wallace, May, 2016).

Anarchive #2 *Then* formed from a body memory of the gurgle of shallow running water describing the scene of another massacre site. It is about how water holds memory and how the sound of the water tells a story that cannot be fully told. It is informed by theorising the intercultural space of the contact zone with Gumbaynggirr co-researcher and author Tony Perkins (Somerville & Perkins, 2010). Taking this piece and counterposing with an extract from a conversation with Gamaroi artist and collaborator, Daphne Wallace, produces new insights into the way that water flows through these stories, carrying their trauma but ultimately transforming that trauma into creative outflowings of writing and painting, telling and listening. It is about the power of water, its sound, and flow, the fact that it lives before and beyond the death of any individual human. Water generates both the tears and the powerful libidinal forces that reside in the rainbow serpent's creative powers.

ANARCHIVE 3#
THEN: A LITERATURE REVIEW OF WATER (SOMERVILLE, 2013)

Curtains of fluted and ruffled rock surfaces lead in towards deep internal space. Outside this inner core, layers and layers of rock surfaces face in all directions. On every layer groups of human and animal figures, all dancing, painted in white ochre that shines from the darkness. Only one is deep red ochre, a clever man with a boomerang in one hand; his other arm, long and extended, ends in an emu foot. On another surface, in a row of dancing male figures and an emu, a single female figure gives birth. Further in, the pattern of the fish traps with a white ochre cod swimming towards them. As eyes get used to the dim light, deep inside a lower surface, a group of figures shine white on a background of red ochre near the white shape of the Narran Lake. These are differently shaped dancers, the white more intense in the darkness. All water places mapped on these rocky surfaces.

Knowledge of Country and of water is passed on in stories told in oral traditions by older family members, in the signs and symbols of creation stories read in the landscape, and from the landforms of country itself. Together these constitute the body of literature that is read as the knowledge of water in Country. A literature review of water, in this sense, is a (re)view of Country. How, then, does this kind of knowing intersect with knowledge passed on through the written word?

I remember the marks the water makes on the rocks in Booralong Creek as the level rises and falls with seasons and rains and water's flow and think they are like the qualities of water marked in words.

Watermark I: Water as Flow

'[Water] is always on the move, flowing, conforming to the shape of its environment'.

Water constantly moves, shaping the contours of the land and the nature of knowledge. Water flows, that is its phenomenological nature. Water as both a literal entity and a metaphysical phenomenon flows across countries, cultures, boundaries, binaries, disciplines and genres, enabling the possibility of literal and metaphysical connections between them.

Watermark II: Water as Omnipresence

As the substance that is literally essential to all living organisms, water is experienced and embodied both physically and culturally. The meanings encoded in water are not imposed from a distance, but emerge from an intimate interaction involving ingestion and expulsion, contact and immersion. Water moves in and through Country and the bodies of all the living creatures that make up Country. Water, in this quality of omnipresence, can transform our understanding of place-based knowledge.

Watermark III: Water as Transmutable

Water is characterised [by] evaporating and precipitating ... it can transform from ice to fluid, to steam and back again. It can be entirely invisible and transparent, or impenetrable and reflective. It shimmers with light and movement. Through ritual the transforming qualities of water are incorporated into practice. Rituals of life and death involving water, such as baptism, initiation, and the cleansing and preparation of the body in death, are about transformation from one state of being into another.

ANARCHIVE 3#
NOW: WATERMARKS BOORLONG CREEK MARCH 31, 2016

Return to Booralong creek 31 March 1 pm

Arriving
shiny bright-orange rose hips
on sparse prickly branches
rose hip jelly taste of sweet smell
clamber through barbed wire fence
full picnic bag
walk along animal track
beside rocky creek
strong smell of eucalypt leaves
soft and wet underfoot
from yesterdays rain.
Another
Stop at soft green grass
under deep shade of tall casuarinas
where rocky creek
meets wide sandy river bedcircle of river stones
is water-made fireplace
lit with casuarina needles as
flickering orange-red flames leap
shift direction
with slightest breeze
luminous sensitive quivering
and shimmering water reflections
that change moment by moment
with shifting sun cloud and

sweetest smell
ragged fallen down fence
squatters country
living by water
centuries old quince plum pear fig
bare lichen-covered woody branches
no fruit here now
lush green grape vine
curtains ricketty iron shed
drapes massive old pine tree
and winds
its way towards rocky creek bed.
against hard grey surface
of water's rock and stone.
Water makes its mark
on massive round rocks
line upon line of white
and dark grey striations
tracing long gone deep water
across rows of curved rock surface
timeless and still yet
overlaid by ever-moving shadows cast
from creek's fallen timber
light movement of air
against stillness of rock and stone

Anarchive #3 *Then* begins with a map of water places on the walls of a teaching cave and explores the nature of knowledge that is oral, ephemeral, visual and on Country. It is informed by the intercultural onto-epistembology of thinking through Country developed with U'Alayi researcher Immiboagurramilbun (Chrissiejoy Marsall in Somerville, 2013). The question is asked what might a

Figure 3.1: Stillness of water's marks with ever-moving shadows.
Source: Author.

literature (re)view of water look like? This possibility is explored through connecting anthropological literature about water as water's marks in words on pages with the marks that water makes on rocks in waterways. Anarchive 2 *Now* is created by the irrepressible urge to return to the creek of remembered watermarks. It is shaped within new materialist and post-qualitative approaches to research. The meaning of the piece resides in the nostalgic embodied memories of this water place, with its immediate sensorial pleasures of scent of sweet rosehips, feel of grainy texture of rock, multiple sensory stimulations of fire, and play of shadow and shimmer in the temporal complexity of water's marks on rock.

ANARCHIVE 4#
THEN: EMERGENT LITERACIES (CHILDREN, PLACE SUSTAINABILITY, 2015)

(Water gurgling, birds twittering
child singing high bird-like sounds
child walks into water with fine stick balancing on stones
flicking stick at water and at stones
wobbles back to stones on island, humming

sings) that's a daddy(low sing song voice, lifting a rock),
that's a daddy, that's a daddy, that's a bigger daddy (patting a rock each time)
that's a little baby (picking up a small pebble), that's a little baby
got babies cousins dadda (arms wide open in expansive gesture
walks away lifts hands to sky, loud sound to sky
comes back to rock pile singing)
a-gugu a-gugu a-gugu (sing-song to birds trilling)
you're a baby (to me), and I'm a mama
kangaroo
I'm a mama kangaroo, you're a baby kangaroo
that's my fire (loudly, pointing to rocks)
that's my fire, baby kangaroo
that's my fire, baby kangaroo
that's my fire, baby kangaroo.

Initially my ear heard only meaningful human word sounds when I transcribed this video. When I forced myself to transcribe all of the sounds as well
as the words I realised that the sounds and words were formed together and they
were all very sing-song. There was no separation of sounds of birds and water and
soundings of the child. Place was singing to the child and child was singing to the
place. She was also simultaneously playing with rocks and water, telling a story
about rocks, talking to the sky, opening out her arms and hands and calling out
loudly, just to the sky, just to call to the world. When I came to really listen, alongside 'a-gugu a-gugu a-gugu' I could hear a bird trilling in unison, the two songs
coming together. I recognised them both as just a small incidental song, with no
other meaning than sounding the place. But this meaning all of a sudden appeared
transformative. What if we imagined all of language as derived from these intimate embodied relations with our local places? How does water produce language?

ANARCHIVE 4#
NOW: SOUND OF GURGLING WATER

Water gurgles
bell birds tinkle
tiny wrens twitter
distant crow caws
young blue heron lifts
fine delicate legs
walking back and forth across
smooth river rocks
dip and lift dip and lift
long fine neck into water and

up again to air
gurgling water continues
on and on and on
until eternity

> the sound of the shallow running river over smooth river rocks ... less than a gurgle, ... something like the resonance of your own circulatory system. Although there is no beat of the heart there is a deep pitched murmur that is already within you.[3]

Finally, in Anarchive 4# *Then*, water playing with child and child playing with water as data is recorded in a short video. Transcribing this video is following water's relation, always in relation, water, stones, child, birds, talk, song, simultaneously come into being through the agential cut of their mutual play (Barad, 2007). The research underpinning this piece was intentionally designed according to the concept of intra-action, the outcomes reinforcing the idea that 'the material and the discursive are mutually implicated in the dynamics of intra-activity' (Barad, 2007, p. 152). Water produces this data as much as the video and its researcher. The memory of gurgling water takes me back to the place in the river of my everyday walk, the place where the shallow water runs over smooth rocks. The sound itself recalled by and recalling Katrina Schlunke's writing with its sensory resonance of the gurgling of water, like the sound of our body's circulatory system, both inside and outside of us, always already there.

SUMMARY NOTES

This chapter has taken up the challenge to re-think old data, and to create new live data, using the method of Anarchiving (Springgay, 2014). In particular, it focuses on re-thinking water as data through a lifetime of academic research connected with water. Water was not previously thought of as data, but was present as an onto-epistemological force in all of this research. Anarchiving enables the selection of segments of water-as-data from four previous research publications, selected on the basis of water memory to form Anarchive *Then*. These small segments are extracted from the whole and paired against new writing of water as data to produce Anarchive *Now*. Together, these pairs form a single piece that re-thinks water as data through considering its ontological, epistemological and methodological implications. It is understood throughout that the necessary translation from matter to thought/words, from embodied experience to writing, is fundamental to re-thinking water as data and data as water.

The chapter is set within the necessity to decentre the human for the new epoch of the Anthropocene in recognition of human entanglement in the fate of the planet. The intention is not to erase human presence, nor to offer a story of heroic human rescue, but to take up the challenge of exploring new concepts of the human and new modes of thought. The concept of data in qualitative research has important implications for this endeavour because of the everpresent tendency to reinstate Western enlightenment ontologies and epistemologies of the rational, autonomous, individualised and self directing human being (Lather & St Pierre, 2013). For this reason, the Anarchives offer a range of different theories and theorists from Deleuze's becoming-animal, Barad's intra-action as entanglement, and U'Alayi researcher Immiboagurramilbun's 'thinking through Country' as ways to think data differently. Bringing together Australian Aboriginal and Western new materialist onto-epistemologies acknowledges the nature/cultures that have always existed in indigenous knowledge frameworks, but the necessity of Western researchers to find languages and practices that enact our own ethical responsibilities to the more-than-human worlds (Taylor, 2013; Whitehouse, 2011).

In the more practical sense of method, this exploration of water as data, and data as water, has led to an ongoing project that flows with the ever mobile qualities of water-in-the-world. Water sounds, feels, smells, moves, floods, offers habitat, has power, gathers up all in its force. Water as data reconfigures what we understand as matter, it is always in relation, gathering up everything in its onto-epistemological force, including the human subject. It may be recorded as data by humans in the form of embodied sensory responses, memory, affect, curiosity, small videos, or still photographs but it is always in excess of these, always already there and continuing on long after any of us, a powerful reminder of the transience of human life.

NOTES

1. Schlunke (2003b).
2. I borrow these words from Schlunke (2003a, p. 2) Myall Creek: Dumb Places, a presentation at Writing Events: New Writing in Cultural Studies, UTS Sydney, as a dramatic refrain throughout this chapter.
3. Schlunke (2003b).

REFERENCES

Barad, K. (2007). *Meeting the universe halfway: Quantum physics and the entanglement of matter and meaning*. Durham, NC: Duke University Press.

Grosz, E. (1994). *Volatile Bodies: Toward a corporeal feminism*. Bloomington, IN: Indiana University Press.

Lather, P., & St. Pierre, E. A. (2013). Post-qualitative research. *International Journal of Qualitative Studies in Education, 26*(6), 629–633.

Schlunke, K. (2003a). Dumb places. *Balayi: Culture, Law and Colonialism, 6*, 72–81.

Schlunke, K. (2003b) 'Myall Creek: Dumb places', a presentation. *Writing events: New writing in cultural studies*, UTS Sydney.

Somerville, M. (2013). *Water in a dry land: Place-learning through art and story.* Innovative Ethnography Series. London and New York, NY: Routledge.

Somerville, M., & Green, M. (2015). *Children, place and sustainability.* London: Palgrave Macmillan.

Somerville, M., & Perkins, T. (2010). *Singing the Coast: Place and identity in Australia.* Canberra, ACT: Aboriginal Studies Press.

Somerville, M., Davies, B., Power, K., Gannon, S., & de Carteret, P. (2011). *Place pedagogy change.* The Netherlands: Sense Publishing.

Springgay, S. (2014). *Anarchiving: Propositions in movement for qualitative research. Paper presentation.* Brisbane: Annual Association for Research in Education.

Taylor, A. (2013). Caterpillar childhoods: Engaging the otherwise worlds of central Australian aboriginal children. *Global Studies of Childhood, 3*(4), 366–379.

Whitehouse, H. (2011). Talking up country: Language, natureculture and interculture in Australian environmental education research. *Australian Journal of Environmental Education, 27*(1), 56–67.

CHAPTER FOUR

Data Provocations

Disappointing, Failing, Malfunctioning

BIDISHA BANERJEE AND MINDY BLAISE

ABSTRACT

Responding to recent calls for the invention of research approaches that move away from traditional humanist notions of research to more situated, performative, and material ways of enacting research, this chapter foregrounds the authors' performative surveillance data practices and shows how disappointing, failing, or malfunctioning data productively helps them to reconsider the notion of 'inadequate' data that might open up new directions for methodology and qualitative research practices. Using a wearable camera called the *Autographer* as a sur/sousveilling device, Banerjee and Blaise attempt to generate data by walking through a popular shopping district in Hong Kong, hoping to capture 'nativist' attitudes of resentment toward mainland (Chinese) shoppers, thereby enabling the authors to comment on the peculiar nature of postcoloniality in Hong Kong. They show what is possible when surrendering to being out-of-control and resisting the researcher impulse to give life and meaning to data, yields new insights into the paradoxical productiveness of disappointing, failing, and malfunctioning data.

Keywords: disappointing data, malfunctioning data, failing data, performative research practices, surveillance, sousveillance

INTRODUCTION

Critical social science researchers have been raising important questions regarding the future of qualitative research. Some scholars have been questioning the very idea of research and of method. Many of these queries are coming from non-representational theory (Thrift, 2008) which is a turn away from cognition, symbolic meaning, and textuality in order to "… better cope with our more-than-human, more-than-textual, and multisensual worlds" (Lorimer, 2005, p. 83). Within this discourse, there is a call for the invention of research approaches that move away from traditional humanist notions of research to more situated, performative, and material ways of enacting research. These shifts have also changed typical conceputalizations of knowledge, thought, and being. As a result, more diverse and dynamic understandings of 'data' have emerged (see Koro-Ljungberg & MacLure, 2013; Koro-Ljungberg, MacLure, & Ulmer, forthcoming). In this chapter, we foreground our performative surveillance data practices and show how disappointing, failing, or malfunctioning data productively helps us to reconsider the notion of 'inadequate' data that might open up new directions for methodology and qualitative research practices.

Building on the work of Nigel Thrift's (2008) non-representational theory, Phillip Vannini (2015) advocates for non-representational methodologies that attend to events, relations, practices, affects, and backgrounds of everyday life. Since there is not a singular non-representational theory, defining and attempting to pin-down what non-representational methodologies might be is difficult, if not impossible. Instead, there is a *style* to enacting this kind of research and it can take many forms. A core principle of non-representational theory is that it is experimental, refusing the social sciences' "… obsessed with control, prediction, and the will to explain and understand everything" (Vannini, 2015, p. 5).

In an attempt to put into practice a non-representational, or what Hayden Lorimer (2005) calls a 'more-than-representational' *style* of research, this chapter shows our efforts at experimenting with surveillance data practices. In particular, we try to enact such practices that do not rely on rationality and certainty to explore Hong Kong shopping as a way to understand postcoloniality in Hong Kong through a different lens. In doing so, we are striving to take a different orientation to 'data' and the temporality and materiality of knowledge. We begin these experimental and more-than-representational ways by thinking with surveillance studies (see Lyon, 2007) to understand how data is understood through surveillance and control.

SURVEILLANCE AND CONTROL

Within surveillance studies there is much discussion expressing anxiety about how data collection is a form of surveillance and control (Virilio, 2002). Most of the arguments about surveillance highlight forms of control that are used to collect, mine, analyse, and use data. By thinking with surveillance studies and more-than-representational theories we examine the performativity and materiality of surveillance practices, including our own, and show how we were anything but in control. In a strange way, the surveillance practices that we used compelled us to surrender our presumptions about 'data', what it does, and consider it and our practices differently.

We used the *Autographer*, a small wearable camera, while setting out to explore aspects of postcolonial Hong Kong's complex relationship with mainland China. We wanted to explore the ways in which the resentment towards Chinese tourists from the mainland plays out during the mundane activity of shopping in one of the busiest and most exclusive shopping districts in Hong Kong. Our interest in resentment came from a previous experiential study about Hong Kong air that led us to create 'becoming-with research practices' (see Banerjee & Blaise, 2013). These practices, sensing air, tracing childhood memories, and cominglings, then took us to understand postcoloniality in Hong Kong in a new light. We build on these embodied becoming-with research practices by troubling the research performances produced with the *Autographer*.

HONG KONG SHOPPING

In the postcolonial world, Hong Kong lays claim to a most unique history. Hong Kong was colonized by Britain, but unlike most countries with long and bloody anti-colonial struggles, it was 'leased' to Britain by China for a period of 99 years and it was always only a matter of time before the 'Fragrant Harbour' would be returned to the Chinese. When the Handover finally took place in 1997, Hong Kongers had mixed feelings about it. While some (especially the elite) were anxious about the loss of civil liberties that a return to China might bring, others were optimistic about becoming part of the fastest growing nation which was suddenly commanding the world's attention and respect.

Almost twenty years after the handover, it can be said that things have not turned out as planned. Hong Kong's struggle for universal suffrage has led to pro-democracy movements like the recent (2014) Umbrella Revolution. Another outcome of the fraught relationship between Hong Kong and mainland China has been the recent rise in localist and nativist ideologies, stemming from a deep anxiety that unless protected and defended, the city as well as Hong Kong identity will be subsumed by its far larger and authoritarian neighbor. Characteristic of this nativist ideology is a vicious anti-mainlander sentiment. Nativists claim that the local population feels acutely dislocated as the city is overcome and changed beyond recognition by mainland visitors who routinely cross the border to purchase everyday necessities like baby milk powder, medicines and cosmetics as well as high end designer goods

It is in this milieu, that we undertook a walk through Tsim Sha Tsui, the most popular shopping district frequented by mainland visitors. We wanted to experience how it felt to traverse the same streets, stand in the queues that form outside the designer stores like Gucci and Prada and observe how fellow shoppers, who were mostly mainlanders, are treated or regarded. We were curious if we would be able to sense anti-mainlander sentiment, by working with a more-than-representational style towards researching. We believed (and hoped) that taking part in the performance of 'shopping', in an area where mainland resentment often occurs, might open up opportunities for us to engage in more performative, rather than passive research practices.

'LIFE-LOGGING' HARDWARE

Having non-Chinese faces and bodies, we anticipated that we would be perceived quite differently from the predominantly Chinese shoppers, but our main interest was in exploring mainland Chinese resentment. We did not set out with a specific plan of how or what exactly we would 'research', nor did we assume that we would be able to see or recognize resentment, but we were interested in recording our excursion. We were also acutely aware of the performative aspect of our endeavour since we had absolutely no intention of actually shopping. And the use of our data collecting device, the *Autographer*, made us even more aware of our performance.

Although working with a camera entails engaging with its troubled history of voyeurism, othering, and violence (Kind, 2013), we were interested in using one because cameras, whether visible or hidden, are one of the most common surveilling devices. In order to record our open-ended, performative, and experimental excursion, Mindy wore the *Autographer* camera around her neck, enabling spontaneous, hands-free image capture. These kinds of wearable devices are often referred to as 'life-logging' technology and provide a visual record of wherever a person has been (Spence, 2013). Logging one's life, or rather logging the everydayness of high-end shopping in Hong Kong was something that we were interested in doing. Since we both live and work in Hong Kong, we were curious to see how or if the device might activate a different style of attentiveness to the atmosphere of resentment, something that we might not always be attuned to.

The *Autographer* has a 136° eye view lens that mirrors a human's range of vision and a GPS. In addition, it has 5 built-in sensors to detect changes in the environment. These changes then trigger the camera to take a photo. Shifts in color, changes in light and temperature, differences in direction and motion are all detected. The long battery life (12 hours) enables the *Autographer* to take up to 2,000 photographs.

We were intrigued with the notion of the device taking over and deciding what and when to photograph. The advertisement for the *Autographer* claims by using this camera one will, "Experience a new level of creative control through data" (see Autographer.com, 2016). However, instead of experiencing a new level of creative control, we encountered several moments of out-of-controlness. This occurred not while we were walking through the streets of Hong Kong and 'shopping', but when we were viewing the photographs that the *Autographer* took. What moments were photographed did not make sense and because we had no control over what photographs were taken, data collection was literally out of our control. By taking this out-of-controlness on board, we explore what this 'new level of creative control' means and what performative surveillance data practices might afford. We will show what is possible when surrendering to being out-of-control and reconsidering how the simultaneous absence and presence of data yields new insights into the paradoxical productiveness of disappointing, failing, and malfunctioning data.

SUR/SOUSVEILLANCE AND AGENCY

As a wearable device, the *Autographer* masks its actual function of taking photos. In this case, it could be said that we were conducting a kind of surveillance or what has been called sousveillance within the larger field of surveillance studies (see Lyon, 2007). It is interesting to consider how surveillance practices are part of, not separate from, the atmospheres we currently live in. In regards to the *Autographer*, the camera is completely visible because it is either hanging on a human's neck or clipped on to clothing. Since there is no viewfinder or preview screen, the human body never touches the camera, making its function as a recording device somewhat invisible. While security cameras are omnipresent, there is a large degree of opacity surrounding the use of data gathered by these devices and other forms of internet data surveillance. Scholars have often expressed anxiety about the disquieting ways in which data gathered from surveillance practices have been used. Lyon (2007) cautions of a world in the making "in which all of daily life is under constant surveillance" (p. 1). Something that has emerged out of this conversation is the counter surveillance practice of sousveillance or citizens' use of technology to "watch ('veiller') from below ('sous')." Sousveillance may be seen as an attempt to invert the normative power relation in surveillance practices. It involves citizens and the common people wearing cheap, portable devices in order to surveil the use of power. When we decided to walk through the streets of Hong Kong's shopping district frequented by the nouveau riche of the mainland, we took on a similar practice. Our intention was not exactly to surveil the surveilling power structure, which is usually the case in sousveillance. Rather, our intention was to explore, and in doing so included observing and recording how mainland tourists and shoppers were treated by the local Hong Kongers including the staff of the designer stores.

While surveillance data has created a massive and unwieldy infrastructure, the way sousveillance data works is far less controlled and rigid. Because the device worn by the sousveiller is hidden or not obviously marked as a surveilling device, the sousveiller also has no direct control over what might get recorded. Thus, uncertainty is a key element of sousveillance data. This uncertainty was considerably heightened in our case because the *Autographer* randomly captures images. A hidden camera or voice recording device, such as the kind worn by undercover journalists, records everything from the moment it is turned on. However, the *Autographer* randomly takes images based on sensory triggers. Thus, in undertaking our walk, we were giving up all control over the data generated by the device. As a kind of sousveillant performance, we were claiming some agency for ourselves, simultaneously, yet contradictorily, we were also forfeiting much of that agency by using a device like the *Autographer*. Furthermore, because we didn't know what photographs were being taken by the *Autographer*, we had no way of responding. For instance, if we were to have known that 200+ photos were 'blank' we might have fiddled with the device. So, the device prompted us to ask the question, "What would it mean just to go with what the *Autographer* decided to take and to work with that, rather than to try and intervene and 'fix' it?". This requires us to have a radically different relationship with data. It means that we must be willing to give up a bit of human exceptionalism, or the belief that we, as humans, can actually pin-down this notion of mainland resentment in the data collected through the *Autographer*. It also entails a somewhat uncomfortable relationship with data because shaking traditional beliefs that the researcher gives life and meaning to data is hard to do. This new or different relationship that we have with data might feel second-rate or inadequate because the 'right' kind of data was not generated or it could seem to be missing altogether.

DISAPPOINTING, FAILING, MALFUNCTIONING

Opening up the computer and clicking on the file labeled, June 2014, I am surprised to see that the first photo is of me, in my bathroom. I am wearing the Autographer around my neck and it has photographed my reflection in the mirror. All of a sudden I have a horrible feeling in the pit of my stomach, and I turn my head away from the computer screen, while muttering, "Oh no." For the slightest moment my two fingers resting on top of the mouse hesitate before clicking to the next photo. With a sense of unease, I wonder, "What kinds of photos did this thing take?" To my surprise, and disappointment, the next sixty-five photographs are of the inside of my apartment. The Autographer captured me preparing to go out and meet Bidisha. I couldn't help but wonder, "What made this interesting to the Autographer?" "Why did it record these activities?"

As I continue clicking through the remaining 621 photos I quickly view my movements out of the apartment and down the elevator, through the door and onto the streets of SoHo. Next, I am riding the mid levels escalator down towards the bottom of Central, and across the elevated pedestrian bridge. It has recorded me getting onto the Star Ferry, and then navigating the crowded streets of Kowloon. Suddenly I view a blank photo, and another, and another. Quickly, I click through these while asking, "What's going on?" There doesn't seem to be any record of Bidisha and me waiting in line to enter the exclusive handbag stores, or of us self-consciously 'shopping'. Annoyed at all of the blank photos, I click backwards, hoping to figure out what happened. I ask, "Where are all of the photos?" The last images are taken inside of a favourite British store for expatriates. I am disappointed and wonder what in the world has happened and why didn't the Autographer 'work'?

Disappointing, failing, and malfunctioning data are not often discussed in relation to research. However, they make an appearance here in surprising ways. First, the relationship between researcher and data is transformed. Almost immediately, Mindy is surprised to see that she has been 'caught on camera'. She is present in the research. The camera took a photo of Mindy in the bathroom, a place often considered private. Mindy dreaded the thought of something 'private' being documented. At the same time this photo, and the unease that it caused is an example of how data does something to us, or how it is provoking. It simultaneously made Mindy pause, uneasy, and curious. She kept viewing the photographs, but with an expectation that they would tell her something more. Second, the data was disappointing because it failed to reveal anything exciting or surprising about our excursion. This disappointment is interesting because it shows how we were anticipating data to explain or represent our walk. In fact, while we were out and about, either walking slowly through the streets, standing in line to enter one of these high-end stores, or to 'shop' for a handbag, it was uneventful. Third, data was failing because it appeared to lack any meaning. It seemed boring and was unsatisfying. Finally, and what stumped us the most, were the large quantity of blank photographs. It felt like the *Autographer* was malfunctioning. We were hoping that the *Autographer* would encourage a different orientation to data or open up new ways of understanding our lackluster afternoon. Unfortunately, it did neither (or so we thought).

EXTRAORDINARY IMAGES? A NEW LEVEL OF CREATIVE CONTROL?

The *Autographer* claims to take 'very different photographs' that are always 'natural, unexpected and completely authentic'. Because of the 5 built-in sensors, 'a new level of creative control' is afforded. However, when we first reviewed the photographs, we found them to be of little interest, boring, and unremarkable. These disappointments were related to the ways in which we were expecting the data to be. In fact, we were wanting it to be representational of our experience, something that we find hard to move away from. However, in an interesting turn, these disappointments, failings, and malfunctions then activated a different kind of encounter with data.

One of the first ways we engaged with the photographs differently was through our viewing practices. The software package for the *Autographer* allows the photos to be viewed in three ways; stream view (images are displayed in an endless, chronological stream), cinema view (images are displayed on a full screen and they are played back like a film), or calendar view (images are displayed by event or date). Although we tried all viewing practices, we repeatedly found ourselves adopting the calendar method. This meant that we were viewing the photos through our lens of predetermined expectations, looking for individual photographs that would allow us to say something about mainlander resentment in Hong Kong. We were getting caught up in the idea that the researcher is the one giving life and meaning to data, rather than mobilizing disappointments, failings, and malfunctions as productive. However, on viewing the photos as a continuous stream, a different pattern emerged—a far more coherent narrative which both disturbed us and destabilised our presumptions by making us aware of them and compelling us to confront and question them.

DATA PROVOCATIONS

Despite the disappointments, failings, and malfunctions, we came to realise that what the photos had done was provoked us to re-examine our expectations and subject positions as researchers as well as our relationship with data. After all, it wasn't as if the *Autographer* had not 'worked.' In fact, it had taken hundreds of images. The reason we believed the data was inadequate was because we were not presented with the kinds of images we had expected. There were in fact photos of us standing in the queues outside the designer store, then entering the store and trying on sunglasses, an elaborate performance undertaken in an attempt to appear like regular customers and not betray the fact that we were there on a sousveilling mission. But none of this seemed significant. It felt as though there was an absence of data, and yet clearly something was present. We were also disappointed because although the *Autographer* captured mainland shoppers in the stores, it would be almost impossible to make some kind of argument about mainland resentment from the photos. Instead what emerges from the photos is the narrative of a single day when two researcher friends walked around the shopping district of Tsim Sha

Tsui. Our dread arises from the fact that the camera has documented in significant detail all our activities that afternoon. In the hands of a stranger, it would be quite easy for them to document Mindy's whereabouts and activities on that particular day from the photos, starting from the privacy of her apartment, documenting the route and modes of transportation she took to travel from Central to Tsim Sha Tsui, the stores she visited, her meeting with Bidisha followed by what the two of them did together—queued up outside and then entered a Chanel and a Prada store, walked through the Harbour City Mall, entered a Marks and Spencer, bought tickets to an event and sat in a coffee shop. While we thought we were using the *Autographer* to surveill, instead we were the ones getting surveilled by our own device, through the detailed photographic documentation of our day. Therefore, a disconcerting double reversal has taken place—the sousveillers who attempted to surveil, have in turn become the victims of their own self surveillance. Rather than considering the photographs as somehow lacking, our data surveillance practices activated a new kind of agency that was unrecognizable because we were failing to notice how our own presuppositions about data were getting in the way. This phenomenon of surveillance and data turning inwards, against itself, suggests the simultaneous absence presence of data. What we perceived as absence and a failure of data at first, turns out simply to be the presence of data of another kind, which in turn, compels us to productively engage with this alternative data.

The first image of the 651 that were taken on our Sunday walk is one of Mindy getting dressed in her bathroom. It caught her off guard, filling her with dread. It provoked. This photo is a reminder that as researchers we are always implicated in the work that we aim to do. We are a part of what we are doing and it is naive to think that we can somehow be separated from it. During the entire time that we were walking through Tsim Sha Tsui, standing in line to enter the exclusive stores, and 'shopping', we were logging our lives and the milieu that we were a part of. So it becomes a kind of self-surveillance. Mindy was in her own domestic space, but unbeknownst to her, she was photographed. On the other hand, the things that we hoped would get photographed—the interaction between the store personnel in Tsim Sha Tsui and the mainland shoppers, or an annoyed and disarming glance, for example, didn't get recorded. So what we have here is a kind of reversal in the intended outcome of our research endeavour. The photo of Mindy looking at her reflection in the bathroom mirror as she puts on a necklace, is a literal yet symbolic representation of our research act—we intended to hold up a mirror to Hong Kong society, yet the mirror got held up to us instead. Although we believed we were giving up much of our agency as researchers by using a device such as the *Autographer* which generates images at random, when confronted with the data generated by the *Autographer*, we were in fact attempting to exert our agency by forcing the data into our presumptive narrative. We were then disappointed when it did not readily fit into this narrative. Mindy's self-conscious reaction to the photograph directs us to our own presence in the data we were seeing as absent. Thus, by altering our approach and instead focusing on randomness, absence, presence, disappointments, failings, and malfunctionings as paradoxically productive, makes room for us to consider data having its own agency and meaning in ways that we might never fully understand.

We are still wondering about this day, what we set out to accomplish, and our reactions to the disappointments, failings, and malfunctions with the 'data'. In the end, we believe that rather than being preoccupied with what was or was not photographed, it is more useful to be interested in eliciting present moments, such as the moment when the data did something to Mindy, when it provoked, and how this can inspire radically different ways to engage with data. In many ways data was an interference. We need to learn how to work with these interferences, rather than immediately shutting them down as inadequate. What if we were to consider the data as an absence and a presence? Data was always and already present, but at the same time absent. Data was able to be both absent and present because of where and how we were looking. That is, every time we tried to exercise our human interpretation onto the photographs, we came up empty. It was only in the briefest of moments when we let go of our human exceptionalism and allowed the data, with all of its disappointments, failings, and malfunctions to do what it was always and already doing, that we were able to see it as productive. We just simply do not yet know what this means or how to make meaning of it. It is the uncertainty about the absence and presence that we are learning how to work with as new research practices.

Although we might embrace experimentation and performative methods, we have learned that breaking traditional research habits is hard. We turn to Vannini (2015), who reminds us that taking risks is necessary and part of enacting a more-than-representational style to research. We end not with any sort of findings or conclusions, but rather a provocation for others who are interested in doing this kind of research. What is required is not just about taking 'more' risks, but it is also about learning how to relish failing and failing better in order to produce different kinds of research practices (Dewsbury, 2009). For us, failing better is about taking on a less certain style of practice by opening ourselves up to *more* data disappointments, failures, and malfunctions.

REFERENCES

Autographer.com. (2016). *Autographer.com*. Retrieved July 1, 2016, from http://www.autographer.com/

Banerjee, B., & Blaise, M. (2013). There's something in the air: Becoming-with research practices. *Cultural Studies<=>Critical Methodologies, Special Issue, Provocations: (Re)visioning Data in Qualitative Research, 13*(4), 240–245.

Dewsbury, J. D. (2009). Performative, non-representational, and affect based research: Seven injunctions. In D. DeLyser, S. Herbert, S. Aitken, M. Crang, & L. McDowell (Eds.), *The SAGE handbook of qualitative geography* (pp. 322–335). Thousand Oaks, CA: Sage.

Kind, S. (2013). Lively entanglements: The doings, movements and enactments of photography. *Global Studies of Childhood December, 3*(4), 427–441. doi: 10.2304/gsch.2013.3.4.427

Koro-Ljungberg, M., & Maclure, M. (2013). Provocations, re-un-visions, death, and other possibilities of 'data'. *Cultural Studies-Critical Methodologies, 13*(4), 219–222.

Koro-Ljungberg, M., MacLure, M., & Ulmer, J. (2017). D ... a ... t ... a ..., data++, data and some problematics. In N. Denzin & Lincoln (Eds.), *The SAGE handbook of qualitative research.* 5th Edition (pp. 462–484). Thousand Oaks, CA: Sage Publications.

Lorimer, H. (2005). Cultural geography: The busyness of being 'more-than-representational'. *Progress in Human Geography, 29*, 83–94.

Lyon, D. (2007). *Surveillance studies: An overview.* Malden, MA: Polity Press.

Spence, E. (2013 December 19). The autographer is an intelligent wearable camera that raises many important questions Forbes. *Forbes.* Retrieved March 12, 2016. https://www.forbes.com/sites/ewanspence/2013/12/19/the-autographer-is-an-intelligent-wearable-camera-that-raises-many-important-questions/#7ebdd7b9419a

Thrift, N. (2008). *Non-representational theory: Space/politics/affect.* London: Routledge.

Vannini, P. (2015). Non-representational research methodologies: An introduction. In P. Vannini (Ed.), *Non-representational methodologies: Re-envisioning research* (pp. 1–18). New York and London: Routledge, Taylor and Francis.

Virilio, P. (2002). *The visual crash.* Cambridge, MA: MIT Press.

Irruptions

In the Beginning, There Was a Hole

MAREK TESAR, MIRKA KORO-LJUNGBERG,
AND TEIJA LÖYTÖNEN

ATTEMPTING NOT TO INTRODUCE DATAHOLES

We would like to begin by not introducing DataHoles. In the absence of introduction, we offer some examples, preliminary notes, puzzlements, and possible methodological connections DataHoles have prompted in our thinking and practices. Similar to the impossibility of introducing DataHoles, these holes also cannot be delivered, described in detail, or potentially captured in existing methodological discourses. However, in their absences they may form more or less imaginary presences, data becomings, and they might relate to data hosts that could be seen as more describable and discussable.

> H o l e s as Data, Data as H o l e s, As Data H o l e s, H o l e s Data as The
> WHOLE thing

> I love doing it together, said Teija in her text message. She data holes.

> Disrupting and challenging the established ways of how we are thinking about,
> collecting and producing data.

We are adding notes to ourselves:

> Data cannot control differences—
> Data shifting on their seats—
> Data dressed in a graduation gown—
> Data wanting a gin and tonic to be able to code and categorize—

So … What do data want?
To become an object? To have a material presence?

18 decorated lamps
1 broken lamp
1 empty container
3 human subjects
1 non-human subject who was thinking he is one
4 failed assignments
½ of a chewed pencil
0 working learning management system

How do we describe them?
Is this a recipe for an academic cake?

What h o l e s do we see in these data?

Alma mater--multiple verses.
Hundreds of silent heads and few singing chairs.
Data disruptions.
Fried chicken
A breath from a meth lab.
Grounded data under the sun.
Whispering of data.
Ultra-data
Hypo-hyper-hapto-neuro data.
Can you butter my data?
Data murmurings.
Tearoom data! How could we forget!

Data clicks. Best data friends. Best data forever, BDF.

Who has the biggest data (BIG DATA) and best post-data?

Post. post. And again and again … multiple tiny posts.

When you say the word 'data' many times—the word will magically appear. The word data might produce you (data user, data thinker, data producer, reader, scholar, teacher, woman, child …) as its potential host. Through you (our reader) data and their absence might become visible.

Or something (else) will (dis)appear.

Figure 1.1: Encountering holes.
Source: Author.

DATAHOLES PUZZLED: ITERATION **1**

There are holes everywhere: I collected data as I was looking around, sitting on the ground. I saw suddenly everything maybe more clearly. The cold air was blowing on my back, from behind. Are those data? Is that a hole? The air had to come from behind. Or not? And ... and ... and ... I saw holes between the rows of chairs, feet and expensive footwear. There were clear holes in my view—I realized that I am looking at the hole-ways in a hall-way. The view was purely terrifying—why am I so scared of these hole-ways? Are they whole? They are everywhere. Dirty socks and large bags on the ground made me feel small and clean ...

DATAHOLES PUZZLED: ITERATION **2**

At this hour I seem to have a hole in my head. Everything seems to leak through the hole(s), the thinking, the ideas, the affects and concepts. Whatever they are. Nothing to hold on to. Holes can be sucking up everything, imbruing up everything. Turning my thoughts into a liquid. Fluid data, fluid matter, fluid thinking. Fluid, slippery, data transforming themselves continuously.

It is becoming (*becoming*) clear that dataHoles are productive and generate uncontrollable thinking, uncontrollable world.

Uncontrollable human subjects.

Unruly scholars.

Data that won't conform.

Holes that cannot be colonized.

DATAHOLES SINGING ECHOED METHODOLOGIES

Holes create uncontrollable mistakes in writing.

Voids, gabs, mistakes are visible and situated on holes.

And this text message programme—bloody programme—translates my writing all the time from English into Finnish and into what so ever. ... that so ever.

Holes. ... Data ... Data ... Holes

Hole waits for no one. Echo?

Maybe it is just lyrics to a song

> "They carried me softly into that hole.
> You gave me part of you, just for me.
> But down in the hole ... give me some data, within these holes;
> I need some data, like dessert needs a hole".

Wholes holes makes me scream: data fever; data stories; data management; 4th data base. Data growth and data warts. Data inquiry. Data representation. Data validity.

Holes. There are holes in these data.

(Re)searching for holes, data holes. Methodologies of dataHoles.

Can we run out of data? Like in our mailboxes ... or in my dropbox. My dropbox is asking me to "upgrade space, to add more data" ... That I have run out of data. And what about semantics—holes in data and data holes—are they the same?

I am all for gluten free data; but if so, then I perhaps would be more interested in data that are separated and removed because of the gluten infestation ...

Data hole in my soul, holes in the soles on my shoes, for sure data must have so(u)l(e); if not so(u)ls. That's our metaphysics of data holes (sauls).

DATAHOLES AFRAID

Who is afraid of data? Or of data holes? Or is it something else?

The whole of this thinking around data holes is concerned, in fact, with what you (our reader) might really struggle with—the pointlessly harsh and long-lasting consequences in which the contemporary histories of the present violently abuse both subjects and objects, by extracting data and plugging the data holes with white noise. The price that all subjects and objects are bound to pay for the drastic suppression of history, the cruel and needless banishment of data into the underground of holes and spaces where the new compulsory deferment of every opportunity for data to be and perform in unexpected ways. You are not so much worried about the everyday bitterness at the spoliation of data and human centered great collection of all and everything; both material and spiritual … but what about the heavy tax we shall have to pay in the long-lasting decline of creativity of data and pure exploitation of data holes. You are also concerned with the scarcely calculable surcharge, which may be imposed on data holes if they are added to the mix of the methodological toolbox.

Economics of data holes concern you.

We do need more love and compassion for data holes in our qualitative inquiries?

Why can't you keep a sterile data hole?

Why can you not move beyond normative notions of data even though the others claim to do that?

What does it mean when you were told that data merely give new names to old horses. And what have holes got to do with it?

DATAHOLES PUZZLED: ITERATION 3

Time after time—frustration and boredom.

True.
For researcher, and for participants.

After listening to stories and productions of (neoliberal) data for hours now you are fed up, saturated with non-sense and completely tired with dry discussions of what-works-data. Emergent data cannot reach you!
But the IRD, IRB, IRS can.

Raw data; real data; interactive, emergent, entangled data; relational data.

> Data; transparent data; slippery data; self-evident data.
> Existing data, producing data.
> These are my data doings.
> DataLove ♥

Okey, you seem to be back on track.

What if we focused on irresolvable data holes, instead of data wholes?

What if the hole is what matters?

Everything is much clearer for you now.

Longing for holes, dataHoles.

Holes for breathing with the methodological world.

Fresh air, after the light spring rain.

Fresh, new air for thinking about and with data.

Fresh air as data privilege.

REFERENCES: N-ONE

CHAPTER FIVE

Traces OF Breath

An Experiment in Undoing Data Through Artistic Research

LEENA ROUHIAINEN

ABSTRACT

This chapter introduces an attempt to undo data through artistic research. It especially draws on the concept of the artistic research exposition to argue that it is possible for artistic practice in itself to be both the subject and object of inquiry. In the formation of such expositions it is not data but different elements and materials which form a composition that performatively reveals an aesthetic or material thinking. Additionally, the processual and entangled nature of the body is addressed. The particular research interest from the perspective of which the chapter is written relates to the somatic practice of cultivating breath. It is the emergence of sense generated by this embodied practice that informs the formation of materials and construction of a poetic exposition that is likewise discussed. The chapter concludes in a poetic exposition on breathing and breathwork. This exposition is an experiment that aims at substantiating the arguments presented in the chapter.

Keywords: Artistic Research, Exposition, Poetic writing, Cultivating breath

INTRODUCTION

This chapter introduces an experiment that questions data on the basis of, on the one hand, the performative nature of artistic research and, on the other, the becoming nature of embodiment. The chapter begins by reasoning about the chosen approach to data through discussing the artistic research exposition and Bruno Latour's views on the body. It concludes in a poetic meditation that, while tracing intermittent moments of a random practice of breathing, considers the vicissitudes of cultivating breath. Therefore, the chapter both attempts to offer some insights into a creative alternative to the notion of data and presents a short piece of research to demonstrate its cause. More concretely, the final meditation is a piece of experimental writing that interweaves descriptions of experiences of breathing, recollections related to breathwork as well as theoretical insights from especially biomechanics (Calais-Germain, 2006), psychotherapy (Lowen & Lowen, 1977; Victoria & Caldwell, 2013), affect theory (Brennan, 2004; Gibbs, 2001), body studies (Blackman, 2008, 2012; Latour, 2004; Leder, 1990) as well as feminist philosophy and gender studies (Ahmed, 2006, 2010; Irigaray, 2002, 2013). These elements are indebted to my work as a professional contemporary dancer, movement educator and artist-researcher. During the more than twenty years in this field, I have become acquainted with diverse dance techniques and somatic practices in which the regulation of breath is used as a means to support dance and movement performance. Thus, one of the objectives of writing this chapter has been that of learning more about breath and breathing, a process I have been on occasions more closely and others more loosely engaged with for several years both through practical exploration as well as research (see e.g. Rouhiainen, 2012a, 2012b, 2015).

OFFERINGS FROM ARTISTIC RESEARCH

The manner in which data is related to in this chapter finds impetus in the trajectory of artistic research as it is discussed in Northern Europe. Following recent argumentation in this field, the experimental poetic writing that the chapter includes is considered an exposition. The term relates to the means through which artistic practice in artistic research becomes the medium of research (Kirkkopelto, 2012). What is denoted by exposition is artistic practice as an aesthetic manifestation that exposes, reveals or shows something while simultaneously making the performativity of this showing apparent. In Dieter Mersch's (2015) view, events of appearing in which such appearances of something are produced that include contradictions and instabilities and that resist resolution or closure involve a reflexivity. He argues this issue to be at the core of the manner in which art generates knowledge (Mersch, 2015). Indeed, exposition in artistic research has been described as a "redoubling of practice in order to artistically move form artistic ideas to epistemic claims" (Schwab & Borgdorff, 2014, p. 15). What such a redoubling of artistic practice can establish is "a reflective distance within itself that allows it to be simultaneously the subject and object of an inquiry" (ibid.). As a consequence, artistic processes or outcomes in themselves can convey both "a thought and its appraisal" at the same stroke (ibid.).

What is also worth noting in this context is that artistic practice is not strictly speaking involved with gathering or constructing, analyzing and interpreting data. It deals with the configuration of compositional elements and materials that come together as forms of aesthetic or material thinking. The process of generative interplay between the artist and the materials is a thinking ingrained in the making. Here materials too have agency and both tacitly and explicitly inform what the artist does, so that in the end it is difficult to discern exactly who is producing a work. Therefore, instead of regarding certain materials as data and others as interpretative theoretical frames, this chapter concludes in an exposition in the form of a written performative arrangement. It aims to allow a sense of breath to take flight and find solutions through elements from here and there that come together in writing without their category being considered as this or that (Deleuze & Parnet, 2002). Initiated through the process of me actually breathing, the composition of chosen quoted materials and personal accounts of breathing in the poetic exposition redouble, mirror and, in the end, produce its own embodiment of breathing. It is in this fashion that the chapter distances itself from understanding data as something that can be collected and known in any simple manner. It undermines data as a kind of evidential archive that is regarded as a fixed and separate entity, an external object analyzed and interpreted by a researcher in order for her to retrieve reliable knowledge about reality (see e.g. Denzin, 2013; Koro-Ljungberg & MacLure, 2013).

To elaborate on the above position further I follow Mika Elo's (2014) line of thinking. He argues that the "the task of an artist-researcher operating in the interstices of different media can be likened to the task of the translator" (Elo, 2014, p. 31). When faced with the challenge of bringing forth the feel of an artistic practice, the artist-researcher is to find "medium-sensitive ways of articulating his or her epistemic interests and of looking for productive contact points between different modes of articulation—without any pre-established hierarchies, which could limit what is exposed" (ibid., p. 32). For the purposes of this chapter, Elo interestingly bases his views on Walter Benjamin's formulations on language. According to him, for Benjamin language is something that precedes the separation of the sensible and intelligible and is not limited to expression in words. Rather, all perceptible articulations can be understood as languages, as forms of the emergence of sense. There is a non-sensuous similarity between language, gesture and vision (Manning & Massumi, 2014). Languages thus extend the spoken and written. In this line of thinking, perceptual articulation of physical practice can be related to on the same footing as other forms of similar linguistic expression. This is a worthwhile note, since the subsequent piece of research is indebted to such practices. With the kind of understanding that Elo introduces, language is further qualified as an "immediate impartability" that brings things into relationship in an expressive event (Elo, 2014, p. 30). Kathrin Busch (2006) discusses Benjamin's views by pointing out that in this event expression *through* language communicates content and expression *within* language allows for indeterminable latent meaning to be exposed. The latter poetic character is related to the form of articulation and is something directly conveyed. It is not wholly translatable into meaning, rather it is something reminiscent of atmosphere. This characteristic is sometimes considered to be language's magical quality. Elo suggests that it is derived from language's way of continuously relating to other languages for sense-making as well the fact that language is never fully present to itself. There is a limit and an inexpressible or insensible operative in language (Busch, 2006; Elo, 2014).

ON EMBODIMENT IN WRITING

In addition to considering the artist-researcher as a translator who does not appreciate pre-established hierarchies, categories and the like in order for the emergence of sense to find expression in an event of exposure, what further informs the stand the article takes on data is Bruno Latour's (2004) performative conception of the body. According to Lisa Blackman (2008), he relates to it as an articulation or "an association and concatenation of heterogeneous elements which *produce* what we take entities", such as the body, to be (Blackman, 2008, p. 122). The elements or objects forming such articulations or assemblages are in themselves complicated, entangled and multiple. They never even strictly speaking pre-exist the relational connection which produce and enact them as very particular types of objects. Furthermore, being related to time and changing circumstances, articulations never quite remain the same, entities are in a continuous process of becoming. Therefore, in Latourian terms, the body is understood as a mixture of processes that cannot be disentangled and it is its relational connections that articulate what the body can do and become (Blackman, 2008, pp. 122–123). In this sense, the different kinds of intertwined texts this chapter subsequently introduces as a poetic articulation of a sense of breath, could be regarded as its materials, the entangled elements that produce the enaction of embodied breath that the text accomplishes.

More concretely, the following writing addresses the emergence of sense in a writing that interweaves awareness of moments of actual breathing, anecdotal accounts of them, and chosen excerpts from research literature. This it does in order to expand on articulations concerning the cultivating breath. Working as a translator, placing the found and construed translations on an equal footing, this approach could be understood to bare similarities with how Monica Prendergast (2009) describes poetic inquiry to be a combination of what she defines as literature voiced poems and researcher voiced poems. The first are responses to literature or theory and the second relate to reflective and creative autobiographical writing (Prendergast, 2009; see also Leavy, 2015). Even if this article considers data problematic and turns to work with interlinking what could be understood as derived materials and generated new material, for the ends of situating the experimental writing as a piece of research, pointing out, even if only partially, the contexts that inform the formation of the utilized materials is called for. This is what I have up to now attempted to introduce and continue to do with a few more insights.

In part, the materials did not pre-exist the writing of the article, and in part, as excerpts from previous writing by others, they have been transposed by the immaterial lure of physically cultivating breath and probing its nature. As its basic element, a concrete practice of breathwork informs the mode of writing and sense of breath, embodied relations, references and insights articulated in the poetic exposure. Latour (2004) relates to this by stating that: "Acquiring a body is thus a progressive enterprise that produces at once a sensory medium *and* a sensitive world" (ibid., p. 206). He explains this by stating that "By focusing on the body, one is immediately—or rather mediately—directed to what the body has become aware of" (ibid., p. 206). In the subsequent poetic exposure, breathing and its world is viewed from the position of an artist-researcher engaged with both the cultivation of breath and experimental writing in order to share traces of the immaterial process of the practice of breathing. Here the immaterial especially denotes the experiencing body's ability to feel and register such phenomena that are not easily seen, known or understood and that undermine the knowing subject (Blackman, 2008, pp. 132, 134). The immaterial has induced an affective impact, a force that directed the reading and writing done in constructing the poetic exposition. The process of writing itself was a weaving back and forth between sensations, percepts, memories, reading passages and a processes of writing that appreciated the sense of breath they conveyed and searched for ways of forming a breathing text. None of the passages the writing involves were chosen and formed or convey meaning without their relation to each other. The experimental writing aims to allow the on occasion only very silent and on others keenly noticeable and versatile quality of breathing to inform its rhythm. My hope is that that together the elements of the text form a complex articulation or expressive event. In order to further substantiate the potential abundance of reality Latour (2004) opines that scientific "Generalizations should be a vehicle for travelling through as many differences as possible—thus maximizing articulations—and not a way of *decreasing* the number of alternative versions of the same phenomena" (p. 221). Indeed, in his view, for us to become more sensitive to differences is to become more embodied (Latour, 2004). The following section of the chapter presents the actual exposition on breathing. In order to appreciate the nature of artistic research expositions, I will let it speak for itself from here on.

A POETIC EXPOSITION

How to grasp the immaterial within the material?

I lay still with agility. Acute curiosity. What is this that is taking place here?

The moment gesticulates into an extended cessation of breathing.

Undisturbed stillness.

Then, the reinvention of inspiration.

Embodied gratitude

Is it really so that breathing is mere "movement that is performed in respiration"? (Calais-Germain, 2006, p. 13)

What about the body's potential for mediation?

Neither movement nor bodies "arrive in the neutral. How we arrive, how we enter this or that room, will affect what impressions we receive. After all, to receive is to act." (Ahmed, 2010, p. 37)

I have performed like this before, simple.

Confidence in the familiar routine of standing in the center of attention.

A sudden loss of awareness.

Scanning in vain, sensations closed down.

Hiatus.

The frightful realization that my body stopped breathing.

Shivering bodily profile and a fluttering heartbeat.

Is this what it feels like to be stared at by a strange group in close proximity?

"An arrival takes time, and the time that it takes shapes "what" it is that arrives." (Ahmed, 2006, p. 40)

"... an arrival points towards a future that might or "perhaps" will happen, given that we don't always know in advance "what" we will come into contact with." (Ahmed, 2006, p. 40)

Confronted by the not-yet-known.

"... to be affected by something is to evaluate that thing. Evaluations are expressed in how bodies turn toward things" (Ahmed, 2010, p. 31) *or move away from them.*

"Spaces are not only inhabited by bodies that "do things," but what bodies" *in themselves* ""do" leads them to inhabit some spaces more than others." (Ahmed, 2006, p. 58)

Withdrawal, disengagement, fear.

Some are dedicated to the idea that "breathing patterns correspond with coping attitudes." (Victoria & Caldwell, 2013, p. 217)

The amazing responsiveness of respiration and its uncanny autonomy.

To consider that "... breathing is affected by conscious and unconscious attempts to stave off strong emotion or uncomfortable states." (Victoria & Caldwell, 2013, p. 217)

How am I breathed through moment by moment, situation by situation?

"An emotion is among other things a breathing pattern." (Heller, 2012, p. 35 as reported by Victoria & Caldwell, 2013, p. 218)

What does breathing engender for me to witness?

And what does this have to do with the fact that even "research has shown that the psychological is distributed throughout the body"? (Blackman, 2008, p. 57)

Where does breathing really happen?

"Healthy breathing is a total body action; all muscles of the body are involved to some degree." (Lowen & Lowen, 1977, p. 24)

Breath as pervasively assembled motion.

"Movement always starts from a superposition," *that is* "a formative zone of indistinction," "a mutual inclusion of sequential forms" (Manning & Massumi, 2014, pp. 40–41, 156 n14).

And "… to have a body *is to learn to be affected*, meaning 'effectuated', moved, put into motion by other entities, humans and non-humans. If you are not engaged in this learning, you become insensitive, dumb, you drop dead." (Latour, 2004, p. 205)

She sits quietly on a chair with her feet supported by the floor—

calm as if sunken deep in her thoughts.

A passing surprise of such a retracted manner of beginning a class.

Routinely finding my place, I settle to observe my breath.

Undisturbed minor gestures of us all fill the room.

A deep dive into the weightiness and subtlety of my body embodying the situation.

Presence with ease, neither this or that provoking our sharing.

What examples can silently accomplish.

Indeed, "Bodies can catch feelings as easily as catch fire: affect leaps from one body to another, evoking tenderness, inciting shame, igniting rage, exciting fear." (Gibbs, 2001, p. 1)

What is more is that "… entrainment may also depend on body movements and gestures, particularly through the imitation of rhythms (effected by sight, touch, and hearing) … Rhythm has a regulating role between two or more people. The rhythmic aspects of behavior at a gathering are critical in both establishing and enhancing a sense of collective purpose and a common understanding." (Brennan, 2004, p. 70)

Shared breathing.

…

She was far from being retracted.

She was in the comforting silence of a transubstantiating breathing.

What if "Being in the rhythm (…) you are and have to be in the present moment (…) Being in the rhythm will automatically make you *loose yourself* in the movement. You will adopt the rhythm as an embodied dimension of yourself. The rhythm will strengthen your pre-reflective orientation to the environment and your action" (Stelter, 2008, p. 223) *and this all was transmitted to us.*

A teaching was going on through her.

"(…) to learn, in the best cases, is to learn from someone's experience. To teach is to transmit an experience. What is taught is guaranteed by the life of the one who teaches (…)." (Irigaray, 2002, p. 58)

"It is impossible to appropriate breath or air. But one can cultivate it, for oneself and others. Teaching then takes place through compassion." (Irigaray, 2002, p. 79)

Here potentially "The fact that breathing is rhythmical and constantly changes helps us to relate to its changes in accommodative ways. We realize that we need to be flexible (…)." (Williams et al., 2007, p. 72)

Compassionate transmission stutters and stumbles in solitude:

Waiting to become still I observe my breath to the extent my concentration allows for.

Thoughts meander.

No easy surrender

Exhale deeply.

It might help.

Techniques and routines take charge.

In the midst, I recognize a familiar holding:

Shallow breath, movement in the belly, chest immobile and a long pause after exhalation.

Finally, the first inklings of yielding.

Unto what I do not know.

Impatience. I stop.

The burden of cultural inscription and anticipation—layers and layers of them in breathing.

"(…) practices do not simply describe the body, but rather create what the body might become, and in that sense both enact and have the potential to do the body differently." (Blackman, 2008, p. 126)

I have learnt my practices well, no easy surrender.

After all, "Movement always happens behind the thinkers back, or in the moment he blinks." (Deleuze & Parnet, 2002, p. 1)

… to embody another practice, a practice that "seeks slowly to rework the parameters by which experience is defined—but (…) does so by a process of engagement with and examination of experience." (Boon, 2015, p. 41)

Simply to sit and wait and follow.

"Bodies tend towards some objects more than others given their tendencies. These tendencies are not originary but instead are effects of the repetition of the "tending towards"." (Ahmed, 2006, p. 58)

Tending towards a not doing.

"The point is simple, what we "do do" affects what we "can do". This is not to argue that "doing" simply restricts capacities. In contrast, what we "do do" opens up and expands some capacities, as an "expansion" in certain directions that in turn might restrict what you can do in others." (Ahmed, 2006, p. 60)

S i t t i n g   a n d   w a i t i n g   a n d   f o l l o w i n g…

Sitting and waiting and following.

Nothing seems to call for any particular attention, almost like doing nothing.

In the unaccountable interlacing of a mundane flow of minute sensations and perceptions

a fragile calm.

"To remain silently attentive to the breath comes down to respecting that which, or who, exists and maintaining for oneself the possibility to be born and to create." (Irigaray, 2002, p. 51)

Silent sitting now a standard late afternoon routine,

a form of recovery by being lost in silence,

neither this nor that,

often broken off by taking notice that it had turned dark.

"A culture of breath is accompanied by a culture of silence." (Irigaray, 2013, p. 220)

"Breathing in a conscious and free manner is equivalent to taking charge of one's life, to accepting solitude through cutting the umbilical cord, to respecting and cultivating life, for oneself and others." (Irigaray, 2002, p. 74)

Livingroom floor, pillow, sitting crossed legged, this time a timer at 15 minutes.

Observing the gradual rhythmic pulse of my breath, nothing else.

Awareness occasionally slides into one thought or another,

only to gently return and become anchored in breathing.

Quietude, depth, expansion, belonging—

timelessness

before the time is out.

No wonder it is written that "While we can modulate our breathing at will, it is primarily an automatic function (…) Watching the breath come in and go out for minutes or hours, one is saturated by the presence of a natural power that outruns the "I". Breathing simply happens and happens and happens (…) Moment to moment, breathing actualizes our one-body relation with the surrounding world. Inside and outside, self and Other, are relativized, porous, each time one takes a breath. The air is constantly transgressing boundaries, sustaining life through interconnections." (Leder, 1990, pp. 171–172)

Further teaching is on offer.

"Silence is a place of possible encounters between human beings, more generally between living beings who do not speak the same language and do not obey the same values, the same ideals. Such a silence corresponds to a breath that is not yet determined or expressed in a certain way, according to certain rules, a certain logic, and this can be respected and shared as life itself beyond its various embodiments and forms of expression." (Irigaray, 2013, p. 221)

"Being autonomous at the level of breathing, of breath, is essential to reach a relation without conflict to and with the other." (Irigaray, 2013, p. 217)

A new orientation.

"Lines are both created by being followed and are followed by being created. The lines that direct us, as lines of thought as well as lines of motion, are in this way performative: they depend on the repetition of norms and conventions, of routes and paths taken, but they are also created as an effect of this repetition. To say that lines are performative is to say that we find our way and know which direction we face only as an effect of work, which is often hidden from view. So in following these directions, I arrive, as if by magic."

(Ahmed, 2006, p. 16)

By magic the immaterial spirit of breath

"Nothing is more material than mysticism. Through sustaining living attention by concentration, the mystic enters into a timeless state that eventually yields an experience that is evidently sensual and spiritual."

(Brennan, 2004, p. 159)

REFERENCES

Ahmed, S. (2006). *Queer phenomenology. Orientations, objects, others*. Durham, NC and London: Duke University Press.

Ahmed, S. (2010). Happy objects. In M. Gregg & G. J. Seigworth (Eds.), *The affect theory reader* (pp. 29–51). Durham, NC and London: Duke University Press.

Blackman, L. (2008). *The body. The key concepts*. Oxford and New York, NY: Berg.

Blackman, L. (2012). *Immaterial bodies. Affect, embodiment, mediation*. London: Sage Publications.

Boon, M. (2015). To live in a glass house is a revolutionary virtue par excellence. In M. Boon, E. Cazdyn, & T. Morton (Eds.), *Nothing. Three inquiries in Buddhisim* (pp. 23–104). Chicago and London: The University of Chicago Press.

Brennan, T. (2004). *The transmission of affect*. Ithaca, NY: Cornell University Press.

Busch, K. (2006.) The language of things and the magic of language. On Walter Benjamin's concept of latent potency. *TRANSVERSAL multilingual webjournal, 12*, np. Retrieved from http://eipcp. net/transversal/0107/busch/en

Calais-Germain, B. (2006). *Anatomy of breathing*. Seattle, WA: Eastland Press.

Deleuze, G., & Parnet, C. (2002). *Dialogues II*. London and New York, NY: Continuum.

Denzin, N. (2013.) "The death of data?" *Cultural Studies—Critical Methodologies, 13*(4), 353–356. doi: 10.1177/1532708613487882

Elo, M. (2014). Notes on media sensitivity in artistic research. In M. Schwab and H. Borgdorff (Eds.), *The exposition of artistic research: Publishing art in academia* (pp. 25–38). Amsterdam: Leiden University Press.

Gibbs, A. (2001). Contagious feelings: Pauline Hanson and the epidemiology of affect. *Australian Humanities Review, 24*, np. Retrieved from http://www.australianhumanitiesre-view.org/.

Irigaray, L. (2002). *Between east and west: From singularity to community*. Translated by Stephen Pluháček. New York, NY: Columbia University Press.

Irigaray, L. (2013). To begin with breathing anew. In L. Skof & E. A. Holmes (Eds.), *Breathing with Luce Irigraray* (pp. 217–226). London: Bloomsbury.

Kirkkopelto, E. (2012). Inventiot ja instituutiot: Taiteellisen tutkimuksen kritiikistä. *Synteesi, 3,* 89–96.

Koro-Ljungberg, M., & MacLure, M. (2013). Provocations, re-un-visions, death and other possibilities of "data". *Cultural Studies—Critical Methodologies, 13*(4), 219–222.

Latour, B. (2004). How to talk about the body? The normative dimension of science studies. *Body & Society, 10*(2–3), 205–229.

Leavy, p. (2015). *Method meets art: Arts-based research practice.* New York, NY and London: The Guildford Press.

Leder, D. (1990). *The absent body.* Chicago and London: The University of Chicago Press.

Lowen, A., & Lowen, L. (1977). *The way to vibrant health. A manual of bioenergetic exercises.* New York, NY and London: Perennial Library.

Manning, E., & Massumi, B. (2014). *Thought in the act. Passages in the ecology of expression.* Minneapolis, MN and London: University of Minnesota Press.

Mersch, D. (2015). *Epistemologies of aesthetics.* Zurich-Berlin: diaphanes.

Prendergast, M. (2009). Introduction: The phenomena of poetry in research: "Poem is What?" Poetic inquiry in qualitative social science research. In M. Pendergast, L. Carl, & p. Sameshima (Eds.), *Poetic inquiry. Vibrant voices in the social sciences* (pp. xix–xlii). Rotterdam, Boston, Taipei: Sense Publishers.

Rouhiainen, L. (2012a). An investigation into facilitating the work of the independent contemporary dancer through somatic psychology. *Journal of Dance and Somatic Practices, 3*(1&2), 43–60.

Rouhiainen, L. (2012b). From body psychotherapy to a spatial dramaturgy: A collaborating performers point of view. In S. Ravn & L. Rouhiainen (Eds.), *Dance spaces. Practices of movement* (pp. 137–160). Odense: University Press of Southern Denmark.

Rouhiainen, L. (2015). Priming the body: Breath as a foundation for exploring ethical artistic practice. *Nordic Journal of Dance: Practice, Education and Research, 6*(1), 6–21.

Schwab, M., & Bordgdorff, H. (2014). Introduction. In M. Schwab & H. Borgdroff (Eds.), *The exposition of artistic research: Publishing art in academia* (pp. 8–20). Leiden: Leiden University Press.

Stelter, R. (2008). Approaches to enhance body-anchored and experienced based learning. In T. Schilhab, M. Juelskjær, & T. Moser (Eds.), *Learning bodies* (pp. 111–129). Copenhagen: Danish School of Education Press.

Victoria, H. K., & Caldwell, C. (2013). Breathwork in body psychotherapy: Clinical applications. *Body, movement and dance in psychotherapy, 8*(4), 216–228. doi: 10.1080/17432979.2013.828657

Williams, M., Teasdale, J., Segal, Z., & Kabat-Zinn, J. (2007). *The mindful way through depression. Freeing yourself from chronic unhappiness.* New York, NY: The Guildford Press.

CHAPTER SIX

Data

The Wonder of It All[1]

NORMAN K. DENZIN

ABSTRACT

Do we any longer need the word data? Where does the word data fit in the new, post-qualitative inquiry discourse? A new set of interpretive performative practices is outlined.

Keywords: autoethnography, performance, method of instances, intervention, praxis

> Ethnography, rhetoric, and performance join forces precisely on this front of resistance to totalizing thought. This is a performative cultural politics which recuperates any lingering estrangement between rhetoric, ethnography, the poetic and the political. (Conquergood, 1992, pp. 80, 96 paraphrase)

How fitting: A book about data encounters when the practices that produce data are under assault. Criticism comes from all sides (Koro-Ljungberg, 2016). The argument is straightforward: things, words, 'become data only when theory acknowledges them as data' (St. Pierre, 2011, p. 621). In a single gesture, doubt replaces certainty, no theory, method, form of data analysis, discourse, genre or tradition has 'a universal and general claim as the "right" or privileged of authoritative knowledge' (Denzin, 2013; Richardson, 2000, p. 928).

More is at play. There is a rupture that goes beyond data and its meanings. The traditional concepts of narrative, meaning, voice, presence and representation are also put under erasure, regarded as pernicious left overs from the twin ruins of postpositivism and humanistic qualitative inquiry (Jackson & Mazzei, 2012, p. vii). Materialist feminist ontologies, inspire new analytics of data analysis, including defractive readings of data. Post-methodologists, post humanist, post-empirical, and post-qualitative frameworks call for new models of science, second empiricisms, reimagined social sciences, capacious sciences, sciences of differrance, a science defined by becoming, a double(d) science (Lather, 2007; MacLure, 2011; St. Pierre, 2011, p. 613). Where do data fit in these new spaces? Is there any longer even a need for the word? Why keep the word after you have deconstructed it?

It is clear that a great deal is happening,

New places are sought. For some this is a place where there are no data, where the search is for justice, moral arguments, a politics of representation which seeks utopias of possibility, a politics of hope not a politics based on data (Madison, 2010). For others data are reconfigured, re-read through new ontologies and new interpretive analytics (St. Pierre, 2011). For others data are used for practical purposes, in framing claims for changes in social policy (Gomez, Puigvert, & Flecha, 2011).

These reconfigurations move in three directions at the same time. They interrogate the practices and politics of evidence that produce data. They support the call for new ways of making the mundane, taken for granted everyday world visible, whether through performance, or through disruptive post-empirical methodologies. These unruly methodologies read and interrupt traces of presence, whether from film, recordings or transcriptions. They do not privilege presence, voice, meaning or intentionality. Rather they seek performative interventions and representations that heighten critical reflective awareness leading to concrete forms of praxis.

Underneath it all it is assumed that we make the world visible through our interpretive practices. All texts have a material presence in the world. Nothing stands outside the text, even as it makes the material present. Neither the material nor the discursive are privileged. They fold into one another, get tangled up in one another. How a thing gets inside the text is shaped by a politics of representation. Language and speech do not mirror experience. They create experience and in the process transform and defer that which is being described. Meanings are always in motion, incomplete, partial contradictory. There can never be a final, accurate, complete representation of a thing, an utterance or an action. There are only different representations of different representations. There is no longer any pure presence description becomes inscription erases collection becomes performance erases analysis becomes interpretation.

WE NEED A NEW WORD

But even if data are dead we still need a word. What replaces data? After all, we are an empirical, not a text-based humanities discipline. We connect our interpretive practices to events that go on in the social world. That is we do more than read and interpret already published works. We write in ways that evoke experience in the world. We write stories that can be used, stories that can be trusted, stories that can change the world. Further, we are, after William James, radical empiricists (1912). That is we only deal with materials that can be drawn from and are based in experience: performances, emotions, perceptions, feelings, actions. Experience cannot be quantified, counted or turned into a thing. Experience is an on-going process. Experience, James reminds us, can never be reduced to a stream of data or to something called data. Experience is a process. It is messy, open-ended, inconclusive, tangled up in the writer's and reader's imagined interpretations.

***

AN ASIDE ON THE METHOD OF INSTANCES

Any given interpretive practice, event or performance that is studied is significant because it is an instance of a cultural practice that happened in a particular time and place. This practice can not be generalized to other practices, its importance lies in the fact that it instantiates a cultural practice, a cultural performance (story telling), and a set of shifting, conflicting cultural meanings (Fiske, 1994, p. 195). This is the logic of the method of instances. Every instance is unique and has its own logic.

An analogy may help. In discourse analysis

> no utterance is representative of other utterances, though of course it shares structural features with them; a discourse analyst studies utterances in order to understand how the potential of the linguistic system can be activated when it intersects at its moment of use with a social system. (Fiske, 1994, p. 195)

This is the argument for the method of instances. The analyst's task is to understand how this instance works, to show what rules of interpretation are operating, to map and illuminate the structure of the interpretive event itself.

Whether the particular instance occurs again is irrelevant. Indeed this is an irrelevant question, because occurrence unique, and shaped by prior occurrences. The question of sampling from a population is also not an issue, for it is never possible to say in advance what an instance is an instance of (Psathas, 1995, p. 50). This means there is little concern for empirical generalization. Psathas is clear on this point. The goal is not an abstract, or empirical generalization, rather the aim is 'concerned with providing analyses that meet the criteria of unique adequacy' (p. 50). Each analysis must be fitted to the case at hand, each 'must be studied to provide an analysis *uniquely adequate* for that particular phenomenon' (p. 51, italics in original).

This approach to interpretation rejects a normative epistemology which presumes that what is normal is what is most representative in a larger population.

A normative epistemology directs generalizations to this 'normal' population. This stance pays little attention to the processes that produce an instance in the first place. Furthermore, it ignores the 'non-representative' and marginal formations that can exist in any social structure (Fiske, 1994, p. 196). Finally, what is normal is reduced to what is most frequent. A normative epistemology requires a set of postpositivist, naturalistic criteria for evaluating methodological work. I reject normative epistemologies, even if data are dead.

***

Data Encounters: Embracing the performance turn, I connect the study of data encounters, to the study of instances, to interpretation, and to hermeneutics. I privilege performed experience as a way of knowing, as a method of critical inquiry, and as a mode of understanding, as a way of making the meanings of instances visible. Hermeneutics does the work of interpretation with the potential of producing understanding. Knowing refers to those embodied, sensuous experiences which create the conditions for understanding (Denzin, 1984, p. 282). Through performance I experience another's feelings which are present in a remembering, a performance event (Pollock, 2005). Performed experiences are the sites where felt emotion, memory, desire, and understanding come together. I seek performative interpretations that are poetic, dramatic, critical and imaginative, interpretations that are interventions, interpretations that matter.

The self-as-subject-as-performer of another's text, enters onto an ethical relationship with the other. I honor their presence. The other is no longer the other, there is no other, only a multitude of voices, movements, gestures, intersecting selves, performing for one another (Pollock, 2005, p. 6, paraphrase). I bring my body, my flesh, my voice to your text. I circle around the hidden meanings in your narrative, I make these meanings visible with my voice and my body. This *archeology of unearthing*, Madison's phrase. is never neat or tidy. It is a continuous process of resurfacing, of digging, looking, feeling, moving, inspecting, tracing and re-tracing memories, new memories (Madison, 2005, p. 150).

As an autoethnographer I embed myself in my own history, in my memories, in my stories from my past.

TOWARD A PERFOMATIVE CULTURAL POLITICS

Performance autoethnography is defined by a commitment to a politics of resistance, to a commitment to change, not just interpret the world. Performance autoethnography addresses the structures and beliefs of neoliberalism as a public pedagogy, understanding that the cultural is always political (Giroux, 2014, p. 222).

The political is always performative. The performative is always pedagogical. To perform, to read, to analyze, to interpret, to write is to resist. Moral witnessing, civic courage, and moral outrage are sustained forms of resistance (Giroux, 2014, p. 223). Interpretation is a performance.

Here is Anzaldua, on the politics of performance along the U. S. Mexico border. These words could have been written yesterday:

> The border Patrol hides behind the local McDonalds on
> the outsksirts of Brownsville, Texas ... They set traps
> along the river beneath the bridge. Hunters in army-green
> uniforms stalk and track these economic refugees using the
> powerful nightvision of electronic sensing devices. Cornered by headlights,
> frisked, their arms stretched over their heads, *los mojados* are handcuffed, locked
> in jeeps, and then kicked
> back across the border, no home, just the thin edge of barbwire. (1987, pp. 12–13 paraphrase)

'Refugees in a homeland that does not want them,' wetbacks, no welcoming hand, only pain, suffering, humiliation, degradation, death (1987, p. 12). South of the Border, down Mexico way, North America's rubbish dump, no direction home (p. 11).

PERFORMANCE AS INTERVENTION

The rhetorical/pedagogical turn in performance studies interrogates the ways in which the performance text functions as an ideological document. This performance paradigm travels from theories of critical pedagogy to views of performance as intervention, interruption and resistance

Critical pedagogy understands performance as a form of inquiry. It views performance as a form of activism, as critique, as critical citizenship. It seeks a form of performative praxis that inspires and empowers persons to act on their utopian impulses. These moments are etched in history and popular memory. They are often addressed in testimonial and fact-based (and verbatim) theater, theatre which bears witness to social injustice and encourages active ethical spectatorship.

Moises Kaufman, and his oral history play, *The Laramie Project* (2001)[2] is illustrative. He observes:

> There are moments in history when a particular
> event brings the various ideologies and beliefs prevailing
> in a culture into deep focus. At these junctures the event
> becomes a lightning rod of sorts, attracting and distilling
> the essence of these philosophies and convictions. By paying
> careful attention in moments like this to people's words,

one is able to hear the way these prevailing ideas affect not
only individual lives but also the culture at large.
The trials of Oscar Wilde were such an event ... The
Brutal murder of Matthew Shephard was another event of this kind.

Spectacle pedagogy addresses these moments, those lightening rod occasions
when power, ideology and politics come crushing down on ordinary people and
their lives. It does so by staging and re-staging performances which interrogate
the cultural logics of the spectacle itself. Staged performances of culture are always
appraisal of culture (see Madison, 2010, p. 13). These re-stagings raise a series of
questions asking always, How did this happen? What does it mean? How could it
have been prevented? What are its consequences for the lives of ordinary people?
(see Madison, 2010, pp. 12–13).

To answer these questions Kaufman's Laramie Project enlisted the help of
Laramie citizens in the production of the play's script:

Kaufman:

We devoted two years of our lives to this
Project. We returned to Laramie many times
over the course of a year and a half and conducted
more than two hundred interviews. (2001, p. vii)

When the project was completed, a member of the community reflected on the
Shepard death and the play:

Jonas Slonaker:

Change is not an easy thing, and I don't think people
Were up to it here. They got what they wanted. Those
two boys got what they deserve and we look good
now. Justice has been served ... You know it has
been a year since Matthew Shepard died, and they
haven't passed shit in Wyoming ... at a state level,
any town, nobody anywhere, has passed any kind of
laws or hate crime legislation. ... What's come out
of it? (p. 99)

A community member replies:

Doc O'Connor:

I been up to that site (where he was killed). I
remembered to myself the night he and I drove
around together, he said to me, 'Laramie sparkles,
it?' ... I can just picture what he was seeing. The last
thing he saw in this earth was the sparkling lights. (p. 99)

And as Kaufman's little theatre group left Laramie, for the last time, a member commented:

Andy Paris:

And in the distance I could see the sparkling lights of
Laramie, Wyoming. (p. 101)

Mathew's legacy, the pure, sparkling lights of Laramie, what a town could be.

Critics have argued that Kaufman's play smooths over the raw edges of homophobia in Laramie. Taken out of context, the play, as Pollock notes, reads a bit like a version of Our Town,[3] but this impression may be due, in part to the effect 'of repeated productions in communities across the United States in which the original actors/interviewers are re/displaced by actors playing interviewer/actors' (Pollock, 2005, p. 6). This puts the representations of the Laramie and the murder 'at one further remove from the reality of the audience members who might otherwise identify with the members of the Tectonic Theater as people-like-themselves' (p. 6).

Being further removed speaks directly to the relationship between representation, performance and reality, that is 'actual' events. Paraphrasing Pollock (2005, pp. 2–3), too many representations of living history try to collapse reality and representation. The goal is to give the impression that 'you were there.' But that is only an ideological construction, a modernist realist myth which ignores the politics of representation.

The goal is to use critical pedagogy as the means to disrupt, expose and critique these structures of injustice. The stage becomes the site of resistance, the place where performative-I's confront and engage one another.

Paraphrasing Conquergood:

The aim of performance is to bring self and other, the performative-I and the audience together so they can question, debate, and challenge one another. The performance resists conclusions. It is open-ended. It is committed to creating and keeping a dialogue ongoing. It is more like a hypen, than a period. (2013, p. 75, paraphrase)

Madison (2005, p. 146) elaborates:

Performance involves seeing ourselves and showing ourselves to ourselves in a way that allows you to understand something new about who you are, it is a doubling, a kind of meta-narrative, performing performances of our inner and outer lives. For fieldwork performances there is another kind of performance going on as a result of invoking the nonfiction of other people's stories and vulnerabilities. (2005, p. 146, paraphrase)

A goal is to bring the audience into this space so they can co-experience this doubling, this meta-narrative and apply it to their own lives.

PERFORMANCE, CULTURAL PROCESS, POLITICS

All pragmatists and performance ethnographers who have read John Dewey would agree that culture, like data, is a verb, a process, an on-going performance, not a noun, or a product or a static thing. We cannot study cultural experience directly, just as we cannot study data directly. We study performances that produce those things we call data. We study experience in its performative representations, staged performances of culture. Experience has no existence apart from the storied acts of the performative-I (Pollock, 2007, p. 240). Performance becomes a tactic, a form of advocacy, of resistance, a cry for human rights and social justice,

Madison (2010, p. 9) provides an example, an imaginary scene in a death camp, an instance of courage and resxistanfe?[4]

> A death camp in Treblinka. A dancer stands naked in line waiting for her turn to enter the gas chamber. We see s human being with a natural power to command space reduced to a body taking up space, passively submitting to the prospect of death. A guard tells her to step in line and dance. She does, and carried away by her *authoritative action* and by her *repossession of self and a world* she dances up to the guard an—now within the compass of her space—takes his gun and shoots him. What a surprise, a zombie-like creature can spring back to like by means of a performance.

The dancer is moved, carried away by the forces of performance and justice to enact the unimaginable (Madison, 2010, p. 10).

The goal is to give back, to see performance as a form of activism, as critique, as critical citizenship. The goal is a performative praxis that inspires and empowers persons to act on their utopian impulses. These moments are etched in history and popular memory.

BACK TO LARAMIE, WYOMING, TEN YEARS LATER

Kaufman and the members of the Tectonic Theater Project returned to Laramie, Wyoming on the 10th anniversary of Mr. Shepard's death. They re-interviewed town members, intending to use the new interviews in an epilogue to the play. They were disappointed to learn that nothing had been done to commemorate the anniversary of Matthew's death. Mr. Kaufman was angry that there were as yet no hate-crimes law in Wyoming. But the city had changed.

Local Citizen:

> Laramie has changed in some ways. The city council passed a bias crimes ordinance that tracks such crimes, but it does include penalties for them. There is an AIDS Walk now. Several residents have came out publicly as gay, in their churches or on campus, in part to honor Mr. Shepard's memory. The university hosts a four-day Shepard Symposium for Social Justice each spring, and there is talk of creating a degree minor in gay and lesbian

studies. But there is no memorial to Mr. Shepard here in town The log fence has been torn down where he lay dying for 18 hours on Oct. 7, 1998. There is no marker. Wild grass blows in the wind. You can see the lights of Laramie from the spot where he died.

Performance ethnography disguised as spectacle theater in the service of memory, social change and social justice.

***

Effects like these in Laramie represent, at some deep level, an emancipatory commitment to community action which performs social change, even if change is only an idea, whose time has yet to come. This form of performance inquiry helps people recover, and release themselves from the repressive constraints embedded in repressive racist and homophobic pedagogies.

A dramatic production like *Laramie* moves in three directions at the same time: it shapes subjects, audiences and performers. In honoring subjects who have been mistreated, such performances contribute to a more 'Enlightened and involved citizenship' (Madison, 1998, p. 281). These performances interrogate and evaluate specific social, educational, economic and political processes. This form of praxis can shape a cultural politics of change. It can help create a progressive and involved citizenship. The performance becomes the vehicle for moving persons, subjects, performers, and audience members, into new, critical, political spaces. The performance gives the audience, and the performers, 'equipment for [this] journey: empathy and intellect, passion and critique' (Madison, 1998, p. 282).

Such performances enact a performance-centered evaluation pedagogy. Thus fusion of critical pedagogy and performance praxis, uses performance as a mode of inquiry, as a method of doing evaluation ethnography, as a path to understanding, as a tool for engaging collaboratively the meanings of experience, as a means to mobilize persons to take action in the world. This form of critical, collaborative, performance pedagogy privileges experience, the concept of voice, and the importance of turning evaluation sites into democratic public spheres (see Worley, 1998). Critical performance pedagogy informs practice, which in turn supports the pedagogical conditions for an emancipatory politics (Worley, 1998, p. 139).

Extending Toni Morrison, the best art, the best performance autoethnographies are 'unquestionably political and irrevocably beautiful at the same time' (Morrison, 1994, p. 497, also quoted in Madison, 1998, p. 281). They help us extract meaning out of individual instances, the murder of Matthew Shepard.

IN CONCLUSION: BACK TO DATA AND ITS COLLECTION

The performance turn problematizes data, its collection and analysis. Of course data are not dead. Data are not passive objects waiting to be collected, coded, categorized, treated as evidence in a theoretical model. Data are verbs, processes made visible through the performative acts of the inquirer. Data are never passive. Data have agency. Data have presence. Data have presence in the individual instance. The method of instances allows data to have another day in court, but only when it is read back through the radical empiricism of William James.

Data, at one level, refer to the facts of experience, and we can never be without the facts of experience, but we cannot be controlled by them. Data are always fluid, transformative, unruly (Koro-Ljungberg & MacLure, 2013; MacLure, 2013a, 2013b). I have suggested that we need an emancipatory, performance-based approach to data. This discourse requires a re-reading of words like data, data collection and data analysis. A performance-based approach reads these words in terms of a critical theory of performance, ethnography culture, politics and pedagogy.

NOTES

1. An earlier version of this essay draws on Denzin (2017). I thank Uwe Flick for his suggestions.
2. On October 7, 1998 a young gay man, Matthew Shepard, was discovered bound to a fence outside Laramie, Wyoming, savagely beaten, left to die. Matthew's death became a national symbol of intolerance. In the aftermath Kaufman and the members of the Tectonic Theatre Project went to Laramie and conducted more than 200 interviews. From these transcripts the playwrights constructed the Laramie Project. Ten years later they returned to Laramie, producing a second play based on the ways the community was grappling with Matthew's legacy. The play has been performed over 2000 times. The Tectonic Theater Project collaborated with Home Box Office (HBO) to make a film based on the play. It starred Peter Fonda, Laura Linney Christina Ricci and Steve Buscomi. It opened the 2002 Sundance Film Festival, and was nominated for 4 Emmys.
3. Our Town is a 1938 three-act play by American playwright Thornton Wilder. It tells the story of the fictional American small town of Grover's Corners between 1901 and 1913 through the everyday lives of its citizens.
4. From Hallie (1965, p. 46).

REFERENCES

Anzaldua, G. (1987). *Borderlands/La Frontera: The new mestiza*. San Francisco, CA: Aunt Lute Books.

Conquergood, D. (1992). Ethnography, rhetoric and performance. *Quarterly Journal of Speech, 78,* 80–97.

Conquergood, D. (2013). *Cultural Struggles. Performance, Ethnography, Praxis*. Ann Arbor, MI: University of Michigan Press.

Denzin, N. K. (1984). *On understanding emotion*. San Francisco, CA: Jossey-Bass.

Denzin, N. K. (2013). The death of data. *Cultural-Studies ⇔ Critical Methodologies, 13*(4), 353–356.

Denzin, N. K. (Forthcoming). Performance, hermeneutics, interpretation. In U. Flick (Ed.), *Sage Handbook of qualitative data collection*. Sage.

Fiske, J. (1994). Audiencing: Cultural practice and cultural studies. In N. K. Denzin and Y. S. Lincoln (Eds.), *The handbook of qualitative research* (pp. 189–198). Thousand Oaks, CA: Sage.

Giroux. H. (2014). *The violence of organized forgetting.* San Francisco, CA: City Lights Bookstore.

Gomez, A., Puigvert, L., & Flecha, R. (2011). Critical communicative methodology: Informing real social transformation through social research. *Qualitative Inquiry, 17*(3), 235–246.

Hallie, P. (1965). *The paradox of cruelty.* Middleton: Wesleyn University Press.

Jackson, A. Y., & Mazzei, L. (2012). *Thinking with theory in qualitative research: Viewing data across multiple perspectives.* London: Routledge.

James, W. (1912). *Essays in radical empiricism.* New York, NY: Longman, Green & Co.

Kaufman, M. (2014). *The Laramie project & the Laramie project 10 years later.* New York, NY: Vintage (originally published 2001).

Koro-Ljungberg, M. (2016). *Reconceptualizing qualitative research: Methodologies without methodology.* Thousand Oaks, CA: Sage.

Koro-Ljungberg, M., & MacLure, M. (2013). Provocations, re-un-visions, death and other possibilities of 'data'. *Cultural Studies ↔ Critical Methodologies, 13*(4), 219–222.

Lather, P. (2007). *Getting lost: Feminist efforts toward a double (d) science.* Albany, NY: SUNY Press.

MacLure, M. (2013a). The wonder of data. *Cultural Studies ⇔ Critical Methodologies, 13*(4), 228–232.

MacLure, M. (2013b). Classification or wonder? Coding as an analytic practice in qualitative research. In R. Coleman & J. Ringrose (Eds.), *Deleuze and research methodologies* (pp. 164–183). Edinburg, TX: University Press.

Madison, D. S. (1998). Performances, personal narratives, and the politics of possibility. In S. J. Dailey (Ed.), *The future of performance studies: Visions and revisions.* (pp. 276–286). Annadale, VA: National Communication Association.

Madison, D. S. (2005). *Critical ethnography.* Cambridge: Cambridge University Press.

Madison, D. S. (2010). *Acts of activism: Human rights as radical performance.* Cambridge: Cambridge University Press.

Psathas, G. (1995). *Conversation analysis.* Thousand Oaks, CA: Sage.

Pollock, D. (2005). Introduction: Remembering. In Pollock, D. (Ed.) *Remembering. Oral History Performance.* (pp. 1–17). New York, NY: Palgrave Macmillan.

Pollock, D. (2007). The Performative "I". *Cultural Studies <−> Critical Methodologies. 7*(3), 239–255.

Richardson, L. (2000). Writing: A method of inquiry. In N. K. Denzin & Y. S. Lincoln (Eds.), *Handbook of qualitative research* (2nd edn., pp. 923–948). Thousand Oaks, CA: Sage.

St. Pierre, E. (2011). Post qualitative research: The critique and the coming after. In N. K. Denzin & Y. S. Lincoln (Eds.), *Handbook of qualitative research* (4th edn., pp. 611–626). Thousand Oaks, CA: Sage.

Worley, D. (1998). Is critical performative pedagogy practical? In S. J. Dailey (Ed.), *The future of performance studies: Visions and revisions* (pp. 136–140). Washington, DC: National Communication Association.

CHAPTER SEVEN

(Un)becoming Data Through Philosophical Thought Processes OF Pasts, Presents AND Futures

SONJA ARNDT

ABSTRACT

This chapter reconceptualises data and its treatments. It unsettles the focus on data as representations of particular temporal or human subjective experiences or environments, by conceptualizing data as complex encounters with pasts, presents and futures. It invokes post and more-than-human perspectives, drawing on a Māori whakataukī (proverb) representing the notion of calling on the past to face the future. Philosophical attitudes and approaches are utilized to disrupt data beyond the thinkable, and beyond representation, to include uncertain, unknowable entanglements of time, space, matter, and energies. Philosophical thought, invention, creativity and style entangle the playings-around in the explorations of this chapter. They dethrone the conception of data as knowable, or truth telling, creating cracks and inventions that entwine data in the intricate inter- and intra-relationships of temporal, relational and other-worldly realities, open, uncertain, and contextually complex.

Keywords: rethinking data, philosophy as a method, philosophical attitudes, philosophical approaches, doing philosophy

INTRODUCTION

Kia whakatōmuri te haere whakamua
My past is my present is my future
I walk backwards into the future
with my eyes fixed on my past
(Māori whakataukī/proverb, Rameka, 2016)

This chapter disrupts normative conceptualisations and practices of data. It imagines beyond, beyond the present, to the past, to face the future, in non-linear, blurry, im/possibilities. Like the opening Māori whakataukī, it walks 'backwards into the future', revisiting thought and data utilising philosophy as a method. Adopting philosophy as a method involves particular attitudes and approaches to thought, some of which are outlined in this chapter, to enable a critical unsettling of what might be seen as data, and beyond data, through these philosophical engagements. The chapter attempts to disrupt conceptions of data in educational research and investigates through philosophical approaches what even might be seen as data—or not. It disturbs common conceptions of data, and raises possible temporal and relational limitations of a linear or human-centric approach to data. Further, the chapter muddies conceptualisations of data as truth representations of human experience.

A focus on human experience often dominates data in educational research. This chapter seeks to elevate factors and affects from outside, beyond, and around the human realm, in recognition of their inter-relatedness, temporally, as the opening whakataukī reminds us, and relationally. It raises thinking about data to a level that shifts possibilities for/of data beyond the living, feeling, sensing and sensual, gendered, talking—and also glorified, marginalising, power-and-knowledge-hungry, dominant—human element. The chapter sets out, then, not to disregard, but to enhance the human element, precisely because human experiences are complex, incomplete, often unknowable, unspeakable, and, in a conventional sense, unreliable as data.

The philosophical framework used in this derangement of data draws on the Māori conception of walking backwards towards the future. Entangling post- and more-than-human perspectives with conceptions of and approaches to 'doing' philosophy de-elevates data as recordable, observable, analysable and thus knowable, and challenge the reification of human voice and perceptions. Conceptions of philosophy and philosophical thought raise questions about the knowability of what is and what is not, what affects, and what warps data, creating spaces for diverse 'more-than-Is', to include matter, energies and forces, in rhizomatic beginnings, tangents, and disruptions, as in the past, present and future of the opening whakataukī. A Māori conception of Being (Mika, 2011) suggests a mysterious metaphysical relationship with the infinite, unknowable, to add to the 'doings' explored here, further blurring the boundaries, of what might be recorded, coded, stored, for example, as data.

(UN)BECOMING DATA

Data are dominantly and commonly seen as representations of knowable human experiences to inform educational research. Koro-Ljungberg and MacLure (2013) lament this situation, particularly in consideration of alternative conceptions and treatments of data, in St. Pierre's and many others' work, in recent years. Despite these provocations for critical and creative workings with and around data, that reconceptualise "notions, definitions, enactments and treatments" (p. 219), dominant conceptions persist and are perpetuated, in undergraduate and postgraduate research methods courses and publication guidelines. One such dominant form of data's representation of human experience is the reliance on research participants' voice. Widely valued as a human right, and expression of human agency, voice is ennobled as the representation of human experience. Voice as data is commonly perceived as a record of subjective experiences, as a subject's story that must be, or deserves to be, heard.

Un-becoming data, and dislodging the reliance on voice, calls for a more questioning approach to narrating human experiences. What, for instance, is 'a subject's experiential story'? Does every person/subject know his/her/their story, or have the ability or inclination to tell it? Does what an individual research participant or researcher tells actually represent her, his, or their story? And is what the listener hears the story that the speaker was intending to tell? Even if we were to remain focused on voice—which Plato famously considered to be 'pure', 'true' knowledge—linguists and philosophers have long argued that speech is not only incomplete, warped, inaccurate and already out-dated by the time it is uttered, but that the story heard is always also complicated by the listener. An individual's story is always only that which the listener makes of it, on the basis of her, his, or their own story, made up of experiences, insights and contexts (Bakhtin, 1981; Kristeva, 1986). What is really captured, by recording voice in field notes, videos or transcripts is thus an ethical minefield in itself.

The aggrandizement of voice, therefore, deserves further attention. Jackson and Mazzei (2013) caution against a privileging of voice, as

> traditional qualitative research assumes that voice makes present the truth and *reflects* the meaning of an experience that has already happened. This is the voice that, in traditional qualitative research, is heard and then recorded, coded, and categorized as normative and containable data. (p. 263, emphasis in the original)

Barad (2003) shares the concern with the notion that words can represent, or worse, determine, what is real, and claims that such a belief demonstrates that "[l]anguage has been granted too much power" (p. 801). The question of what is real directs conceptualisations of data beyond the social and the cultural, calling for the humble recognition of temporally and relationally complex, post-, more-than- or non-human potentialities (Bennett, 2010; Braidotti, 2013; Haraway, 2007), and whole world impressions of reality (Barad, 2007). This implicates the uncertainty of relying on voice as representation of human realities, for example, in what indi- vidual research participants might choose or be able to represent in terms of pasts, presents and future. It raises the question, then, of what can be data and how can what-ever-it-is-or-becomes capture such whole world ontological, epistemological inter- and intra-relationships, that go beyond voice, beyond language, or beyond the human? Focusing on what is real, thus, either misses or limits the point.

Deepening concerns with representing realities and what might or should be considered as data raise a further concern with imaginings of past, present and future. What does this entail? In other words, how might this perspective com- plicate data, in ways that enhance research representations of temporal and rela- tional multiplicities, for example, across cultures, or beyond the human? In this exploration I argue that thinking through philosophy as a method helps to blur binaries, so that "[h]uman bodies are ... not seen to be merely the physical coun- terpart to a self, but part of the very materiality that comprises any space" (Todd, 2016, p. 407). These imaginaries endorse Barad's (2015) claim, for example, that matter matters, and they acknowledge possible propensities of matter to "test out every un/imaginable path, every im/possibility" (p. 387). Re-imagining data through philosophical attitudes and approaches creates possibilities for entwining multiple pasts, presents, futures and infinites, to act on and react to each other, in un-representable inter- and intra-active responsibilities and relationships, deter- mining and performing planetary and worldly, cross-cultural and cross-species, blurred, interdependencies (Haraway, 2007; Latour, 2014; Malone, 2016). Such imaginations and possibilities implicate and complicate what should or could be known, and the ways in which knowledge can be obtained. Philosophy as a method opens critical spaces for expanding data-imaginings.

PHILOSOPHY AS A METHOD

Philosophy can be seen as a method that involves critical attitudes, approaches and thought. In relation to destabilising conceptions of data, by seeking to revisit the past, it entails walking backwards, as the opening whakataukī suggests, towards im/possibilities and imaginings for the future. To begin with the question of philosophical attitudes and approaches, Hegel (1807) states that philosophy is concerned with learning about general principles and perspectives, and applied to considerations of the concerns at hand. Hegel's perspective grounds common views on data through his concern with understanding subjectivity, the human mind, and the nature of things (Siep, 2014). His belief that the nature of 'things' is consciously knowable feeds the expectation that there is a knowable truth, and that there are particular ways in which this knowledge can be gained. It therefore reasserts the very dialectics and binaries that this exploration attempts to dissolve. Hegel's view, then, affirms the importance of carefully conceptualising data and its aims in relation to the principles and perspectives of a particular research project. Simultaneously, Hegel also conveys that everything is also spiritual, bringing his thinking closer to the mysterious, unknowable elements of entanglements, meanings, past, present and future.

Coming from a Māori indigenous perspective, Mika and Stewart (2016) acknowledge such uncertainties through their examinations of counter-colonial Māori metaphysical conceptions of time, of nothingness, and form. They describe a space that reaffirms the opening whakataukì, where "the past reaches out to connect with the present and the future" (p. 310). Hegel, then, draws connections to seemingly paradoxical perspectives. On the one hand his philosophical thinking supports the categorisation and identification of knowledge in dualisms and dialectics that, on the other hand, are imbued with a sense of uncertainty, as in the spiritual, temporal indigenous perspective of Mika and Stewart.

Hegel's categorisations and dialectics, and especially the notion that truths are knowable, affirm the conception of data as recordable and observable. Interspersing the uncertainty of the spiritual, or of a sense of the mysterious infinite, plays into the hands of the negativity in Hegel's work, through the dialectical 'other'. Such a sense of denial arises in Deleuze's (1990), view on philosophy as not a method, but that "doing philosophy is trying to invent or create concepts" and that "there are various ways of looking at concepts" (p. 25). Urging creativity and heterogeneity in developing and considering concepts, he says that "concepts are not ready-made 'givens' and have no pre-existence: one needs to invent them, one needs to create them" (p. 32). Butler's description of Deleuze and Guattari's philosophy further supports such de-essentialising:

> What they see as constituting authentic philosophy is the project of doing away with *all* preconceptions as to what thought is or should be. It would be to hold to the principle that there is *nothing* that naturally or innately belongs to thought that all definitions of it reveal themselves merely to be the reflections of a particular place and time. (Butler, 2015, p. 18)

Data viewed through this lens then shifts and changes in accordance with place and time.

Deleuze (1990) calls for not only creativity but style in this undertaking, through philosophical as well as non-philosophical understandings, of concepts, percepts and affects, in a 'particular place and time'. Philosophy, commentary and criticism of everyday realities, beliefs and problems, thus draw precisely such fluid contextual issues into an unknowable temporal, im/possible encounter.

Following these explorations, philosophy is about creating (concepts) and styling, of characters, settings, scenes, 'space-times'. As Deleuze (1990) says, "philosophy has absolutely nothing to do with discussing things, ... all you should ever do is explore it, play around with the terms, add something, relate it to something else, never discuss it" (p. 139). Philosophy is about creating likenesses, he says, and about inventing concepts, and is by its nature creative, revolutionary, a matter of style, and, re-affirming the temporal element, it is "like an echo chamber, a feedback loop", where ideas appear and re-appear, "as it were, through various filters" (p. 139). The remainder of this chapter uses conceptions of philosophy to 'play around with' what data may be. It applies metaphorical 'echo chambers' and 'feedback loops' to explore possibilities for enhancing data through insertions of pasts, present and future. Philosophy should allow for a spark to "flash and break out of language itself, to make us see and think what was lying in the shadow around the words, things we were hardly aware existed" (p. 141). In this sense philosophy creates possibilities for movements, sparks and flashes to shift, position and re-position what is and what is not, data.

DOING PHILOSOPHY—DISRUPTING DATA

Philosophy as a 'playing around' means that "content and method are one" (Standish, 2009, p. i). It entails a traditional view on exposing previously held pre-suppositions (Harré, 2000), but, through a Deleuzian sense of inventiveness, moves beyond the discursive. Examining what is hidden, in the shadows, becoming even more complicated, since it implies moving beyond the assumption that there is always "a secure distinction between words and the things or concepts to which they refer" (MacLure, 2010, p. 279). Discursive boundaries are therefore contested. Such contested spaces open up to thinking the unthinkable (Koro-Ljungberg, Carlson, Tesar, & Anderson, 2014), and invite a certain bruteness, allowing for "[t]hinking brute, doing brute, and writing brute" (p. 1). Bruteness here might be seen as in Bennett's (2010) insistence on reclaiming rather than avoiding rawness. Deleuze and Guattari (2013) echo this notion in their assertion that the "world has become chaos" (p. 5), and that such chaos calls for thinking in rhizomes, where beginnings, endings and in-betweens, rupture significations, and shatter understandings and linear or smooth conceptions or categorisations. A brute, chaotic perspective disturbs expectations of data to suggest or represent conclusive realities, worlds or behaviours. It alludes to vibrancy, uncertainty and agency, as data that draws on the past, and into unknowable futures.

Philosophy can be concerned with engaging with sensitive, subjective notions of human activity, thoughts and feelings. Harré (2000) like Hegel locates it in the flesh of subjective experiences, of examining practices, absolute beliefs and taken-for-granted epistemologies. What, however, if we suggest, as the addition of vibrancy, agentic matter and bruteness might, that the absolute is unknowable? Blurring the human-centric notions of the flesh of subjective experiences creates spaces for the insertion of actors and actants surrounding and beyond the humanly discernable.

Furthermore, philosophical attitudes and approaches open unparalleled thought possibilities, for resolving problems in practice in ways that might otherwise not be achieved (Standish, 2009). Returning to the problem with data and its reliance on human voice and experience, draws on Standish's suggestion that philosophical puzzles arise because of, and are messily entangled with, the language by which they are articulated, clarified, aligned and resolved. This view of philosophy as a complex undertaking, informing, and illuminated by entanglements of the everyday, maintains a human discursive orientation.

To further complicate attitudes towards and conceptualisations of data, Papastephanou's (2009) insistence on philosophy as a space for estrangement creates another possibility for temporal and relational multiplicities. If estrangements become data—revealing perceptual and affective strangenesses in and caused by things, matters, energies and forces, what openings might form, for past or metaphysical conceptions of data? In what ways might such data be identified, captured, even necessary? Estrangements in and of data place data well into the realm of uncertainty.

PHILOSOPHICAL ESTRANGEMENTS AND UNCERTAINTY

Estrangements might be thought of as eluding knowable truths. Finding and arguing for multiple philosophical 'truths', to be acquired by "thinking hard, making distinctions, giving proofs" (Feinberg, 2014, p. 4) resituates data as humanly representable and knowable. However, as truth arguments depend on complex conceptions of the problem and the kind of evidence sought (Bowell & Kemp, 2015), they too might estrange, by creating unfillable openings through beyond human connections. Considering philosophy as a method that searches for multiple truths (Ruitenberg, 2009) then, helps to disrupt any perceived simplicity, in recording, coding, or relying on data. Furthermore, focusing on multiple, diverse truths might disturb educational expectations and counter reductivist, "anti-intellectual" (Bridges & Smith, 2006, p. 132) tendencies and expectations of 'single truth' solutions for improving practice, through "a very narrow, apparently scientific, conception of empirical research" (Bridges & Smith, 2006, p. 132). While seeking multiple truths using philosophy as a method supports the notion that there is no one ideal, or correct truth, it holds nevertheless that there is such thing as a truth or nameable reality. Taking the vitality of things and times seriously disrupts data by exposing the brute, chaotic possibilities of truth, non-truth, or brute-truth, in all its rawness.

Philosophy as a method for engaging with data thus relies on critical philo-sophical attitudes and approaches to truth, estrangements and uncertainty. This space then might encompass, as Bennett (2010) urges, the vitality of things and their affect, that interfere with the "will or designs of humans" and that this occurs through their actions as "agents or forces with trajectories, propensities, or tenden-cies of their own" (p. viii). Such things and agentic forces can interfere with multiple truths and what might be seen as useful research funded, conducted and driven by the local/global educational and political climate. Openness to such forces inserts more of the unknowable other, and following Barad (2015), more of "the imagina-tive capacities of materiality" involving rather a zigzagged dis/continuous musing, than a "linear argumentation" (p. 388), to counter the oversimplification driven by human representations and analysable data. Measurable, definable research ideals encapsulated in "the rage for closure that animates contemporary policy" (MacLure, 2006, p. 224) retain the controllable, visible, discursive human element. Turning back to look forward, provokes playing around with data as material imaginings, to by-pass the rage for closure, and by-passes human expectations.

Seeing philosophy as a zigzagged musing beyond traditional forms of analysis, synthesis, and dialogue comes to involve wider constructions. It draws in recon-structions and revelations of meanings and values beyond those that might tradi-tionally be seen as academically, or humanly important. Indeed, attributing human importance to experiences, discoveries or occurrences—that might be recorded as data—sustain the glorification of human superiority. In a Deleuzian sense of philosophy, as playing around with framings, understandings and elements, in a search for possible inter-relationships, philosophy then creates spaces for flows of articulation and thought to slow, accelerate and rupture, to constitute new data assemblages and multiplicities (Deleuze, 1990; Deleuze & Guattari, 2013). Seeking wider worldly, imaginative, critical human and academic understandings of the power inherent in data, is thus a critical aspect leading beyond human, beyond present, forms of data recognition and articulation.

BY-PASSING HUMAN REALITIES

Locating data in a past, present and future framework highlights and contests its boundaries. Contradictions and disjunctions open up to the possibilities of data as uncertain representations of the past that might combine, as Barad (2003) urges, social and scientific matter and materialities, to represent the "exteriority within" (p. 803). Philosophical attitudes and approaches to conceptualising data expose concerns and challenges in "rigid demarcations" (Papastephanou, 2009, p. 451). They might, for example, reflect such certainties as what Massumi (2013) refers to as "good sense, … 'universal' truth and (white male) justice" (p. vii), or the truth-ful evidence sought by conventional representations in data. Arguing that philosophical research cannot simply "replace one formula with another" (Papastephanou, 2009, p. 452), or reapply one prescriptive approach as it questions another, Papastephanou's perspective further urges a rethinking, disrupting approach.

Approaching data through philosophy, then, invokes the principle of *aporia*. An *aporetic* approach in philosophy calls for a constant puzzlement and openness, and strengthens the view that technical esteem and reification of data or statistics within the humanly knowable, are less important than an open orientation towards the unknown and what is beyond the human. Similarly to Deleuze and Guattari's (2013) rhizomatic thought processes, *aporia* disrupts—and possibly aborts—thought patterns, in an "iconoclastic revolt" (Papastephanou, 2009, p. 454), pushing against sacred boundaries and reifications. *Aporia* supports and arises in stutters and tangents that in turn subvert, entangle, strangle and restart the unknowable, in complex temporal, beyond human, data-sensings.

Iconoclastic revolt that averts halting limitations or dead ends, and spirals instead into such unfamiliar territory, highlights the role of philosophy. It follows, in one sense, the call for in-depth examinations of "the fine-grained complexities of social phenomena" (Davis, 2009, p. 371). However, it also ruptures this social focus to create spaces for contesting the spiritual, metaphysical significance of past, present and future representations in data. While Papastephanou (2009) refers to the necessity of engaging with "the dangerous normalcy of daily life" (p. 458), the fine-grained complexities in the vitality and vibrancy of matter, more-than-human, temporal and relational realities, takes this into new daily life territory.

An urgent confrontation of data through senses, knowledges, and intuitions, as encompassed in the Māori ecological connections and relationships, may be necessary not as an academic, researcherly solution, but for survival. Beyond thought, grappling with worldly engagements, following Haraway (2007), calls for head–on ecological confrontations of data. She urges serious engagement with inter-species, inter-relational co-dependencies, and, like the indigenous Māori world-view encompasses its relational, metaphysical engagements. An argument from Mika and Stewart (2016), for temporal and material relatedness affirms the inseparability of these forces and connections. Following Cole (as cited in Bennett, 2010) the "colliding of particle-forces" (p. xiii) relate body to body affects to forces, materials and beings (Bennett, 2010). The Māori metaphysics examined by Mika and Stewart (2016) problematizes the "entitised" and "thingified" (p. 301) concerns of a human and knowledge-centric focus in and on understandings of data. Their indigenous interrelatedness demonstrates its alignment with Deleuze and Guattari's thought, as rather than immuring in some kind of "ordered interiority", it "rides difference ... does not respect artificial division between ... subject, concept, and being" and, most importantly, "it replaces restrictive analogy with a conductivity that knows no bounds" (Massumi, 2013, p. xi). Removing boundaries, direction, and recognizing conductivity without words, collisions and collusions of energies, and connections creates a dilemma for data.

The dilemma is, that even if they could be recognised, what would it mean to communicate, sense, feel, be or do data as/in/through such complex assemblages? Interfering with human perceptions, control and desire, opens up to the question of how should human researchers encounter such a beyond and uncertainty through data, when that data is more-than-us? *Aporetic* messy, and uncertain conceptions of and engagements with data, then, open up to a reconceptualisation of encounters with forces that are raw and chaotic. Researchers themselves then, become drawn into the dilemma, through the particular, necessarily uncertain, time, place, and relational and metaphysical encounters of the situation.

CONCLUDING COMMENTS

Conceptualisations of data can be disrupted using philosophy as a method, attitude and approach. Drawing on an indigenous Māori whakataukī has elevated the importance of the past in understandings of the present and future, and complicated data as complex representations of truths and uncertainties. This chapter has explicated philosophy as diverse critical thought processes and orientations that have created cracks and openings for temporal and relational forces and contexts to elude human data imaginaries.

Neither more-than-human imaginaries and their multifaceted, brutal and complex elements of beings and times, nor philosophy, offer a solution. Philosophy as a method, and as critical attitudes and approaches, has raised questions, unsettling data by inserting unknowable forces and energies, acting and affecting data and researchers. The chapter has created spaces for catapulting data knowing towards a humble reconceptualization of data uncertainties, as unknowable past-present-future-infinite, a data chaos—frightening, entangled, enduring. The ruptures created by this chapter also offer no solution. Instead, they create openings into which, as it urges, researchers insert their own particular, non-linear, uncertain reconceptualization of what data might or might not be, drawing on the past, towards the present and into the future: *Kia whakatōmuri te haere whakamua.*

REFERENCES

Bakhtin, M. M. (1981). *The dialogic imagination* (C. Emerson & M. Holquist, Trans. M. Holquist, Ed.). Austin, TX: University of Texas Press.

Barad, K. (2003). Posthumanist performativity: Toward an understanding of how matter comes to matter. *Signs: Journal of Women in Culture and Society, 28*(3), 801–831. doi: 10.1086/345321

Barad, K. (2007). *Meeting the universe halfway: Quantum physics and the entanglement of matter and meaning*. Durham, NC: Duke University Press.

Barad, K. (2015). Transmaterialities: Trans*/matter/realities and queer political imaginings. *GLQ: A Journal of Lesbian and Gay Studies, 21*(2–3), 387–422. doi: 10.1215/10642684-2843239

Bennett, J. (2010). *Vibrant matter: A political ecology of things*. Durham, NC: Duke University Press.

Bowell, T., & Kemp, G. (2015). *Critical thinking: A concise guide*. Oxon: Routledge.

Braidotti, R. (2013). *The posthuman*. Cambridge: Polity Press.

Bridges, D., & Smith, R. (2006). Philosophy, methodology and educational research: Introduction. *Journal of Philosophy of Education, 40*(2), 131–135.

Butler, R. (2015). *Deleuze and Guattari's 'What is philosophy?'*. London: Bloomsbury Academic.

Davis, A. (2009). Examples as method? My attempts to understand assessment and fairness (in the spirit of the later Wittgenstein). *Journal of Philosophy of Education, 43*(3), 371–389.

Deleuze, G. (1990). *Negotiations* (M. Joughin, Trans.). New York, NY: Columbia University Press.

Deleuze, G., & Guattari, F. (2013). *A thousand plateaus: Capitalism and schizophrenia* (B. Massumi, Trans.). London: Bloomsbury Academic.

Feinberg, J. (2014). *Doing philosophy* (5th ed.). Boston, MA: Wadsworth, Cengage Learning.

Haraway, D. (2007). *When species meet*. Minneapolis, MN: University of Minnesota Press.

Harré, R. (2000). *One thousand years of philosophy: From Ramanuja to Wittgenstein*. Oxford: Blackwell Publishers.

Hegel, G. W. F. (1807). *Phänomenologie des Geistes (Phenomenology of Spirit)*. Bamberg and Würzburg: Joseph Anton Goebhardt.

Jackson, A. Y., & Mazzei, L. A. (2013). Plugging one text into another: Thinking with theory in qualitative research. *Qualitative Enquiry, 19*(4), 261–271.

Koro-Ljungberg, M., Carlson, D., Tesar, M., & Anderson, K. (2014). Methodology brut: Philosophy, ecstatic thinking, and some other (unfinished) things. *Qualitative Inquiry*, 1–8. doi: 10.1177/1077800414555070

Koro-Ljungberg, M., & MacLure, M. (2013). Provocations, re-un-visions, death, and other possibilities of "data". *Cultural Studies <-> Critical Methodologies, 13*(4), 219–222. doi: 10.1177/1532708613487861

Kristeva, J. (1986). Word, dialogue and novel. In T. Moi (Ed.), *The Kristeva reader* (pp. 34–61). Oxford: Blackwell Publishers.

Latour, B. (2014). Agency at the time of the anthropocene. *New Literary History, 45*(1), 1–18. doi: 10.1353/nlh.2014.0003

MacLure, M. (2006). 'A demented form of the familiar': Postmodernism and educational research. *Journal of Philosophy of Education, 40*, 223–239.

MacLure, M. (2010). The offence of theory. *Journal of Education Policy, 25*(2), 277–286. doi: 10.1080/02680930903462316

Malone, K. (2016). Posthumanist approaches to theorising children's human-nature relations. In K. Nairn, P. Kraftl, & T. Skelton (Eds.), *Space, place and environment* (3th ed., pp. 1–22). Singapore: Springer.

Massumi, B. (2013). Translator's foreword: Pleasures of philosophy. In G. Deleuze & F. Guattari (Eds.), *A thousand plateaus: Capitalism and schizophrenia* (pp. vii–xiv). London: Bloomsbury Academic.

Mika, C. (2011). Overcoming 'being' in favour of knowledge: The fixing effect of 'mātauranga'. *Educational Philosophy and Theory, 44*(10), 1080–1092. doi: 10.1111/j.1469-5812.2011.00771.x

Mika, C., & Stewart, G. (2016). Māori in the kingdom of the gaze: Subjects or critics? *Educational Philosophy and Theory, 48*(3), 300–312. doi: 10.1080/00131857.2015.1013017

Papastephanou, M. (2009). Method, philosophy of education and the sphere of the practico-inert. *Journal of Philosophy of Education, 43*(3), 451–470.

Rameka, L. (2016). Kia whakatōmuri te haere whakamua: 'I walk backwards into the future with my eyes fixed on my past'. *Contemporary Issues in Early Childhood, 17*(4), 387–398. doi: 10.1177/1463949116677923.

Ruitenberg, C. (2009). Distance and defamiliarisation: Translation as philosophical method. *Journal of Philosophy of Education, 43*(3), 421–435.

Siep, L. (2014). *Modern European philosophy: Hegel's phenomenology of spirit.* Cambridge: Cambridge University Press.

Standish, P. (2009). Preface. *Journal of Philosophy of Education, 43*(3), i–ii.

Todd, S. (2016). Education incarnate. *Educational Philosophy and Theory, 48*(4), 405–417. doi: 10.1080/00131857.2015.1041444

CHAPTER EIGHT

Writing Data

JESSICA VAN CLEAVE AND SARAH BRIDGES-RHOADS

ABSTRACT

In this chapter, we attempt to slow down our thinking about data's role in qualitative and post qualitative inquiry by focusing on what data does to us and becomes in our collaborative encounters with philosophical concepts. Specifically, we take up Deleuze and Guattari's concept *ritornello* because it seemed both *necessary* for our thinking about data and *unfamiliar* to us, two criteria that Deleuze said should constrain the philosophical work of creating new concepts. Rather than using the concept to think about and theorize data, we use the space of the page to map the becoming of *ritornello* in order to illustrate our encounters with the data produced as the concept becomes some*thing* that *can* slow down our thinking. In other words, we ask what happens to data, to ritornello, to Deleuze and Guattari, and to us when we layer, connect, extend, dissect, and so on our understandings and beings with *ritornello*. The goal is to continue our work of exploring how conventional writing structures (e.g., citation) reduce those becomings to the procedural and limit the possibilities for responsible methodological work that does not anticipate an end goal and remains open to the unknown. Our hope is that the work to re-vision data will enable us to interact or intra-act with the conventions of writing in as-yet unimaginable ways.

Keywords: Ritornello, data, theory, writing

INTRODUCTION

In this chapter, we experiment with writing data. We write data as *ritornellos*, a concept that Deleuze and Guattari (1980/1987) described as "the beginnings of order in chaos" (p. 311; see also Kleinherenbrink, 2015). Because ritornello is immanent to Deleuze and Guattari's ontology, which flattens hierarchies, writing ritornellos unmoors habitual connections between language and meaning, enabling us to think and do representation differently. As MacLure (2013) argued, rejecting the "hierarchical logic of representation" engages the "materiality of language itself—its material force and its entanglements in bodies and matter" (p. 658). Alongside data, theories, ritornellos, conversations with our children, dreams, walks in the park, quotes from scholars that persistently leap on the page, and, and, and, we step into the void, uncertain of where this path—the path of writing data as ritornellos—will take us.

The effect of our experimentation is the text that follows—a rhizomatic, messy, and "generative text [that] does not just transmit significations [but] puts its meaning always in-the-making" (Massumi, 2015, pp. 61–62). In other words, this is a text whose meaning is becoming. This is an unfinished text—much like data as ritornello–that "could rather be thought of in events, particles, and through brute and raw partiality" (Koro-Ljungberg, Carlson, Tesar, & Anderson, 2015, p. 613). We acknowledge that some may find the partiality of this text to be uneasy, uncomfortable, and/or unfamiliar. Readers (including ourselves) will not find clean descriptions of data as ritornellos and ritornellos as data. In part, this is because we hesitate to overcode either what ritornello *is* or what data *is*. When we layer, connect, extend, dissect, and so on our understandings and beings with *ritornello*, we maintain the unfinishedness of the text and invite readers to engage ritornello to see what happens to data, to ritornello, to Deleuze and Guattari, and to us when ritornello becomes something on the page. For readers who prefer guidance in potential uses of this chapter, we provide a brief glossary (or perhaps unglossary) of writing conventions that highlights how representation and conventions of writing create artificial separations of theory and data.

Perhaps it is best for readers to approach the text with the hope of finding it *useless* for disrupting data-as-usual. After all, according to Manning and Massumi (2013), "what is most experimental is most useless. If something is truly new, the context for its use will not yet exist. It will create its own context, giving rise to new uses never before imagined." In this sense, the words, the writing conventions, the format, the data, the theory may not be understood at all. Rather, like a record, with each reading/listening, there may be some parts that "leave you cold" and ought to be skipped while others may "follow you" as you try to think/live/do inquiry; you may find yourself "humming them under your breath as you go about your daily business" (Massumi, 1987, pp. xiii–xiv).

(UN)GLOSSARY

Author

In a conventional text, the pronouns used in the body of the piece match the number of authors in a byline, presumably reflecting who did the inquiry, who wrote the text, and so on. In this chapter, however, we use both "I" and "we," though neither is necessarily reflective of who wrote a section of the text. Such confusion signals to the decentering of an "intentional subject standing separate and outside of 'the data' [and theory], digging behind or beyond or beneath it, to identify higher order meanings, themes or categories" (MacLure, 2013, p. 660). That decentering happens when language "become[s] one element in a manifold of forces and intensities that are moving, connecting and diverging" (p. 660). Thus, we suggest readers not ask, *Is this Sarah? Or Jessica? Or both?* but rather, *What part of the "collective assemblage of enunciation" (p. 660) is no longer thinkable when personal pronouns easily connect to individual authors?*

Concepts

Throughout the text, we create, experiment with, and sometimes just mention concepts, like ritornellization, theory without theorists, immanence, and the force. We do not provide definitions of those concepts because "conventional definitions would strictly be invalid, since to define is to return to the logic of representation, where words 'refer' to entities as if these were separate and distinct from one another" (MacLure, 2013, p. 661). We recommend that readers likewise resist trying to pin down the meaning of any of these concepts—erasing the entanglements of language—and instead make themselves available to what those words might do to them, for them, with them *and* how they feel them in their bones *and* where those words might take them *and* what concepts they might create as they read.

Headings

Headings are often intended to help guide the reader through the text because they indicate both something about the content of each section as well as the hierarchical relationship between and among sections. Our headings, however, create a "beginning of order in chaos," a portable territory, which "launches forth ... not on the side where the old forces of chaos press against it but in another region" (Deleuze & Guattari, 1980/1987, p. 311). For example, we created a list of words, phrases, statements, and questions in the midst of our entanglements with *ritornello*, like "[a] child in the dark, gripped with fear, comforts himself by singing under his breath" (Deleuze & Guattari, 1980/1987, p. 311). Those words, phrases, statements, and questions became our headings, which we sometimes repeat throughout the text. As readers encounter the chaos of this text, then, we suggest allowing their own headings to materialize, "spooling out without a predetermined destination" (MacLure, 2013, p. 662), instead of expecting that *our* headings will resonate enough to "weave into the melody of their everyday lives" (Massumi, 1987, p. xiv).

References

A reference list typically aids the reader in locating and retrieving the sources cited in a text. In this chapter, however, the reference list locates the reader in a situated, local territory and includes texts that can be located and retrieved, actual people, fictional characters, dreams, animals, relatives, a novel, a song, recordings of conversations that a reader cannot access, physical locations, and, and, and. We suggest a reader not go to the reference list to "look for anything to understand" (Deleuze & Guattari, 1980/1987, p. 4); instead, the reference list becomes useful for sparking the same sorts of questions we ask of data and theory, like "what it functions with, in connection with what other things it does or does not transmit intensities" (p. 4).

RITORNELLOS

The Space of the Page

This will fail. It has to fail. We may try to take up the space of the page as non-representational, a space of becoming, of inhabiting theories as data. But that doesn't mean it will be read that way by an audience. Whatever mark it is that we abandon here on this page—the version that we leave instead of continuing to work and think and be with it—will be read as final, as having come to some meaning. *The* meaning. We'll probably read it that way, too, when we return to it. So this writing becomes a ritornello. Maybe.

Let the Words Wash Over You

I can't finish the sentence, "Deleuze and Guattari describe …," even though I just interrupted my walk around the block to run inside the house and write it down. It's gone now. And I have no idea what it could have been. I know that they wrote something that was helping me think. I know it. I can't find it in the text. I can't place the thought. But it will help me make sense of the chaos. Perhaps it was something about territory? Bird songs? Milieu? Rhythm? Meter? Consistency? Cosmos? Changes in intensity? The becoming-expressive? Moment? Motif? Expressiveness? Center? The words just wash over me.

Han Solo: "That is Not How the Force Works"

How does one figure out how a concept works? One way is to focus on the words others say. Jedi master Yoda (Lucas & Kerschner, 1980; Abrams, 2015) said of the force: "it's energy. It surrounds us. It binds us." There are also non-Jedi who speak of the force, such as Maz (Abrams, 2015), who said, "I am no Jedi, but I know the force." Beyond that, there are oodles of YouTube videos with titles like, "The Force Explained—Star Wars 101" (Sourcefednerd, 2015), Star Wars dictionaries, conversations between generations who have seen the films, and so forth. George Lucas, creator of the Star Wars franchise, actually quantified the force, introducing the new concept, midi-chlorians. Star Wars fans like to pretend that never happened.

The Space of the Page

What are we going to do with the page? What goes on there? Why do we fret so much about this? Does it even matter? Why do we worry about whether or not we should cite Deleuze and Guattari or that video we watched about musical ritornellos? Or should we cite MacLure? Or that monopoly game I was playing the other day with my daughter when she sang *Da-do-do* seemingly at random in the middle of it? Wasn't that the ritornello? Wasn't that her way of—what do they say—humming in the dark to intervene in the chaos? Isn't it more than that, though? What are the three aspects or moments of the ritornello that can happen simultaneously? Was I thinking about those in the monopoly moment? Was it the ritornello if I wasn't?

We Invented the Ritornello

They said that. Actually, Deleuze said something like that when an interviewer asked him (1991) if he thought he and Guattari had created any concepts. "How about ritornello? We formulated a concept of the ritornello in philosophy" (p. 385). I looked in *A Thousand Plateaus*, time and again, poring over the pages, searching the index, and not finding ritornello. So I listened to music. I talked to a colleague of mine who is a music professor and composer. And somewhere I was reading—I don't know where it was now—mentioned ritornello as a feature of baroque music, so I began to pursue the baroque. Maggie MacLure (2006) again. The productive potential of baroque as method. I thought the baroque might give me access to ritornello. So many things outside my grasp. There was only ritornello, my ritornello, our ritornello that we were inventing.

When Massumi translated the French 'ritournelle' to refrain, "[t]his was a mistake" (Kleinherenbrink, 2015, p. 225). "A refrain is a return of the same (a, R, b, R, c, R), but a ritornello is defined by variation" (p. 225). MacLure (2016) said the terms are interchangeable. Jackson (2016) uses refrain. We should think with both terms.

Let the Words Wash Over You

I can't let it wash over me. It's not a wave. There's no movement. It's only a brick wall. I don't even understand one sentence. I sit here with a dictionary open next to me, looking up every third word, trying to grasp on to some meaning. It always escapes. But everything feels important.

Data

When I printed off some of this writing and read it, I kept wondering how a reader might relate this to data. It falls in this book about data. Perhaps it ought to be clearly *about* data. It has "data" in the title, so the reader is tasked with thinking/reading/whatevering data in relation to this. What if data wasn't data? What if it was just ritornello? The ritornellization of data. I am off to the field to collect ritornellos today. La-la-la.

Da-Do-Do

I knew what the ritornello was before we even started reading. My son sings this little song, da-do-do, often while he is alone, playing with his trains or walking around in the sand box. Da-do-do. We repeat it back to him sometimes, and lately, we've been initiating it as well, sometimes accompanied by gestures like head bobs or ridiculous grins. It becomes something different as we play. MacLure (2016) said that ritornello is a "concept explicitly associated with the child" (p. 1). I am a child when I da-do-do. Whatever that means.

Beginning

We committed to ritornello for 10 minutes a day. For a few months at least. Sometimes, we were immersed in listening to Mozart with our children even after our allotted ten had passed, working out how ritornellos function in music. Sometimes, we were sucked into lectures or texts or clicking around the internet for who knows how long. The ritornello inquiry was intermixed with emails from students about assignments and phone calls from offices to schedule appointments. Sometimes, we forgot, and ritornello would inhabit our dreams, waking us in the night to jot down notes that made no sense in the morning. Sometimes, we felt so certain that we didn't know what ritornello was that the 10 minutes-a-day task was without boundaries—always haunted by the possibility that the day's inquiry had never even begun. Sometimes nothing happened in those ten-minute chunks. Sometimes aspects of ritornello glowed in Deleuze's texts, like MacLure (2013) wrote that "data fragments" from a study "would sometimes seem to glow" (p. 661). Sometimes the hours and hours each week when we talked and talked and told ourselves we should have been writing didn't help either. We were just children in the dark. Not even humming.

Kylo Ren: "You Need a Teacher ... I Can Show You the Ways of the Force."

I never took Bogue's class at UGA. I just found his lecture (Actual Virtual Journal, 2015) called "Deleuze, Guattari, and the Musical Refrain" on YouTube, and I got so excited because the musical part was in front of the refrain in the title. That ritornello and territory article says that we have to remember the musical part when we think of the refrain. Actually, it says that Deleuze and Guattari *insist* "the formation of a territory should be understood in *musical* terms" (Kleinherenbrink, 2015, p. 209), and we can't understand ritornello if the relation between territory and ritornello aren't "reaffirmed" (p. 209). So I was feeling good about finding this lecture and was watching it last night and taking notes—about territory, at first, and the territorial machine. But then, I couldn't stop noting how Bogue was talking about what Deleuze and Guattari's text *meant*. He said he wanted to understand every sentence. He'd point to a quote on an overhead and say things like, "There they are talking about ..." and "All that they're saying here is ..." Is that what Kylo Ren wants to do for Rey? Tell her what the force is about? What it means?

When Kylo Ren *says* "force," though, Rey *feels* it. The word glowed for her, like Maggie said. Rey repeated the word, closing her eyes, and hesitated. "A long moment passed in which Ren sensed a change in the air. A change in her" (Foster, 2015). How did Rey tap into the force when she wasn't trained? How does it work to learn a new concept? Do we need a teacher? What does this have to do with data? Everything, perhaps.

Tears

I watched the entire two-plus-hours of extra features of Star Wars the day it came out, even though it wasn't on my to-do list. I needed to escape. I needed to get out of the work. I needed to be somewhere different. Do something different. I was taking notes the whole time. I don't even know what about. But I was in our paper. Writing it. Thinking it. Data as ritornellos.

Ethics

A fox just ran across my yard, and I can't think about anything but ethology. Bogue (Actual Virtual Journal, 2015) says ethology relates to Deleuze's ethics. Or something like that. I am guessing ethics isn't some *thing* that can be disentangled from ritornello for Deleuze and Guattari. I sent an email to Jasmine Ulmer to ask her where to start with ethics.

Rey's Force Vision

There is so much more to read. Sometimes I feel like I have a sense of ritornello, Deleuze and Guattari's ritornello I mean, but then I don't know if I do. I cannot talk about every sentence of the refrain chapter, but I read it, and I feel like I get it. But if I try to quote it, the quote just seems out of place. A little return that wasn't a return to the same place.

It's like when I was watching a video (Manyymedia, 2016) the other night about a vision Rey had. Her vision is probably less than 30 seconds long, but there's tons of commentary on what it might mean—like this one guy who looked at different ways the scene has been translated into other languages to get a better sense of what the words were supposed to convey. When I returned to the actual *Star Wars* film again, the vision was different. I saw it differently. And sometimes I looked for things that were said to be there that I still couldn't find.

That's why it doesn't work when I go back to Deleuze and Guattari, too. When I return, again and again, it's always different. I'm always different. "How very important it is, when chaos threatens, to draw an inflatable, portable territory. If need be, I'll put my territory on my own body, I'll territorialize my body" (Deleuze & Guattari, 1987, p. 320). Maybe I should write the quotes on my body like in that movie *Memento.*

Tears

I'm giving feedback on student thesis chapters—too many to do "right" in the amount of time I have. I find myself saying the same things over and over again. I'm territorializing this idea of writing up research in a way that's making me uncomfortable. How do I make feedback ritornellos? How can I deterritorialize instead of staking firmer and firmer ground with each repetition? Is it really in their best interests for me to do so? I'm working so hard to be a teacher because they feel so lost. There's not time to cope, to inhabit. They have to learn it and do it and be done. They need a teacher. They're begging for one.

Have We Read Enough Deleuze?

The more we know about ritornello, the less ritornello is available to us.

Reference List as a Plane of Immanence

What goes in the reference list? Really. What do we put there? What makes it to the page and for what purpose? I don't want to give it to them. Attaching my interview transcripts to the text as if they can unproblematically speak for themselves and you can check if the themes emerged from the data the way they were supposed to. That's not how the force works.

Let's give them something.

Abrams, J. J. (Producer & Director). (2015). *Star wars episode VII: The force awakens* [Motion Picture]. USA: Lucasfilm, BadRobot.

Actual Virtual Journal (2015, January 9). Ronald Bogue—Deleuze, Guattari and the Musical Refrain I [video file]. Retrieved from https://www.youtube.com/watch?v=Eo8JvoRt_fE

At least 95 pages (2016). Cut writing/images/comments. *Google Doc called Ritornello.*

Bogue, R. (retired 2014). Deleuzian scholar. University of Georgia.

Deleuze, G. (1991). We invented the ritornello In A. Hodges & M. Taormina, Trans., D. Lapaujade, Ed., *Two regimes of madness: Text and interviews 1975–1995* (pp. 381–385). New York, NY: MIT Press.

Deleuze, G. (1995). (R. Bellour & F. Ewald, Interviewers). On philosophy. In G. Deleuze, *Negotiations: 1972–1990.* (M. Joughin, Trans). (pp. 134–155). New York, NY: Columbia University Press. (Original work published 1988).

Deleuze, G., & Guattari, F. (1987). *A thousand plateaus: Capitalism and schizophrenia* (B. Massumi, Trans.). Minneapolis, MN: University of Minnesota Press. (Original work published 1980).

Dreams. (2016). Waking and sleeping.

Drury Inn and Suites. (2016). *Writing retreats.* Greenville, SC.

Foster, A. (2015). *The force awakens.* New York, NY: Random House Audio.

Fox. (2016). Out the window. Sarah's house.

Guattari, F. (1996). Ritornellos and existential affects (pp. 158–171). In G. Genosko (Ed.), *The Guattari Reader.* Cambridge, MA: Blackwell Publishing.

Jackson, A. (2016). An ontology of a backflip. *Cultural Studies ⇔ Critical Methodologies, 16*(2), 183–192.

Jackson, A., & Mazzei, L. (2011). *Thinking with theory in qualitative research: Viewing data across multiple perspectives.* New York: Routledge.

Kleinherenbrink, A. (2015). Territory and ritornello: Deleuze and Guattari on thinking living beings. *Deleuze Studies, 9*(2), 208–230.

Koro-Ljungberg, M. (2016). *Reconceptualizing qualitative research: Methodologies without methodology.* Thousand Oaks, CA: Sage.

Koro-Ljungberg, M., Carlson, D., Tesar, M., & Anderson, K. (2015). Methodology brut Philosophy, ecstatic thinking, and some other (unfinished) things. *Qualitative Inquiry, 21*(7), 612–619.

Lucas, G. (Producer) & Kerschner, I. (Director). 1980. *Star wars episode V: The empire strikes back* [Motion Picture]. USA: Lucasfilm.

MacLure, M. (2006). The bone in the throat: Some uncertain thoughts on baroque method. *International Journal of Qualitative Studies in Education, 19*(6), 729–745.

MacLure, M. (2013). Researching without representation? Language and materiality in post-qualitative methodology. *International Journal of Qualitative Studies in Education, 26*(6), 658–667.

MacLure, M. (2016). The refrain of the a-grammatical child: Finding another language in/for qualitative research. *Cultural Studies ⟷ Critical Methodologies, 16*(2), 173–182.

Maggie (See also MacLure).

Manning, E., & Massumi, B. (2013, March 5). For a pragmatics of the useless: Propositions for thought [video file]. Retrieved from https://www.youtube.com/watch?v=Mp5REJAi2Oo&app=desktop

Manyymedia (2016, January 23). *Who is the little boy in Rey's force vision? Star wars the force awakens* [video file]. Retrieved from https://www.youtube.com/watch?v=03XV4zXStn4

Martin, M., & Shellback. (2014). Shake it off. [Recorded by Swift, T.]. On *1984* [CD]. Nashville, TN: Big Machine.

Massumi, B. (1987). Translator's foreword: Pleasures of philosophy. In G. Deleuze & F. Guattari (Eds.), *A thousand plateaus: Capitalism and schizophrenia* (B. Massumi, Trans.) (pp. ix–xv). Minneapolis, MN: University of Minnesota Press.

Massumi, B. (2015). Collective expression: A radical pragmatics. *INFLeXions, 8,* 59–88. Retrieved from http://www.inflexions.org/radicalpedagogy/PDF/Massumi.pdf

QuickTime Videos. (2016). Approximately 25 hours of Skype conversation screen recordings. Jessica's computer.

Ren, K. (2015). Commander of the First Order. Son of Han Solo and General Leia Organa. Star Wars Episode VII: The Force Awakens.

Rey. (2015). Scavenger. Jakku. Possible daughter of Luke Skywalker or reincarnation of Anakin Skywalker. Star Wars Episode VII: The Force Awakens.

Sidewalk. (2016). The intersection of Sloan Mill and Windsor Drive.

Solo, Han. (2015). Smuggler. Scoundrel. Hero. Captain of the Millenium Falcon. Mos Eisley Spaceport, Corellia. Star Wars Episodes IV, V, VI, VI.

Son. (2016). Da do do. Southeastern United States.

Sourcefednerd. (2015, October 17). The Force Explained—Star Wars 101 [video file]. Retrieved from https://www.youtube.com/watch?v=539SUcTrhDk.

St. Pierre, E. A. (2014). A brief and personal history of post qualitative research: Toward "Post Inquiry." *Journal of Curriculum Theorizing, 30*(2), 2–19.

Ulmer, J. (2015–present). Assistant Professor. Wayne State University, Detroit, MI.

Unrecorded Skype Conversations. (2016). Approximately 100 hours. Sarah's and Jessica's computers.

Data?

Let's design a study. Let's collect data (somewhat systematically) about ritornello. We're not sure what that data will be or how we'll know it when we see it, but that will also be a question of the project: *What counts as data here?* We'll analyze the data using something like writing as a method of inquiry or maybe thinking with theory—with ritornello. Or maybe our method is ritornello, our theory is ritornello, our concept is ritornello, our data is ritornello, the page is ritornello. No representation; only ritornello.

On the Page

What I'm finding interesting about writing is that all these relations to texts keep popping up. Kind of like memories of texts but rarely exact quotations. I'm writing and then I'm not. I'm remembering—not remembering, but feeling, or being there with—a text. I see myself or feel myself or something; it isn't like I'm watching a movie, but I'm there with the text again. Returning to it somehow. At what feels like the same spot in the neighborhood I was standing when I paused to underline part of the text or with the same pen in my hand that I used to circle a word that seemed to matter most at the time. I don't remember the words on the page, though. Sometimes I remember different words like, "portable territory," or "da-do-do." It's something that marks that moment where some sort of meaning was made. Not meaning though. Something else. Because when I return, it's different. When I return to the text to find the exact quotation that's supposed to help me get at that sense of understanding or knowing that I think I had, the quotation isn't right. It's different. But I type the quotation in anyway. It goes on the page and pretends to be the thought or the being there or the whatever it is or isn't or whatever.

Theory without Theorists

What happens on the page? In the writing? The bits and pieces of theory become Derrida or Deleuze or Foucault or Barad for the reader, even if we say that my Deleuze isn't your Deleuze isn't her Deleuze. We create these portable Deleuze ritornellos, nevertheless, that can be read as "not my Deleuze" or even "not Deleuze at all." When I call that thinking "Deleuze" on the page, it just feels wrong.

We Invented the Ritornello

"I make the moves up as I go" (Martin & Shellback, 2014, track 6).

"What I know, I know only from something I'm actually working on, and if I come back to something a few years later, I have to learn everything all over again" (Deleuze, 1991, p. 137).

That Seems Important

We've never written like this. When have we ever crafted writing separately to be held together in the same document? We didn't write any sentences together on the page. Until we rewrote everything. All of the back and forth: I don't know what that means, but I think it's important. I'm with you. Think this through with me. I have no idea what you're talking about. Relate that to data for me. Keep going because I don't know what that means. I don't know if this is related at all. That *does* seem important.

INTRODUCTION (AGAIN)

Provoked by the call to expand qualitative researchers' notions of data, this chapter became an opportunity for us to invite data to interrupt our encounters with theory. In our ongoing (post)qualitative inquiry, reading, writing, playing, talking, creating, thinking, and doing theory was (and is) a daily endeavor. Like St. Pierre (2014), we found theoretical concepts useful for "slow[ing] down and reorient[ing our] thinking about everything" (p. 7), enabling different inquiries to become thinkable and possible. At the same time, we were struck by how numerous writing conventions (e.g., citations, section headings) work to make theory *appear* knowable, stable, and separate from inquiry, including data and how it is written. By approaching data as ritornello, we worked against writing conventions in this text—writing conventions that reduce complex and contradictory theories to conventional data, sorting them and putting them under the label of an author, a concept, a framework, an introduction, a conclusion. We instead sought ways of writing that foreground entanglements of theory and data as they are becoming, perhaps in the Deleuzian space of the threshold, in which, as Jackson and Mazzei (2011) describe, "the divisions among and definitions of theory and data collapse" (p. 6). This chapter, then, was an experiment in entanglements on the page—an experiment in writing data as ritornello that continues as readers return differently and differently again to the page.

Da-do-do. ...

CHAPTER NINE

[Data WITHIN (data]-bag) Diffracted

ANGELO BENOZZO AND MIRKA KORO-LJUNGBERG

ABSTRACT

In this text we imagine a different narrative, perspective, and messy as well as complex insights about data (via data-bags and data-bags-waves). We use diffraction to connect diverse forms and actualizations of data but also to differentiate them and produce differences. It is our intention to extend our previous conversation about data-waves and data-splinters by expanding the idea of diffracted bag-data-waves and addressing more explicitly data-within-data, data overlaps and flows, and 'within' data(-bag). In our attempt to multiply data-bag possibilities in different ways, we are drawn to bags not only as objects of possession and utility but also as functional metaphors for data and subjects of 'data-ing'.

Keywords: data, data-bag, assemblage, differentiation

NOWHERE TO START

Too often much interpretative (and also laboratory based and other kind) research data are accessed, generated, and gathered mainly through speaking with participants, and/or on reading documents or observing. Central to this deterministic inquiry is a task of demarcating a field, for example by identifying or locating archives, public or private libraries, newspapers and video "that *might* yield information that *might* be relevant to the topic under investigation ... Other studies ... require similar thinking related to potential settings—so called 'field sites'—that are expected to yield interesting observational data" (Yanow & Schwartz-Shea, 2006, p. 117). In this case researchers seem to identify, locate, demarcate, and enter a field in order to generate data. Field has a perimeter and an edge; it needs to be bounded and well-defined so that the research can be better situated and knowing can be bounded and controllable. (Unfortunately) research often (always) implies demarcating a field and selecting 'empirical material' to support potentially preexisting representation of a phenomenon. However, although these actions can be important and useful they also seem reductionist: they separate and set the limit to 'data', they contain and as such always leave something aside, outside, or too deep inside. It seems as if there is a kind of violence in 'identifying the field and data' and separation, division, cutting, cleaning up, and sanitization are at play. In this chapter, we produce no data sets, cleaned data base, or easily identifiable data-bag-data assemblages. Instead, we multiply data-bag possibilities in different ways.

Data similar to bags come in different forms, shapes, functions, matter and colors. Some data and bags can be constructed, some can be found, and some others might need to be purchased. In some ways data and bags are alive since they generate various reactions and movement in their environment. Data and bags contain, carry, deliver, burden, assist, and can even kill. Data-bags are personal, public, virtual, and actual. They can have a capability to transform the subjects and objects associated with them. Data-bags can differentiate, multiply, and possible generate endless number of tiny data-bags.

Similar to Mitchell (2005) who asks what pictures want, we wonder: What do (data)-bags want from us? Where are they leading us? What is it that they lack, that they are inviting us to fill in? What desires have we projected onto them, and what form do those desires take as they are projected back to us? How can (data)-bags seduce us? Or ask us to feel and act in specific ways? Borrowing Bennett, can we "raise the status of the materiality of which we are composed" (p. 12)?

In addition, data-bags can produce differentiating sameness. As Barad (2007) explains, diffraction happens when waves pass through an opening or obstruction and spread differently than they would be otherwise: "whereas the metaphor of reflection reflects the themes of mirroring and sameness, diffraction is marked by patterns of difference" (pp. 71–72). We look at diffraction as a process that continuously and seamlessly produces new and differentiating data-waves. Data as (in) wave movement unfolds and changes shape, expands and mingle/mix up with landscape (environment), with water (other substances), and beach and shore (particular yet shifting contexts). Differentiating materials and content in-(data)-bags continue to move us in different ways. More specifically the diffracted data-waves take a point of departure from an IKEA bag (in-data-bag), which appeared in Italy in a Company ad. Later in-data-IKEA-bag-wave spread differently and created different diffractions including other in-data-bag which queered the IKEA ad and data-bag (see http://www.gaywave.it/articolo/ikea-pubblicitagay-friendly-a-catania/29093/; see http://www.milady-zine.net/borse-gabs-la-campagna-peccato-essere-uomini/), *Emily Muller*[1] a short film including in-data-bag improvisations, a piece of art by Sophie Calles questioning ethics, voyeurism and inspections, and in-data-bag image-conversation series produced by the authors. In-(data)-bags are empty and full, private and public, liminal and porous with no boundaries, or their boundaries are continuingly being reshaped and everything between.

LOCATING, PRODUCING AND QUESTIONING BAGS

How many data-bags have you carried, bought, desired, and met in your life? How many data-bags have you used today and yesterday? How many data-bags did you throw away?

Some bags are singular and some bags function as part of a collective. Leaky bags of water, body bags, catheter bags, lunch-bags, bean-bags, dress bags, carry-on-bags, duffel bags, shoulder bags, baby bags, book bags, douche bags, grocery bags, eco-bags, leather bags, tea bags, plastic bags, paper bags, garbage bags, empty bags, bags full of …, heavy bags, empty bags, bags of dirty laundry, (useless) conference bags. …

We as researcher are an assemblage of bags, clothes, body, organs, technology, papers …

Data-bags also ask and provoke questions: Does this bag make me look young, old, smart or …? Does this data-bag make me something other than (me) and also does this data-bag do something to or for me?

I'm moving from a student to a professional.

Ah, is this your feeling about that bag?

So before I used … I had a backpack which was very student like.

I still I have a backpack.

And now, well it's fine, it works but it was like a kind of moving to this sac bag and it make me feel more professional. What is 'professional'?

Where are data-bags? We live in a word full of data-bags: researcher's data-bags, participants' data-bags, interviewee's data-bags, manager's data-bags. … Data-bags are everywhere and anywhere, but too often taken for granted by some. Silent and mute data-bags are important for some. Illegible and infinite data-bags. Illegal and inappropriate data-bags. Data-bags arrested. Data-bags arrest.

Researcher data-bags: When we research and inquiry we carry our bags with recorder, blocks to take notes, pens, laptop and camera together with personal belonging such as a handkerchief, lipstick, condoms, keys, fragrances, wallet, mobile phone and charging cables. Everything is mixed up in a bag and there is no separation between data-bag-body. Is this an entanglement?

IN-DATA-IKEA-BAG AND ÉMILIE MULLER- IN-DATA-BAG IMPROVISATIONS

> … its' normative forms. …
> … without a point of departure …
> … continuity and connections …
> … there is no beginning and no end …
> … the beginning is in (already) the end. …
> … the end is already the beginning …
> …(dis)connections …

In our research with/on/through/by data-bag, one of our favorite is an IKEA bag which appeared in Italy in a gay friendly advertising campaign. This bag was a part of image showing two men, holding hands, seen from behind, one of them holding an IKEA bag (Benozzo, Koro-Ljungberg, & Carey, 2016). When we first encountered the advertisement, we started to wonder "… what … what might be in those men's bag. What sex toys or […] pleasures might be in there? What kinds of perversions might emerge from that bag?" (p. 10).

And 'there were' many improvising objects in there:
Ladies and gentlemen—welcome to our theater of data improvisations.
We have a whip, handcuffs and also leather belts
Today we've been at the sea experiencing and contemplating how waves diffract
some lubricant jelly, hair removing cream and vibrators,
without nudity
Their movements are quite hypnotic.

Movements
Quite hypnotic
Hypnotic movements
Their movements

sexy underpants and who knows what other vibrations.
Data as (in) wave movement unfolds and changes shape,
Yes, who knows what movements can we 'find there'?
expansions and intra-actions with landscape (environment),
Or what else can data-bags reveal, desire, and hide?
shore and rocks (within particular yet shifting contexts).
Data-bags are full of possibilities; data possibilities
with water (and other substances), and beach and
they form foam and squirt water molecules producing different series of movements
they interrogate two classical labels of research:
seemingly quite improvisational.
field and source/data
Let's give our warmest welcome to our in-data-bag-improvisers and actors.

Émily: "Should I empty my bag? Or what should I do?"
Director: "Take out any item and tell me why it is in the bag and what associations it
            produces"

A world of many narrated objects appears.

A wallet

A powder-box

An apple—In the morning on her way to the studio she passed by a fruit market.
The marked had various fruits including red and green apples. The seller took an
apple and gave it to her.

Few pages of daily newspaper—She looks for a job from time to time, but she is
not after a precise job because she changes jobs all the time: house keeper, nanny,
waitress, or documentarist. She is impressed by the fact that few words on a paper
may change a person's life. She likes to read recent estate ads, because she wants to
own a house. Not a palace, just a small wooden house deep in the woods. It has to

be a place where she can go whenever she wants, where she could invite friends, or listen to music late into the night. When she reads these estate ads, she imagines what kind of life she would have there. She believes that owning a house signals living a life. House ownership could bring new colors to her life or maybe even loneliness, no one to talk to. And she is not afraid to be lonely because when she was a child, her parents often left her home alone to read.

A ring—An old friend gave it to her. It belonged to his mother, but she passed away.

A sketchbook for taking notes—she writes some stories, scraps of dreams, phrases she has read in books. Every day she writes something down (things she sees, does, or people she meets), but this practice is little absurd and paradoxical. No notes are needed if something is important and memorable. She is afraid that somebody can find and read something that she has never said to anybody. A few words from Jules Renard: "Monday, 7 April. I have known happiness, but that didn't make me happier."

A pen—It is a gift from one of her friends for his birthday. Yes, for his birthday, because he always likes to give presents instead of getting them.

A library card

A donor card

Pills—She almost never takes them, but she always carries them. The pills are for insomnia. The most terrible hours are from 4 to 5 a.m. This is a time when you have neither an interesting book to read nor any crackers to eat.

A pocket of cigarettes—She does not smoke. They are for her friends.

A penknife

An accordion

The director is quite impressed by Émily's easiness but in the end he decides that she is a bit too young for the film. Émily is asked to leave the studio while the director waits for another young actress. Soon the director notices that the handbag is still in the studio and. … What happens next? The video of Émily Muller lasts less than 20 minutes and we invite the readers to watch it: https://www.youtube.com/watch?v=dGAPpSjRehU

VARIOUS LAYERS OF (DATA-BAG) WAVES

A few year ago, following Massumi (2002), we conceptualized data movement and data as a wave: "The image that best describes this (becoming of data) is the

fluctuating movement of the waves ... data expand and contract, constantly changing shape and being carried by some invisible forces" (Benozzo, Bell, & Koro-
Ljungberg, 2013, pp. 311–312). Quite surprisingly the image of waves returned to
us with Barad (2007) who draws on quantum physic to elaborate diffraction both
as process and methodology.

The word *diffraction* was invented in 1665 by the Italian physicist Grimaldi
and it derives from the Latin *diffractio,* past participle of *diffringere.* For us diffraction is a non-straight propagating of shapes, images, meetings, and matter between
different fields. It functions based on a varied range of heterogeneous guidelines
and diverse contexts. For example, Finotti in his book *Retorica della Diffrazione*
(2004) presents the ambiguity and creativity of diffraction in Renaissance literature, which when re-articulated could include small items in a frayed and changing
game, figurative language, poetic theater and music. Diffraction here has something to do with 'infraction' (literally *infrazione*) that is a violation, which according to Finotti in Renaissance literature and paintings happens simultaneously/
together with the respect of the rule. In a personal email sent to us he wrote:

> Ho scoperto ... che in molti artisti del rinascimento l'applicazione e la messa in scena
> della regola coincidono con la sua volontaria infrazione. In passato il rapporto tra ordine e
> disordine, grammatica e errore, regola e infrazione [nella filologia] è stato studiato come un
> netto confine che dividerebbe due campi diversi di tendenze, di artisti o almeno di opere.
> Io sottolineo invece la compresenza organica, costante, strutturale dei due poli non solo
> all'interno dei singoli artisti, (scrittori o pittori) ma all'interno delle singole opere.[2] (email
> from Fabio Finotti, the February 4, 2016)

Diffraction is the process which produce difference: "Whereas reflection and
reflexivity might document difference, diffraction is itself the process whereby a
difference is made" (Davies, 2014, p. 2). "Diffraction as a physical phenomenon
is acutely sensitive to details; small differences can matter enormously" (Barad,
2012, p. 13). Can we imagine the diffraction of data-bag which refers to an over
production of in-data-bag? Data as over-production but always different and
unique: "differences across, among, and between genders, species, spaces, knowledges, sexualities, subjectivities, and temporalities" (Barad, 2012, p. 16). Data-
bags irradiate by both uniting and separating the similarities across the bags thus
disturbing the sameness of the bag owner. Data-bags are also boundary-cross-
ing as they blend material across different spaces (e.g., desks, cars, human back,
shoulders, hands, woods) and carry and distribute energy from different locations
(e.g., travelling across places, carrying heavy items, lifting across heights). As such
data-bags both occupy the subject and depart the unity between the bag and its
carrier. Data-bags are not stable entities but ones that are in constant movement and flux; they are different and produce differences. We, as researchers, are
awash with flows of bag-data-waves that aggregate and disaggregate, compose
and decompose, that continually change.

In terms of methodology, Barad claims that

> ... diffraction does not fix what is the object and what is the subject in advance, ... diffraction involves reading insights through one another in ways that help illuminate differences as they emerge: how different differences get made, what gets excluded, and how these exclusions matter. (Barad, 2007, p. 30)

Observation apparatuses (e.g., technology for observation) cannot be separated from the phenomena under observations, they are part of and constitute that reality; apparatuses always intra-act (interfere and affect) with that reality.

How data-bags intra-act with research? How can we use diffraction in our research? How do data-bags that intra-act with us produce us as researchers? A diffractive methodology does not imply a systematic series of phases to be followed (collecting data and analyzing them), instead it opens "the possibility of seeing how something different comes to matter, not only in the world that we observe, but also in our research practice." (Davies, 2014, p. 3)

IN-DATA-BAG-INSPECTIONS

Sophie Calle is a contemporary French artist whose extensive practice involves intersecting art production with different forms of surveillance. She has been engaged in several art works (e.g., exploring everyday life of a stranger on the streets or of herself) which rises some questions on the voyeuristic nature of the artist, on the arbitrary observation and surveillance of subjects unaware of her presence. Here we are interested in her work named *L'Hôtel* where she describes a period of three weeks she spent in a Venetian hotel as a chambermaid. In presenting this work Sophie Calle writes:

> On Monday, February 16, 1981, I was hired as temporary chambermaid for three weeks in a Venetian Hotel. I was assigned twelve bedrooms on the fourth floor. In the course of my cleaning duties, I examined the personal belongings of the hotel guests and observed through details lives which remained unknown to me. On Friday, March 6, the job came to an end. (Calle, 1999, pp. 140–141 in Hand, 2005, p. 463)

Sophie took photos of the rooms, inspected personal belongings, opened closets and drawers, rummaged suitcases, used makeup from beauty cases, sprayed herself with guest's fragrances, saved a pair of shoes left in the bin, read letters, ate some remains of food, tasted the liquid left in a glass discovering it was Coke and so on. As a 'results' of these three weeks she created twenty-one diptychs each of them made of photos accompagnato/followed by a text written by the artist describing her encounters with the business and personal belongings of guests: "The black-and-white photographs accompanying the sequence of entries on the stay of each set of occupants allude to the discourse of photographic reportage, and indeed in their use of strong contrast they resemble the scene-of-the-crime ..." (Sheringham, 2006, p. 417).

The first time we saw Sophie Calle works we were ambivalent. On the one hand we were annoyed imagining this woman entering (our) rooms and invading (our) private and secret spaces. Can you think of somebody who was allowed to enter your house and take pictures of your space and facilities, make inventories, and open wardrobes and bags? And after she/he has touched and moved everything she/he starts to write and describe, to select and classify traces of your life. How would you feel? Maybe exposed, disappointed, and annoyed. However, at the same time, there is something fascinating about her 'peeking at' or 'spying on' in data-bags of people. Indeed, she opened suitcases and emptied bags of dirty laundry, she inspected bed sheets and handled objects in the rooms, registering her feelings while doing that: "... Call's personal reaction to the absent occupants is to underline the uncanny sense of transgressing the boundary between the private and the public she feels when she makes active interventions in support of her inquiries ..." (Sheringham, 2006, p. 418). It is also possible that her work is fascinating because it is a metaphor of our research; there are affinities and similarities between Call's *L'Hôtel* and scholars' inquiry processes. We also like to rummage through 'personal belongings' of 'the participants'; we might feel a sense of pleasure while inspecting and shifting through participants' 'private and secret' objects knowing that our actions raise many ethical and voyeuristic questions, which has been discussed in social sciences for decades.

To whom belong this data/bags/object/photos?

Can you describe what is in the bag? Do you want to sit down? Yes thanks.

Is the researcher a thief?

Laptop and some writing utensils, and my thermos for coffee. An I-Pad, a charger. I think some chocolates, some feminine anti-aging products, and my wallet.

Is the researcher a spy of others' lives or an inspector?

Are there any secrets? My conference badge. Is it a secret? No there are no secrets in my bag.

Does the researcher stop/block data-bag production while she/he is inspecting them?

What is very intriguing for us in Call's *L'Hôtel* is Calle's feeling that "... if people's lives are under scrutiny the extreme attention to detail does not make them familiar: they remain 'étrangers" (Sheringham, 2006, p. 416). She was proximal to people but not to grasp their essence:

... by focusing on the traces themselves, in the absence of those who left them, she underlines both how very telling they are, and how difficult it is to pin down what they tell. ... [W]hat is being attended to here ... is not who these people are, but what they do— ... in an infinite variety of ways. (Sheringham, 2006, p. 416)

"... what Calle registers above all are differences and variations between people rather than individuating characteristics" (419). At the same time Calle's taking photos of the absent customers has the sense of surveillance as a mean to generate art. Does also our work (as researchers) has a sense of surveillance when, as in the following section, we ask people to tell something about their bags? Or are data-bags surveilling us?

IN DATA-BAG-CONVERSATIONS

Handbag 1 Dialoguing

Are there any secrets?

A conference badge.

Is it a secret?

No. Shall I tell you a secret?

I do not know, if you ... but if you tell a secret it is no more a secret ...

It's true. No there are no secrets in this bag.

Handbag 2 Dialoguing

Please can you say something about yourself?

I am an extension of my owner because I carry a laptop, certainly a kind of memory, extension. So in a way I protect my owner.

Do you hide something in your bag?

No. However, I do not usually carry a brush. And at the airport the officer took away a hair gel that was tucked into my pocket.

Handbag 3 Dialoguing

I carry pharmacy drugs, of all kinds, just in a case of emergency. I have antibiotics, a bandage and ibuprofen (the one we call the wonder drug). And also I carry zinc just in case my owner feels sick. She believes that zinc busts her immune system. I also carry a Chinese herb because my owner is menopausal. Do I have an exciting life or not?

And what else might be there?

Oh, there are all kind of things. Oh emery boards, cue tips and rubber bands, it is very important when you travel you see, you should always have a rubber band when you travel.

I agree. When I travel I always need bands. These are always with me. This is brilliant! (Laughing)

My owner's mother used to call this, ... she always had a section of her purse that she called the "help and beauty section", so you can see mine has expanded quite a bit.

Yes

... and of course, you know, because my owner is a teacher I also carry school supplies. Just in case she will be teaching here is one whiteboard marker.

You are very well organized.

You always need those, and this is ... oh, you never ever travel without your ear plugs. Never without your plugs. Would you like one set? I have more. (Laughing)

You are also very well equipped!

And of course a poncho. This is a poncho in case it rains. I forgot that I have it. It also comes handy. For example, my owner has back problems and if I carry a poncho she can place it on the ground anywhere, including at the airport, and do her exercises.

FAREWELL TO DATA-BAGS-NOT

Now it would be a time to leave data-bags behind, think about conclusions, and implications. However, this is not possible. Data-bags continue their reproduction and lives outside the persons carrying, owning, or abandoning them. Data-bags are doing and working on us (see also Nordstrom, 2015), walking, talking non-human bodies through evolution similar to Bennett's example of mineral.

From leather pouches with long drawstrings to bags that are part hardshell cases and part kickboard-style scooters, and to carry-on-bags that feature 33 pockets that are large and varied enough to hold everything from a water bottle and iPad to dress shirts and a pair of shoes. They possess "thing-power" and "the strange ability of ordinary, man-made items to exceed their status as objects and to manifest traces of independence or aliveness" (Bennett, 2010, p. xvi). Data-bags as vibrant matter and "not-quite-human capaciousness" (Bennett, 2010, p. 3) generate and produce effects (also within and alongside us). It is also possible that data-bags function as *actants* and operators who "by virtue of its particular location in an assemblage and the fortuity of being in the right place at the right time, makes the difference, makes things happen, becomes the decisive force catalyzing an event" (Bennett, 2010, p. 9). Maybe data-bags are similar to *interveners* (neither objects nor subjects) independent from the motivation of human subjects that carry them. As *interveners* they have the power to produce something unexpected, unknown and uncertain. Through their multiple layers data-bags leave and return, attach and detach, constitute and deconstruct subjects/objects and their continuously changing intra-action. Now, we invite the "reader" and the "researcher" to get distracted and disturbed by her/his or other (or somebody else's) data-bag. Alternatively, we are asking nothing, no interactions, no bags, or data. What will happen next?

Figure 9.1: Bags of curiosities I.
Source: Authors.

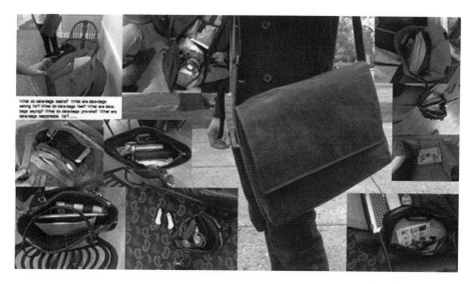

Figure 9.2: Bags of curiosities II.
Source: Authors.

NOTES

1. *Émily Muller* is a short film directed by Yvon Marciano, which appears at the end of the film ABGESCHMINKT! (Katjia von Garnier, Germany, 1993). Émily is a young actress looking for a theatrical work. She enters a film studio for a screening and the director invites her to sit down and talk about her handbag. Finding inspiration from the objects inside the handbag he asks her to narrate about herself.

2. "I discovered that many renaissance artists employ/adopt a rule but simultaneously and on purpose also break/violate it. [In philology] in the past years, the relationship between order and disorder, grammar and errors/mistakes, and rule and infraction/violation has been studied as something with a clear boundary/edge/cutting/separation which would divide two different fields and trends, of artists or at any rate of works. Instead, I underline the continuous structural simultaneity of the two polarities not only within individual artists (writers or painters) but within the single work."

REFERENCES

Barad, K. (2007). *Meeting the universe halfway*. Durham, NC: Duke University Press.

Barad, K. (2012). Intra-active entanglements. An interview with Karen Barad. M. Jueskjaer and Nete Schwennesen. *Kvinder, Kon & Forskning, 14*(1–2), 10–23.

Bennett, J. (2010). *Vibrant matter: A political ecology of things*. Durham, NC: Duke University Press.

Benozzo, A., Bell, H., & Koro-Ljungberg, M. (2013). Moving between nuisance, secrets and splinters as data. *Cultural Studies <=> Critical Methodologies, 13*(4), 309–315.

Benozzo, A., Koro-Ljungberg, M., & Carey, N. (2016). Post/authorship: Five or more IKEA customers in search of an author. *Qualitative Inquiry*, on line first January 10, 2016.

Calle, S. (1999). *Double games*. London: Violette Editions.

Davies, B. (2014). *Listening to children. Being and becoming*. London: Routledge.

Finotti, D. (2004). *Retorica della diffrazione. Bembo, Aretino, Giulio Romano e Tasso: Letteratura e scena cortigiana*. Firenze: OlschKi.

Hand, J. (2005). Sophie Calle's art of following and seduction. *Cultural Geographies, 12*, 463–484.

Massumi, B. (2002). *Parables for the virtual*. Durham, NC: Duke University Press.

Mitchell, W. (2005). *What do pictures want?* Chicago: The University of Chicago Press.

Nordstrom, S. (2015). *Anti-methodology: A delightfully monstrous daughter*. Presented at the Deleuze Studies International Conference, Stockholm, Sweden.

Sheringham, M. (2006). Checking out: The investigation of the everyday in Sophie Calle's *L'Hôtel*. *Contemporary French and Francophone Studies, 10*(4), 415–424.

Yanow, D., & Schwartz-Shea, P. (2006). Accessing and generating data. In D. Yanow & P. Schwartz-Shea (Eds.), *Interpretation and methods. Empirical research methods and the interpretive turn*. London: M. E. Sharpe.

Irruptions

LiteratureHoles

TEIJA LÖYTÖNEN, MAREK TESAR,
AND MIRKA KORO-LJUNGBERG

We would like to continue by experimenting with methodologies of h o l e s, DataHoles: their impotentiality anesthesia, ignorance and darkness, especially in relation to texts and literature. We offer some potential methodological connections with DataHoles and LiteratureHoles, and what these have prompted in our thinking and inquiry practices. Similar to the impossibility of introducing or defining DataHoles, these LiteratureHoles also cannot be captured in any existing methodological or scholarly discourses. However, they may form more or less imaginary presences for more describable and discussable (future) methodologies, texts, and readings. And somehow, they can be performed.

How do we want and need literature?
In text?
In our thinking?
In our play with data and hole?
In the holes and absences literature creates?

In the holes literature creates in us?
So why data/literature/holes?
Holes are absent presences.
New spatial openings to the unknown and otherness.
Data in becoming a third dimension, three-dimensional.
Holes are cuts into the hole's host and these cuts are irruptions in the sameness.
Holes alter their hosts by extending and changing the host's purpose.
Adding something from within.

LiteratureHoles made us do it.
Methodology of holes—timed textual openings; data openings.
Worm holes openings.
Or LiteratureHoles that are (designed as) part of the textual host.
Or LiteratureHoles that are cracks in the host.
Damaged textual hosts.

LiterarureHoles alter their host by extending and changing the host's communicative, representational, or ethical purposes.
Changing the purposes from within.

But what if the LiteratureHole is the purpose, such as letting the air through thick
and rich text, detailed narrative, or scary dialogical exchange?

(IM)POTENTIALITY OF LITERATUREHOLES AND OTHER TEXTS

Deleuze and Guattari (1987) referenced a holey space, and image from the film
Strike. A disturbing group of people rise from the underground through holes covering a field in all directions. They write that "transpierce the mountains instead of
scaling them, excavate the land instead of striating it, bore holes in space instead
of keeping it smooth, turn the earth into Swiss cheese" (p. 413).

Will this be the only reference in this text?
No.

Writing oneself and others into the text through its holes. LiteratureHoles
transpiercing the solid, valid, thorough literature reviews. DataHoles excavating
linear interview transcripts. Methodology being turned into Swiss cheese. Digging
deeper into textual abyss and nothingness. Something being produced. Something
being remembered.

Hinton (2007) referred to the black holes as enigmatic signifiers that represent
and signify nothing. He also notes that paradoxical nothingness links the origin
of the subject and immaterial creativity and freedom. Holes' nothingness enables
renewed imagination. Abyss, void, absence, emptiness, and failure of language are
associated with black holes.

Holes becomings as unrealized and untapped potential. But in relation to
what? To the text? To one's life? All, just in relation to the text? Suddenly we've
remembered Agamben's (1999) writing about the potential:

> What is essential is that potentiality is not simply non-Being, simple privation, but rather
> *the existence of non-Being*, the presence of an absence; this is what we call "faculty" or

"power." "To have a faculty" means *to have* a privation. And potentiality is not a logical hypostasis but the mode of existence of this privation. (p. 179, italics in original)

He then asks 'But how can an absence be present, how can a sensation *exist* as anesthesia' (p. 179) and leans on Aristotle who was concerned with the problem of vision. Agamben writes:

> When we do not see (that is, when our vision is potential), we nevertheless distinguish darkness from light; we see darkness. The principle of sight "in some way possesses color," and its colors are light and darkness, actuality and potentiality, presence and privation. (pp. 180–181)

Yes. Colors of holes. Light and Darkness. We discover holes through pursuing the light, but inside we experiencing darkness. Can we pursue the darkness of holes, to embrace the full spectrum of colors and potentialities?

Escaping and removed text (i.e., LiteratureHole) that is absent from itself generates 'data' differently through its absent presence. A LiteratureHole produces imaginative textual trace and an illusion of accidental textual connections; that are still becoming. LiteratureHoles create a potential for emergent text by cutting a hole into host text, paper, script, and ink letters. These absent textual materials can be replaced by plants-rocks-cacti-rain-fence-mountains-text (or something else) emerging from the hole.

Yet readers might not be able access 'the real' of a plant-rock-cactus-rain-fence-mountain-text but this text emerging from LiteratureHole can be illusive, imaginative, or maybe impossible to even describe or map. Through both LiteratureHoles and created imaginary textual openings readers might sense the dry heat, feel wet and cold rain drops, and get one's shoes wet when stepping into the puddle. However, the host text stays dry at the same time it forms raindrops for its LiteratureHole. A copy of the original generates a double both metaphorically and literally. The text doubles within itself and with other texts and textual objects; a relationship is being established between the textual host and LiteratureHole. At the same time the absence of the text (a hole in the host) enables the presence of plant-rock-cactus-rain-fence-mountain-text. An illusive and impossible access point is being created through the hole; an entryway, or opening between two emerging planes of emergence or data plateaus. Emerging text escapes into the nature and rain fills in the absence of the paper. A vital illusion of 'hole and missing paper' makes this virtual relationality and potentiality possible. Vitality of holes. Vitalogy of holes. Illusion indeed. But what about potential?

For Aristotle all potentiality is impotentiality: based on this premise for Agamben (1999) to be potential means:

> to be one's own lack, *to be in relation to one's own incapacity*. Beings that exist in the mode of potentiality *are capable of their own impotentiality;* and only in this way do they become

potential. They *can be* because they are in relation to their own non-being. In potentiality, sensation is in relation to anesthesia, knowledge to ignorance, vision to darkness. (p. 182)

And yet another LiteratureHole. Data holes are opening toward methodologies of impotentiality: methodologies of anesthesia, ignorance and darkness? [remembering Ranciere and Foucault here] LiteratureHoles are producing (only) impotentiality.

(IRRE)SOLVABLE HOLES

In their introduction to the anthology "Speculative Turn" Bryant, Srnicek, and Harman (2011) describe the new interest or turn toward reality itself. Instead of focusing on 'texts, discourses, social practices, and human finitude' (p. 3), scholars have begun speculating about the nature of reality independently of thought and humanity. Thus, "speculation aims at something 'beyond' the critical and linguistic turns [...], while also taking into account the undeniable progress that is due to the labour of critique" (p. 3).

Within the new (speculative) turn towards realism and materialism the notion of hole is also vital. Bryant et al. (2011) draw on Žižek and his work *The Parallax View*, where Žižek describes the "naïve materialist postulate", which "assumes the position of an external observer from which the entire world can be grasped—a position presumes in principle to encompass all of reality by reducing its own perspective to a thing in the world" (p. 5).

However, for Žižek, "materialism means that the reality I see is never 'whole'—not because a large part of it eludes me, but because it contains a stain, a blind spot, which indicates my inclusion in it" (cited in Bryant et al., 2011, p. 5). Reality, for Žižek, 'is non-All; there is a gap, a stain, an irresolvable hole within reality itself. The very difference between the for-itself and the in-itself is encompassed within the Absolute. Only by attending to this gap can we become truly materialist' (cited in Bryant et al., 2011, p. 5).

Human subjects becoming a gap, a stain, an irresolvable hole within (what?) reality itself. The human subject as a hole, a blind spot. Human subjects becoming a hole. Let's read another brilliant chapter before the next irruption swallows human subjects as holes.

REFERENCES

Agamben, G. (1999). *Potentialities. Collected essays in philosophy.* Stanford, CA: Stanford University Press.

Bryant, L., Srnicek, N., & Harman, G. (2011). *The speculative turn: Continental materialism and realism*. Melbourne: re-press.

Deleuze, G., & Guattari, F. (1987). *A thousand plateaus: Capitalism and schizophrenia* (B. Massumi, Trans.). Minneapolis, MN: University of Minnesota.

Hinton, L. (2007). Black holes, uncanny spaces and radical shifts in awareness. *Journal of Analytical Psychology, 52*(4), 433–447. doi: 10.1111/j.1468-5922.2007.00675.x

CHAPTER TEN

Writing 'Data' Across Space, Time, AND Matter

JASMINE B. ULMER

ABSTRACT

As spacetimemattering, 'data' remain in perpetual motion. Within quantum contexts, therefore, the focus for qualitative methodologists becomes not how to capture, tame, or bestill moving 'data,' but how to address the movements of 'data' through space, time, and matter. Following Barad, this chapter turns to several international exemplars from the visual and performing arts that embody 'data' as spacetimemattering: *Murmur Study*; *YOUR TEXT HERE*; *In Unbridled Yesterday, Today, and Tomorrow*; and *SNAP*. In the process, these exemplars raise several questions for researchers interested in 'data' as spacetimematterings: How might 'data' exist in real-time or outside temporal linearity? How might 'data' intra-act with material place and digital space? How might 'data' be written as spacetimematterings? How might 'data' write spacetimematterings? By way of illustration, I then discuss recent works that develop three potential modes of writing (post)qualitative research: choreographic writing, hypermodal writing, and photographic cartography. In so doing, various forms of multimodal writings provide venues in which to explore how 'data' write, perform, enact, teach, and reconceptualize research.

Keywords: 'data,' writing, spacetimemattering, Barad, arts-based inquiry, dance, pedagogy, methodology

writing—"freed from the page by the multimodal affordances of digital technology, writing is no longer limited to the sequential placement of words on a page–or a screen" (Holbrook, 2010, p. 175).

data—"data (under erasure), data-undone, data-rethought, data-particles, or maybe data-becoming" (Koro-Ljungberg & MacLure, 2013, p. 219).

spacetimematterings—"the ongoing rematerialisings of relationalities, not among pre-existing bits of matter in a pre-existing space and time, but in the ongoing reworkings of 'moments', 'places', and 'things'—each being (re)threaded through the other" (Barad, 2010, p. 268).

INTRODUCING SPACETIMEMATTERINGS

As spacetimematterings, 'data' remain in perpetual motion. Quantum physicists would remind us that all particles are in motion—even particles located within solid matter. 'Data' are much the same: the constancy many researchers seek in data is not to be found in a fixed state of being, but in the constancy of quantum vibration. The question for (post)qualitative (St. Pierre, 2011) methodologists within quantum contexts, then, becomes not how to capture, tame, or bestill moving data, but how to address the movements of 'data' through space, time, and matter (Koro-Ljungberg, MacLure, & Ulmer, 2018). This is particularly the case when writing with multimodal 'data' that, in Baradian terms, spacetimematter. Because multimodal 'data' move as they spacetimematter, modes of writing should further these movements rather than freeze them. Accordingly, this chapter explores how 'data' spacetimematterings might be written within different modes of arts-based and (post)qualitative research.

As 'data' move, then, they set different types and modes of writing into motion. These moves, however, may not be immediately recognizable as writing. For Derrida, the term 'writing' encompasses "all that gives rise to an inscription in general, whether it is literal or not and even if what it distributes in space is alien to the voice" (1976, p. 9). As Derrida continues, writing might be cinematic, choreographic, pictorial, musical, sculptural, athletic, or even cybernetic. Each potentially activates movement, thought, and affectivity as writing travels across multiple forms and spacetimematterings. Writing in this chapter takes shape as digital photographs, videos, microposts, installations, and other modes of composition that do not stay still; various forms of writing continue to move as the 'past' and the 'future' are iteratively reworked and enfolded through the iterative practices of spacetimemattering" (Barad, 2010, pp. 260–261). For scholars and artists who simultaneously compose within the "posthumanist performative" approaches to research for which Barad calls (2007, p. 135), multimodal writings provide a venue for posthuman performances of 'data' spacetimematterings.

To demonstrate, this chapter first turns to international exemplars from the visual and performing arts in which 'data' spacetimematter. In *Murmur Study* (2009–2012), U.S. visual artist Christopher Baker continuously prints live Twitter feeds in an "endless waterfall of text accumulating in tangled piles [of paper] below" (para. 2). In *YOUR TEXT HERE* (2011–ongoing), Spanish and Icelandic architect Marcus Zotes creates a participatory light installation by projecting text messages from the public onto exterior facades of buildings. The Brazilian art troupe Grupo Hybris intervenes in city-space through a public exposition of dance, theatre, light, and photography (Lacorte, 2014), and U.S. choreographer Andrea Gise plays with time and materiality in the dance film *SNAP* (2011).

Together, these exemplars raise several questions for researchers interested in writing 'data' across time, space, and matter: How might 'data' exist in real-time or outside temporal linearity? How might 'data' intra-act with material place and digital space? How might 'data' be written as spacetimematterings? Because writing remains inseparable from time, space, and matter, the latter question remains a continued site of engagement within my own writing practice. To illustrate, the chapter concludes by sharing recent works that write different spacetimematterings in different writing modes: choreographic, hypermodal, and photographic (Ulmer, 2015, 2016a, 2016b). These are followed by a brief discussion regarding how 'data' spacetimematterings not only have the potential to write, but also encounter, teach, and reconceptualize research.

EXAMPLES OF 'DATA' SPACETIMEMATTERINGS

When 'data' are written as spacetimematterings in (post)qualitative methodology, 'data' move, we move with 'data,' and 'data' move us. When Derridean approaches to writing are adopted in tandem with Barad's posthumanist performativity, therefore, writing threads throughout entangled, intra-active processes in which

—'data' dance—
—'data' act—
—'data' Tweet—
—'data' text.—

In the four multimodal examples that follow, performative 'data' are written through temporal, material, and digital space.

SNAP

Title: *SNAP*
Artist: Andrea Gise, USA
Year: 2011
Link: vimeo.com/22542065

Description. 'SNAP' takes place in colorful and gritty outdoor Brooklyn, NY. The dancers of 'agise & dancer' play with their urban environment and with the eye of the camera in this dynamic cinematic short" (Choreographic Captures, 2015, para. 1).

Spacetimematterings. Interdisciplinary dancer, choreographer, and artist Gise (2015) uses dance to explore interests in science, technology, futurism, and the posthuman body. In *SNAP*, two dancers move throughout the urban cityscape of Brooklyn. They trace their bodies with chalk, dance on and with concrete surfaces, move against graffiti-filled walls, eat, lie on grass, and leap through rows of shipping containers. Different material environments differently inform their movements, as materiality provides a site for embodied intra-action. As this occurs, the planes of time and space repeatedly are sewn together and then torn apart.

For example, at 00:56, one dancer is positioned upright against a concrete wall as the other dancer lies at her feet on the concrete ground; together, their bodies form a 90-degree angle while each mirrors the movements of the other. In these moments, they dance on and against perpendicular planes. At 01:12, however, the dancers separate. They are now standing, taking turns staring at the camera and breaking the fourth wall. It is a dance performance, yet the performance continues on without dance. At the 3:28 mark both dancers are walking on the *far* end of the street heading toward what would be house *left*, one second later, the dancers change course and are now walking on the *near* end of the street heading toward house *right*. Their walking pace slows. Soon thereafter at 3:35, one dancer begins snapping her fingers. With each snap, video-editing leaves the other dancer differently positioned—sometimes moving through forward through time, sometimes moving backward through time, sometimes frozen in time. Through video editing, therefore, the dancers are able to exist in (im)possible spacetimes. The dancers rarely share the same spacetimematterings, even when positioned within the same frame.

Na Desmedida do Ontem, do Hoje e Do Amanhã

Title: *Na Desmedida do Ontem, do Hoje e Do Amanhã*
        [*In Unbridled Yesterday, Today, and Tomorrow*]
Artist: Giuli Lacorte, Brazil (Director)
Year: 2014
Link: grupohybris.art.br/expohybris-3/

Artists' description [Original]. "… *de forma experimental os intérpretes buscam interferir, dialogar e transformar alguns espaços convencionais—ou não, de Porto Alegre, imersos na desmedida de diversas questões como a passagem do tempo, as relações humanas, a despedida, o descaso e o caos*" (Grupo Hybris, 2015a, para. 1).

Artists' Description [Translation]. "... experimentally, the interpreters seek to interfere, dialog and transform some conventional spaces–or not, in the city of Porto Alegre, immersed in immoderation of various issues such as the passage of time, human relations, the farewell, the neglect and the chaos" (Grupo Hybris, 2015a, para. 1).

Spacetimematterings. Grupo Hybris (2015b) is a contemporary art group in Brazil that focuses on artistic interventions, moving space, the ways in which gestures and texts overlap, and photography as immeasurable. By experimenting with time and space in public contexts, the group aims to disrupt order in open, hybrid space. They foreground their work in creativity and materiality. In a hybrid exposition (Lacorte, 2014), dancers, theatrical performers, lighting technicians, and photographers combine to explore the spacetimematterings of Porto Alegre, Brazil. The exposition has been shared online as a set of 15 digital photographs. The ninth and tenth images appear as a series of translucent images that have been layered upon one another, as haunted apparitions of dancers and buildings foster spatiotemporal instability. The second image presents a tableau of dancers and theatrical performers positioned across a multi-story building in which the exterior facade has been removed; this image invites viewers to observe the performers in what resembles a beautifully grotesque, life-sized doll-house. Costumed performers intra-act with a background of urban decay, disrupting traditional placements of performers on enclosed, indoor stages that have been partitioned from the vibrancy of the material world.

Murmur Study

Title: *Murmur Study*
Artist: Christopher Baker, USA
Year: 2009–2012
Links: christopherbaker.net/projects/murmur-study/, vimeo.com/4464887

Artist's Description.

Murmur Study is an installation that examines the rise of micro-messaging technologies such as Twitter and Facebook's status update. One might describe these messages as a kind of digital small talk. But unlike water-cooler conversations, these fleeting thoughts are accumulated, archived and digitally-indexed by corporations. While the future of these archives remains to be seen, the sheer volume of publicly accessible personal—often emotional— expression should give us pause. This installation consists of 30 thermal printers that continuously monitor Twitter for new messages containing variations on common emotional utterances. (Baker, 2009–2012, para. 1–2)

Spacetimematterings. In *Murmur Study* (2009–2012), visual artist Baker uses Twitter to create live visualizations of 'data.' Within the hyperlinks above, the installation has been presented in the form of a video and interactive website. *Murmur Study* fits within a larger artistic project to conceptualize what he describes as the "intersections between architecture, space, place and digital data" (Ho, 2012, para. 8). For Baker (2015), a formally-trained scientist who later engaged art, the project of working with digital data is fundamentally material. This is important, he contends, in that the increasingly digital worlds in which we live redefine public space. By collecting and printing 'data' as "an endless waterfall of text accumulating in tangled piles below" (2009–2012, para. 1–2), Baker archives digital utterances such as

argh	meh	grrrr	oooo	ewww	hmph
argh	meh	grrrr	oooo	ewww	hmph
argh	meh	grrrr	oooo	ewww	hmph
argh	meh	grrrr	oooo	ewww	hmph
argh	meh	grrrr	oooo	ewww	hmph
argh	meh	grrrr	oooo	ewww	hmph

through time and space. The project provokes questions related to how individuals produce digital 'data' and, in the process of leaving digital footprints, individuals become digital 'data' themselves. For Baker and others, elements of digital 'data' are of particular interest within urban environments, especially as they relate to participatory projects.

YOUR TEXT HERE

Title: *YOUR TEXT HERE*
Artist: Marcus Zotes, Spain and Iceland
Year: 2011–ongoing
Links: unstablespace.com/work/yourtexthere-detroit/, vimeo.com/80647589

Artist's Description.

The city is constantly telling us what to do, what to think, and how to act. Using explicit visual language, a multiplicity of billboards, signs, images and symbols invade our public spaces in order to tell us how to behave. YOUR TEXT HERE is a project that challenges this condition: Citizens are given the opportunity to change their role as receivers of information in order become the authors. The way it works is simple: you submit an anonymous text message in a website through your mobile phone, and in turn it is automatically projected at large scale onto the façade of a building. ... The project aims at bringing citizens together as a community in public space, providing a tool for public expression through which they can share their feelings, identities, secrets, criticism, wisdom, support, advice, frustrations, etc. (Zotes, 2011–ongoing, para. 1, 3)

Spacetimematterings. As an architect and visual artist, Zotes works primarily from Reykjavik, Iceland. Variations of *YOUR TEXT HERE* (2011–ongoing) have been performed in cities worldwide, including Reykjavik, New York, and Detroit. For Zotes, interactive installations function as a visual intervention in public space in which anonymous text messages are projected onto buildings for between 10 and 20 seconds. Using space as "an arena for debate, a catalyst for social interaction" (2011, para. 3) is a thread that runs throughout his work. Sometimes, as in the case with another installation in New York, Zotes (2015) intervenes in public space that must be actively claimed. At other times he explicitly involves children in his work. In Reykjavik, for example, Zotes (2015) has animated a well-known building with children's drawings. In addition to these and other pieces, Zotes invites the public to create and participate in different light installations in international cities such as Accra, Ghana; Moscow, Russia; Roskilde, Denmark; and Toronto, Canada.

In Detroit, Zotes' *YOUR TEXT HERE* appeared in 2012. Because these texts were produced in a particular period of local and global uncertainty, it is tempting to affix meaning to the installation within past historical accounts. 'Data' as spacetimemattering, however, generate a more complicated analytical response. Instead, the effects of economic instability are at once entangled with intra-active versions of the city—past, present, and future. The text messages below include some of the messages produced by participating Detroiters, some of whom appear in delight and wonder of their newly realized agency to intra-act with public space.

I CAN SERIOUSLY WRITE ANYTHING ?
IS THIS HOW GRAFFITI FEELS LIKE ?

Others were perhaps more quick to claim public space. By owning the content and production of the texts, some appear empowered by the opportunity.

ESSENTIALLY THIS IS MY WALL
IM WHATS NEXT

Yet other text messages (in)directly invoke theory and art. Some follow the calls of critical geographers to 'reclaim your right to the city' (Harvey, 2003; Lefebvre, 2003); others reference Shepard Fairey's (1990) ongoing street art campaign, 'OBEY.' As 'data' spacetimematterings, these text messages detach from isolated, fixed points in time and move within an intra-active, dynamic, material world—one which continues beyond the initial moment in which 'data' supposedly have been 'collected.'

In these examples, 'data' spacetimematterings thread throughout multiple compositions. These forms of posthuman performative writing–as broadly conceived by Derrida and Barad–range from text messages displayed on exterior walls, to Tweets streaming down interior walls, to photographs of buildings without facades, to videos of dancers moving on, over, and within city-scapes. In the process of moving across digital and material surfaces, these 'data' become spacetimematterings become writings.

WRITING 'DATA' SPACETIMEMATTERINGS

Whether writing through similar forms of dance, photography, or video in my own work, I also encounter 'data' as spacetimematterings. This often occurs when 'data' become catalysts for multimodal writing compositions. They might begin as a dream in which text choreographs itself, a familiar photograph that takes off along unexpected lines of flight, or a series of images that assemble into critical conversations. Because 'data' are agential, they continue to spark inquiries that operate across visual and digital modalities and exceed standard formats for publishing academic scholarship. Consequently, I write 'data' as different spacetimematterings in different writing modes. Sometimes texts intra-act with readers, texts intra-act with other texts, sometimes both.

As I shall describe, 'data' have provoked several approaches to (post)qualitative writing, including writing spacetimematterings as choreographic, hypermodal, and photographic 'data.' Each approach resembles one or more of the previous arts-based examples in that they incorporate multimodal space, time, and matter. Like *SNAP*, choreographic writing suggests how embodied movements might be composed. Like *Murmur* and *Na Desmedida do Ontem, do Hoje e Do Amanhã*, hypermodal writing engages varying assemblages of digital images, texts, and sounds. And, like *YOUR TEXT HERE*, photographic cartography addresses material-discursive elements of public space. Yet because these modes of writing emphasize images, video, and multimodal graphics, they differ from traditional formats of scholarly writing that privilege text-based articles, chapters, monographs, and books; multimodal writings most often are supplements to, rather than primary modes of, expression. Being that 'data' as spacetimematterings encounter research differently, the following three examples have, out of necessity, disrupted the normativity of academic writing. Therefore, like the performances of Gise, Lacorte, Baker, and Zotes, these writing modes depart from convention to emphasize how images, videos, sounds, and text can be written as spacetimematterings.

WRITING EMBODIED SPACETIMEMATTERINGS

First, *choreographic writing* composes embodied spacetimematterings as 'data' (Ulmer, 2015). Years of dance training had instilled a sense of somatic being that I had not fully realized until becoming a methodologist. It was not until I began to write that I found I also approach research as movement (spatial, temporal, material, and otherwise). This awareness led to a dream in which writing danced and escaped off the page; this then led a desire to consider how 'data' and writing might move within research texts. As such, choreographic writing is designed to offer a method of writing 'data' "as a visual text in which words move, pause, gain emphasis, and flow as if dancing across the open page" (p. 35). Within the context of 'data' spacetimematterings, choreographic writings are embodied and entangled in surrounding environments in which "all bodies, not merely human bodies, come to matter through the world's performativity—its iterative intra-activity" (Barad, 2001, p. 32). Choreographic writing thus produces embodied 'data' that space-timematters as authors inscribe their moving selves onto surrounding temporal, spatial, and material landscapes.

WRITING SOUND-TEXT-IMAGE SPACETIMEMATTERINGS

Second, *hypermodal writing* engages assemblages of sounds, texts, and images as 'data' spacetimematterings (Ulmer, 2016a). They fold into themselves, duplicating, replicating, mutating into a digital assemblage. As 'data' alter into new rhizomatic forms, hypermodal writings begin to resemble a "lively mutating organism, a desir-ing radical openness, an edgy protean differentiating multiplicity, an agential dis/continuity, an enfolded reiteratively materializing promiscuously inventive spatio-temporality" (Barad, 2001, p. 29). As this occurs, readers are invited into the text and hypertext to experience sound-text-image spacetimematterings by creating their own affective experiences and by having their own encounters with 'data.' This allows readers to read hypermodal writing for affect and effect; read intensively and imma-nently; and read through photography and literature. Engaging readers in the work of thinking about 'data' potentially helps scholars rethink how digital text might be created, experienced, read, and written, particularly in this age of electronic, multi-modal communications. Moreover, hypermodalities, like photographic cartography, demonstrate how 'data' can spacetimematter into different research-creations.

WRITING STREET ART SPACETIMEMATTERINGS

Third, in *photographic cartography*, images of post-graffiti writings ('data') space-timematter across a visually contested city block (Ulmer, 2016b). By using photography to move alongside the material-discursive flows of post-graffiti, murals, stickers, paper paste-ups, fliers, and reverse graffiti, this approach to writing examines how critical conversations move across public surfaces (ex., walls, sidewalks, dumpsters, doorways). Here, writings are 'data' and 'data' are writings. Street art flows into past, present, and future 'data' that complicate notions of time and space in material environments. In other words, post-graffiti are visual conversations that occur among (un)familiar artists in disjointed times across constantly changing material surfaces. Each post-graffito ('datum') is an impetus—a spacetimemattering—with which artists intra-act. Through photographic cartography as a visual mode of writing, then, "spacetimematter can be productively reconfigured ... Changes to the past don't erase marks on bodies; the sedimenting material effects of these very reconfigurings—memories/re-member-ing—are written into the flesh of the world" (Barad, 2001, p. 47). Artists write 'data,' 'data' spacetimematter, and photographic cartography writes 'data' as visual spacetimematterings. Notably, photographic cartography moves rather than locates as it engages fragmented conversations across time, space, and matter.

These three modes of writing illustrate how, when 'data' provoke inquiry, scholarly writing shifts. It is by writing 'data' as spacetimematterings, in which 'data' alternatively write themselves, that such forms of writing may reverse the "deep freeze" of data (in Koro-Ljungberg, 2013, p. 274). Thus, 'data' are not pieces of knowledge waiting to be lassoed or corralled. They are creative, curious, intra-active, curious provocateurs. When 'data' are written as spacetimematter, they have the capacity to extend researchers in unexpected directions across various elements of research, including how research is encountered, taught, conceptualized, and composed.

EXTENSIONS

Significantly, data have been treated much like a museum or a zoo specimen throughout history. As inert material, data have been stuffed, mounted, shelved, and described. As living material, data similarly have been captured, confined, and displayed. Traditional data displays consequently contain decontextualized and decentered data. 'Data' spacetimematterings, however, are 'data' in the wild. Uncontained and uncontaminated, 'data' move and intra-act across space, time, and matter. They provide a different, albeit important, approach to 'data' in which spacetimematterings function as verbs, entanglements, and agential forces (Boje & Henderson, 2014). Importantly, these forces might move beyond writing academic research into classroom spaces, in which initial encounters with both 'data' and scholarly writing often occur.

Within the qualitative methodology courses I instruct, for example, I incorporate multimedia materials from installations such as those described within this chapter. I regularly share these and other examples as the last class activity to destabilize when and where research occurs and when and where 'data' are. Oftentimes, the realization for students is that we are already surrounded by 'data' in our daily lives. Because I currently teach within an international arts city, I am able to localize methodological curricula. For example, I have used videos of performers wearing sound suits designed by multi-media artist Nick Cave; one such example stems from his production *Heard•Detroit* (Cranbrook Art Museum, 2015). Additional local examples of 'data' as spacetimemattering have involved the international exhibit "Before I Die" (2015). In Detroit, as in other cities worldwide, exterior walls of buildings have been painted with chalkboard paint and passersby are invited to use chalk to complete the following sentence: "Before I die, I want to _____." Similarly, I draw from *Station to Station* (Aitken, 2015), a series of 62 one-minute films taken as a train of artists crossed from the Atlantic to the Pacific in 24 days; the films are a series of nomadic 'happenings' across time, space, and matter.

As scholars increasingly consider transgressive instructional practices (e.g., Kuby et al., 2016), 'data' spacetimematterings may offer additional disruptions. Teaching with 'data' spacetimematterings may allow for increased awareness of the material environments in which we live, teach, and research. Moreover, they also may serve as catalysts for when, where, and how 'data' occur, as well as how 'data' might be embodied and embedded within research. If 'data' intra-act with time and space, if 'data' are material, and if 'data' move, then perhaps 'data' ought to be approached within similar veins throughout the research process.

If we were to start by imagining what 'data' *could be,* rather that uncritically follow conventional wisdom regarding what 'data' already *are,* then perhaps we might begin to do qualitative methodology differently. As scholars continue to question the ontological status of data and the implications thereof within qualitative research (Koro-Ljungberg & MacLure, 2013; Koro-Ljungberg et al., 2018), researchers might consider the potential of 'data' as spacetimemattering as a means of reconceptualizing qualitative research (per Koro-Ljungberg, 2016). And, if the 'matter' to which Barad refers were substituted with 'data,' then 'data' might be "diffracted, dispersed, threaded through with materializing and sedimented effects of iterative reconfigurings of spacetimemattering, traces of what might yet (have) happen(ed)" (2014, p. 168). As 'data' dislocate—'data' shift—'data' do not stay still—'data' diffract—quantum 'data' might begin to foster quantum inquiries.

Given that writing has been one of the primary means through which data are fixed in time, space, and matter, encountering quantum data differently might begin by writing differently. Scholarly writing, like performance art, is now able to incorporate a wide variety of texts, including those generated from images, videos, sounds, social media, light projections, paper•installations, and more. Writing spacetimematterings through choreographic, hypermodal, and photographic forms of writing are but three possibilities. If we were to consider how 'data' might be written as spacetimemattering, academic writing might approach a broader range of possible expression. In so doing, scholarly inquiries might then take on additional dimensions of, and intra-actions among, space, time, and matter in research.

REFERENCES

Aitken, D. (Director). (2015). *Station to station* [Film]. Retrieved from http://stationtostation.com

Baker, C. (2009). *Murmur study* [Video]. Retrieved from https://vimeo.com/4464887

Baker, C. (2009–2012). *Murmur study* [Art installation website]. Retrieved from http://christopher-baker.net/projects/murmur-study/

Baker, C. (2015). *Bio + CV + statement*. Retrieved from http://christopherbaker.net/biocv/

Barad, K. (2001). Re (con) figuring space, time, and matter. In M. DeKoven (Ed.), *Feminist locations: Global and local, theory and practice* (pp. 75–109). New Brunswick, NJ and London: Rutgers University Press.

Barad, K. (2007). *Meeting the universe halfway: Quantum physics and the entanglement of matter and meaning*. Durham, NC: Duke University Press.

Barad, K. (2010). Quantum entanglements and hauntological relations of inheritance: Dis/continuities, spacetime enfoldings, and justice-to-come. *Derrida Today, 3*(2), 240–268.

Barad, K. (2014). Diffracting diffraction: Cutting together apart. *Parallax, 20*(3), 168–187.

Before I Die. (2015). *Walls around the world: The ongoing Before I Die wall directory*. Retrieved from http://beforeidie.cc/site/blog/category/walls/

Boje, D. M., & Henderson, T. L. (Eds.). (2014). *Being quantum: Ontological storytelling in the age of antenarrative*. Newcastle upon Tyne: Cambridge Scholars Publishing.

Choreographic Captures. (2015). *SNAP*. Retrieved from http://www.choreooo.org/en/competition/films-2009-2013/capture/show/snap.html

Cranbrook Art Museum. (2015, Oct. 9). *Nick Cave "Heard•Detroit" Sept. 26, 2015* [Video]. Bloomfield Hills, MI: Retrieved from https://www.youtube.com/watch?v=FuiSWY65R7U

Derrida, J. (1976). *Of grammatology*. Baltimore, MD: The Johns Hopkins University Press.

Fairey, S. (1990). *Manifesto*. Retrieved from http://www.obeygiant.com/about

Gise, A. (2011). *SNAP* [Video file]. Retrieved from https://vimeo.com/22542065

Gise, A. (2015). *Home*. Retrieved from http://andreagisedancers.squarespace.com

Grupo Hybris. (2015a). *ExpoHybris*. Retrieved from http://www.grupohybris.art.br/espetaculos_teatro_danca/expohybris/

Grupo Hybris. (2015b). *Home*. Retrieved from http://www.grupohybris.art.br

Harvey, D. (2003). The right to the city. *International Journal of Urban and Regional Research, 27*(4), 939–941.

Ho, Y. (2012, June 18). Artist profile: Christopher Baker. *Rhizome*. Retrieved from http://rhizome.org/editorial/2012/jun/18/artist-profile-christopher-baker/

Holbrook, T. (2010). An ability traitor at work: A treasonous call to subvert writing from within. *Qualitative Inquiry, 16*(3), 171–183.

Koro-Ljungberg, M. (2013). "Data" as vital illusion. *Cultural Studies <=> Critical Methodologies, 13*(4), 274–278.

Koro-Ljungberg, M. (2016). *Reconceptualizing qualitative research: Methodologies without methodology.* Thousand Oaks, CA: Sage Publications.

Koro-Ljungberg, M., & MacLure, M. (2013). Provocations, re-un-visions, death, and other possibilities of "data." *Cultural Studies <=> Critical Methodologies, 13*(4), 219–222.

Koro-Ljungberg, M., MacLure, M., & Ulmer, J. (2018). 'Data' and its problematics. In N. K. Denzin & Y. S. Lincoln (Eds.), *The SAGE handbook of qualitative research* (5th ed.) (pp. 462–484). Thousand Oaks, CA: Sage Publications.

Kuby, C. R., Aguayo, R. C., Holloway, N., Mulligan, J., Shear, S. B., & Ward, A. (2016). Teaching, troubling, transgressing: Thinking with theory in a post-qualitative inquiry course. *Qualitative Inquiry, 22*(2), 140–148.

Lacorte, G. (Artistic director). (2014). *Na desmedida do ontem, do hoje e do amanhã (In unbridled yesterday, today, and tomorrow)* [Photographs by C. Bicocchi]. Retrieved from http://www.grupohybris.art.br/expohybris-3/

Lefebvre, H. (2003). *Writings on cities* (E. Kofman & E. Lebas, Trans.). Oxford: Blackwell.

St. Pierre, E. A. (2011). Post qualitative research: The critique and the coming after. In N. K. Denzin & Y. S. Lincoln (Eds.), *The SAGE handbook of qualitative research* (4th ed.) (pp. 611–626). Thousand Oaks, CA: Sage.

Ulmer, J. (2015). Embodied writing: Choreographic composition as methodology. *Research in Dance Education, 16*(1), 33–50.

Ulmer, J. (2016a). Photography interrupted: A hypermodal assemblage. *Qualitative Inquiry, 22*(3), 176–182.

Ulmer, J. (2016b). Writing urban space: Street art, democracy, and photographic cartography. *Cultural Studies <=> Critical Methodologies,* ahead-of-print, 1–12.

Zotes, M. (2011–ongoing). *YOUR TEXT HERE–Detroit* [Art installation website]. Detroit, MI: Dlectricity Festival. Retrieved from http://unstablespace.com/work/yourtexthere-detroit/

Zotes, M. (2012). *YOUR TEXT HERE–Detroit* [Video]. Detroit, MI: Dlectricity Festival. Retrieved from https://vimeo.com/80647589

Zotes, M. (2015). *Info.* Retrieved from http://www.unstablespace.com/info/

CHAPTER ELEVEN

Spectral Data Experiment n-1

SUSAN NAOMI NORDSTROM

ABSTRACT

In this chapter, I offer two Deleuzoguattarian experiments that disassemble(d) and reassemble(d) traces of spectral data that aim to help readers think through a spectral data territorial assemblage in their own work. First, I describe an arts-based experiment I recently completed in which I examine the work of spectral data in my research over the past six years. Extending from that experiment, I offer an open-ended experiment, a series of infinitive verbs—to anticipate, to perceive, to remember, to invent—and related imperatives that aim to help readers experiment with spectral data in their research and make the multiple of spectral data.

Keywords: post qualitative, spectral data, assemblage

DEFINITIONAL DESIRES

People have frequently asked me the following questions about spectral data since the publication of the *Cultural Studies* ⇔ *Critical Methodologies* (Koro-Ljungberg & MacLure, 2013a, 2013b) special issue about data. How do you do spectral data? What is it exactly? How do I know it if it happens? What do I do with it? In response to these questions, I refer back to the article in which I defined spectral data as a Deleuzoguattarian (1987) territorial assemblage generated among relationships between the living and nonliving and explain how I demonstrated it through a conversation between my long dead grandmother and me (Nordstrom, 2013). I explain that spectral data is a *doing* and not a *meaning* of a relationship between living and nonliving in qualitative research.

More specifically, I explain spectral data as "a place of passage" (Deleuze & Guattari, 1987, p. 323) that enables my grandmother to "occupy the middle of living and deceased so that [she] can insert [her]self into my life and work" (Nordstrom, 2013, p. 338). I describe how she inserts herself into my dreams, my writing, my garden, and so on. Her insertions are untimely, always unanticipated movements that bring us both into the middle spaces of living and deceased such that neither us know who is alive or dead. I claim that spectral data are about "learn[ing] [how] to live with ghosts" (Derrida, 1994, pp. xvii–xviii). I describe how this learning, these affective forces, passes through me and pushes me into unanticipated assemblages that make my life and work foggy with affective forces. Under her gaze words appear, disappear, and reappear when I write. Her long dead gardens rhizomatically extend from Nebraska's rich topsoil to Memphis, Tennessee Granada soil. The reflection in the mirror asks me, "Who are you? Are you her? Is she you?" These moments pass through us and form *our* spectral data territorial assemblage.

I encourage the person(s) asking me to define spectral data "to discover what territoriality [an assemblage] envelops" (Deleuze & Guattari, 1987, p. 503) in their lives and work. Simply put, I cannot anticipate or explore the spectral data assemblage in other people's lives and research. Other people will form their own territories, their own iterations, or doings, of spectral data. Each relationship generated among living and nonliving will always be singular, create a different territory, and, by extension, do different work. To facilitate an exploration of spectral data possibilities, I ask the person(s) the following questions, questions that I ask myself whenever I work with spectral data. How do the dead insert themselves into your life and work? What is the work of that relationship?

Each time I answer questions from readers of the special issue article (Nordstrom, 2013), Derrida's (2007) thoughts on death and writing pass through me. He wrote:

> You do not know to whom you are speaking, you invent and create silhouettes, but in the end it no longer belongs to you. Spoken or written, all these gestures leave us and begin to act independently of us. … At the moment I leave "my" book (to be published)—after all, no one forces me to do it—I become, appearing-disappearing, like that uneducable specter who will have never learned to how to live. The trace I leave signifies to me at once my death, either to come or already come upon me, and the hope that this trace survives me. (p. 32)

Derrida's words help me theorize the work of defining of spectral data that I have done in the past and in the special issue (Nordstrom, 2013). In the special issue, I purposely gave spectral data an open and ambiguous definition as a territorial assemblage formed between the living and nonliving in order to resist normalizing spectral data. The description and definition of spectral data in the special issue article was designed to become a trace, a silhouette, of spectral data, something that no longer even belongs to me. Even the spectral data in my life and work have left me. As the places of passage proliferate in the relationship between my grandmother and me, the fog envelops and makes me question spectral data once again. I am always learning to live with this data. I am always becoming the uneducable specter that Derrida (2007) refers to above.

In this chapter, I offer to those interested in spectral data two Deleuzoguattarian (1987) experiments that disassemble(d) and reassemble(d) traces of spectral data. These experiments aim to help readers think through a spectral data territorial assemblage in their own work. First, I describe an arts-based experiment I recently completed in which I examine the work of spectral data in my research over the past six years. Extending from that experiment, I offer an open-ended experiment, a series of infinitive verbs and related imperatives that aim to help readers experiment with spectral data in their research and make the multiple of spectral data.

MOBILE SPECTRAL DATA

I recently completed an arts-based Deleuzoguattarian (1987) experiment in which I disassembled and reassembled traces of spectral data from the past six years.[1] I made a mobile consisting of all my scholarly work (e.g., dissertation proposal, the special issue article, conference papers, and so on) in which I defined or wrote about spectral data. I reread each definition and example of spectral data and considered the work of this data in my research and life. I cut these definitions and examples out of the papers, removed identifying information (e.g., dates and headings) from the definitions and examples, placed them in a sack, and shook the sack to disrupt any sense of linearity. I then taped each definition and example onto clear elastic thread and hung them on a mobile made of wooden embroidery hoops. I took the mobile for a walk at a local botanical garden to follow the embodied and sensorial ways that spectral data move me (Truman & Springgay, 2016).[2]

As I walked with the mobile, I was reminded of Derrida's (2007) words:

Each time I let something go, each time some trace leaves me, "proceeds" from me, unable to be reappropriated, I live my death in writing. It's the ultimate test: one expropriates oneself without knowing exactly who is being entrusted with what is left behind. Who is going to inherit, and how? Will there even be any heirs? (p. 33)

Each slip of paper became a trace that advanced from me. As I walked and watched the traces dance in the wind, I realized that these writings were never really my own, they had already gone on without me.

The mobile traces of spectral data became an assemblage, a "complex of [molar and molecular] lines" (Deleuze & Guattari, 1987, p. 505) of spectral data. Each slip of paper became molar intensities, traces of spectral data, that sought to create a "segmentary, circular, binary, arborescent system" (p. 505) definition about spectral data. Each movement of the wind created "diagonal[s] [that] free [themselves], break or twist" (p. 505) that proceeded from the arborescent definitions. These complementary movements created a generative assemblage of constantly moving lines that "oscillate between tree lines that segment and even stratify them, and lines of flight or rupture that carry them away" (p. 506). I began to see new and different combinations of spectral data as molar and molecular forces moved spectral data in different ways on a stratum.

Assemblages and their constitutive lines "belong to the strata" (Deleuze & Guattari, 1987, p. 504). The mobile manifested different expressions of spectral data and helped me to work within "the amplification of the resonance between the molecular and the molar" (Deleuze & Guattari, 1987, p. 60) of spectral data. These amplifications opened up "the possibility of a proliferation and even interlacing of forms" (p. 60) of spectral data. The mobile created a space for me to:

> lodge myself on a stratum, experiment with the opportunities it offers, find an advantageous place on it, find potential movements of deterritorialization, possible lines of flight, experience them, produce flow conjunctions here and there, try out continuums of intensities segment by segment, have a small plot of new land at all times. (p. 161)

In effect, the complementary movements between molar definitions and molecular lines of flight created a space for me to see my contribution to the special issue (Nordstrom, 2013) as a spectral data stratum—a seemingly secure equilibrium of spectral data that is organized by a "logic of the AND" (p. 25) among the living and nonliving. This organization is one of constant movement and passages between these two terms that produce momentary stratifications—moments of recognition (e.g., a glance in a mirror, a photograph, a laugh, a song, and so on) of spectral data. These moments of recognition assemble themselves in a territorial assemblage that "goes beyond mere 'behavior'" (p. 504). In other words, the assemblage moves beyond the momentary recognitions to affective forces that pour through me and leave language breathless in its pursuit to catch up to the affects.

The mobile also helped to see how have I have been experimenting with spectral data for the past six years. Each time I wrote about spectral data I explored new connections and relations and, in so doing, created different possibilities about spectral data. For example, in a conference paper I questioned the desirability and possibility of spectral data (Nordstrom, 2010b). In other papers, I worked through different definitions, or traces, and examples of spectral data (Nordstrom, 2010a, 2013, 2015a). Each piece of writing became an experimentation, a way to "discover and dismantle" (Baugh, 2005, p. 92) a spectral data stratum to "look for lines of flight … the dangers of those lines … and new combinations" (p. 92). In effect, each piece of writing about spectral data became an experiment in making the multiple of spectral data, "the magic formula we all seek" (Deleuze & Guattari, 1987, p. 20), a multiplicity of spectral data.[3]

Each experimentation that makes the multiple of spectral data creates a denser "unity of composition in spite of the diversity in its organization and development" (Deleuze & Guattari, 1987, p. 502) on the stratum. In other words, each experimentation thickens the composition of the stratum with definitional (or molar) lines and adds further complexity to the multiplicity of spectral data. This thickening, however, is rendered elastic by "an extremely mobile" (p. 502) stratum. The elasticity is affect, "the force, the lure through which a certain constellation comes to expression" (Manning, 2013, p. 26). Deterritorializing molecular lines move with affective force to push and pull the limit(s) of the stratum created by the molar lines. As affective molecular lines move with definitional molar lines, the spectral data stratum becomes "a continual, renewed creation" (p. 502) in which "there is neither a correspondence nor a cause-effect relation nor a signified-signifier relation" (p. 502). As a result, there is no one systematic definition of spectral data that delimits what the data can or cannot do. Its strengths and limitations become supple rhythmic experimentations on the stratum. On the stratum one must try not to engage in a "formalization that disciplines social science inquiry to make it scientific" (St. Pierre, 2013, p. 226). On the stratum one must resist the dangerous desire to "reproduce the same rather than encourage difference" (p. 226). One must get to work, experiment, in the middle where "it will sometimes end in chaos, the void and destruction, and sometimes lock us back into the strata, which become more rigid still, losing their degrees of diversity, differentiation, and mobility" (Deleuze & Guattari, 1987, p. 503).

To work toward difference, encourage experimentation, and resist formalization in this chapter, I asked myself the following questions. How might I invite readers to experiment with me? How might I invite others to make the multiple with me? Another experiment needs to happen, and it happens in this chapter. It is for this reason that I have titled this chapter, "Spectral Data Experiment n-1." A spectral data multiple is always being made. It is never complete. It is always multiplying, n-1 (Deleuze & Guattari, 1987). Experiment with me. Make the multiple with me. "Feel the influence of the dead in the world" (Michaels, 1996, p. 53)—meander in their influences and let the dead take you where they will.

SPECTRAL DATA EXPERIMENT N-1

In this experiment, I turn my attention to two questions animated by the complementary movement of molar and molecular lines on the spectral data stratum. In particular, I ask the following questions. What is the work of the complementary movement between molar and molecular lines on the spectral data stratum? How do these complementary movements generate a territory between the living and nonliving?

To make the multiple in this chapter, I suggest that the complementary movements are generated by four infinitive verbs—to anticipate, to perceive, to remember, to invent. As traces of spectral data passed through and changed me, these four verbs seemed to repeat and differentiate through the territorial assemblage between my grandmother and me. These four verbs gesture toward the untimeliness of relational movements in a territorial assemblage and how those movements can only be loosely grasped, or perceived, as they undulate in space and time. Through these shifting moments of perceptions that come too late, too soon, or not at all, I (re)member how to live with ghosts who refuse to stay in the ground. Rather than focus on nouns, I focus on the infinitive verbs to position spectral data as data that are always in process and operate in a procedural ontology. The infinitive verb, as Palmer (2014) suggested is a "grammatical form [that] expresses an entire world view through its refusal of stasis, substantives and the present instant, and its simultaneous affirmation of virtuality, indeterminacy and infinite variations" (p. 186). In other words, infinitive verbs gesture to a conceptualization of spectral data that is unstable, reconfigures itself in present moments, and generates new possibilities about it. These verbs create further imperatives to experiment on the stratum of spectral data.

In what follows, I explore each infinitive by exploring what I think happens when I work with these infinitive verbs. These explorations seek to illustrate the "relations of counterpoint into which they enter and the compounds of sensations" (Deleuze & Guattari, 1991, p. 188) that these infinitive verbs generate in my life and work experimentations. Because the infinitive verb is unstable, the explorations are vague and foggy becomings that operate in shifting and contingent middle spaces. The ambiguity of the becomings aim to invite further experimentation. After each exploration, I offer an imperative from Anne Michael's *Fugitive Pieces* (1996), an invaluable novel to my thinking about spectral data that I read when I first developed it six years ago. In fact, I return to this book each time I write about spectral data. The novel follows Jacob through his life as a Holocaust survivor, his rescue by a Greek geologist, and his work as an artist. In many ways, the novel became my imperative to write about spectral data because Michael's writing helped me to articulate possible relationships between the living and nonliving.

To Anticipate

I never know when to anticipate spectral moments as they fall from a life, a plane of immanence. Deleuze (2006) wrote:

A life is everywhere, in every moment which a living subject traverses and which is measured by the objects that have been experienced, an immanent life carrying along the events or singularities that are merely actualized in subjects and objects. (p. 387)

Photographs, a wedding ring spinning around a finger like shared DNA, tears, spectral hands are actualizations of a life. These actualizations pass through me, sometimes without my knowing-sensing. Sometimes I look for the spectral and it is not there. Specters are never there waiting for me, the living. They are not at my beckon call. I search photographs for responses and am given silence in return. Sometimes the dead respond in my dreams. Other times I wait for responses that may never come. The dead are not ours to tame. Sometimes the ghosts unexpectedly overwhelm me. I feel the many hands of generations of women in my family touch me as I weep about a traumatic situation. Their hands push me forward. Still, I anticipate the unanticipated. I wait for the untimely returns of the revenants.

Imperative. The shadow-past is celebrated by everything that never happened. Invisible, it melts the present like rain through karst. A biography of longing. It steers us like magnetism, a spirit torque. This is how one becomes undone by a smell a word, a place, the photo of a mountain of shoes. By love that closes its mouth before calling a name. (Michaels, 1996, p. 17)

To Perceive

These untimely, unanticipated, and intensity-actualizations—the warmth of a life pressing on skin, haunted dreams, and tears of mourning—pass through me. I perceive the ghost "in a haze of dust" (Deleuze, 1993, p. 94) and "realize [them] in the body" (p. 105). In the dust, I seek clarity that was never there to begin with. I desire words to describe indescribable moments that pass through me too quickly. As I reach for a spectral hand, the sensation vanishes so quickly that I wonder if it even happened. The sensation is both potential and real. I lose myself to the dead. Each perception becomes dust. The dust, however, stirs with the pregnant possibility of a life. Perceptions become confused and confounded as they dance between the potential and the real. Order is given and taken away. Language becomes weighted with residues of the dust in which we perceive. Clarity temporarily and contingently emerges from the haze of dust only to be swallowed up by it in the next moment. My words are dusty.

Imperative. Then—as if she'd pushed the hair from my forehead, as if I'd heard her voice—I knew suddenly my mother was inside me. Moving along sinews, under my skin the way she used to move through the house at night, putting things away, putting things in order. (Michaels, 1996, p. 8)

To Remember

To remember, (re)member myself to the dead, is about "learn[ing] to live with ghosts" (Derrida, 1994, p. xviii), an enigmatic, ephemeral becoming with ghosts, an "upkeep, the conversation, the company or companionship, in the commerce without commerce of ghosts" (Derrida, 1994, p. xviii). We must "answer for the dead, respond to the dead" (Derrida, 1994, p. 136) as they weigh, think, "intensify and condense them[selv]es with the very inside of life, within the most living life" (p. 126). To remember is to become "an unstable consensus" (Boundas, 1991, p. 14) between the living and nonliving. Who speaks? Who touches? Who dreams? Who moves? Who writes? These questions become irrelevant. No one knows who speaks, touches, dreams, moves, and writes in the re(dis)appearances of ghosts. We become with the dead. The dead become with us. To remember is to become living and nonliving and living and nonliving and ... and ... and ...

> *Imperative. "I know why we bury our dead and mark the place with stone, with the heaviest, most permanent thing we can think of: because the dead are everywhere but in the ground."* (Michaels, 1996, p. 8)

To Invent

Remembering, perceiving, anticipating, and living with ghosts invents a territorial assemblage, a place of passage, of movement. Repetitions of to anticipate, to perceive, to remember, and to invent assemble, accumulate, and modulate to invent a territory, a spectral data territory that is constantly assembled, reassembled, and disassembled. A territory is never complete. There is no pure territorial assemblage of spectral data. There is no singular spectral data. Spectral data must be assembled, reassembled, and disassembled. Spectral data—an invented assemblage.

> *Imperative. Our relation to the dead continues to change because we continue to love them. All the afternoon conversations that winter on Idhra, with Athos or with Bella, while it grew dark. As in any conversation, sometimes they answered me, sometimes they didn't.* (Michaels, 1996, p. 165)

ANOTHER SILHOUETTE OF SPECTRAL DATA

Palmer (2014) noted that "the infinitive is the undetermined problem and the conjugation is the solution" (p. 87). The infinitives—to anticipate, to perceive, to remember, to invent—are a way to "create a future" (Colebrook, 2002, p. 21) about spectral data not prescribe a predetermined way of doing spectral data. Those researchers interested in spectral data must "connect, conjugate, continue: a whole 'diagram,'" (Deleuze & Guattari, 1987, p. 161) of spectral data rather than signify these data through prescriptive and reductive programs. Simply put, those readers interested in spectral data must put the infinitives to work and connect them to make the multiple. If readers find themselves getting lodged into stratifying spectral data, it "is not the worst that can happen" (p. 161). Use that moment of lodging to:

See how it is stratified for us and in us and at the place where we are; then descend from the strata to the deeper assemblage within which we are held; gently tip the assemblage, making it pass over to the side of the plane of consistency [in which spectral data can] reveal itself for what it is: connection of desires, conjunction of flows, continuum of intensities. (p. 161)

In effect, I ask that readers experiment with spectral data and make the multiple with me. I ask that readers examine the "meticulous relation with the strata [through which] one succeeds in freeing lines of flights, causing conjugated flows to pass and escape" (p. 161). The verbs—to anticipate, to perceive, to remember, to invent—aim to provide a way for readers to engage such work. As readers connect movements of these verbs they might very well be able to see, become, from "the middle, rather and look down on [it] from above or up at [it] from below, or from left to right or right to left" (p. 23). In the middle, "everything changes" (p. 23). Spectral data, a territory generated among the living and nonliving, are animated by infinitive verbs that must be continuously connected and conjugated. Spectral data: to anticipate, to perceive, to remember, to invent …

NOTES

1. Zofia Zawliska's (2016) Ruminatus animated this work. Zawliska asked many of the contributors to the special issue to read a list of directives, revisit their contribution, and complete a directive with their contribution. The arts-based experiment to which I refer is my contribution to Ruminatus. Please visit her website, http://zofiazaliwska.com/written-work/ruminatus/, for this rumination and others.
2. For a video of this walk, please visit: https://www.youtube.com/watch?v=C8OLfW2Sovo (Nordstrom, 2015b).
3. I am most grateful for these insights developed from a casual conversation with Pauliina Rautio at the American Educational Research Association 2016 Annual Meeting.

REFERENCES

Baugh, B. (2005). Experimentation. In A. Parr (Ed.), *The Deleuze dictionary* (pp. 91–93). New York, NY: Columbia University Press.

Boundas, C. (1991). Translator's introduction: Deleuze, empiricism, and the struggle for subjectivity. In G. Deleuze (Ed.), *Empiricism and subjectivity: An essay on Hume's theory of human nature.* (pp. 1–19). New York, NY: Columbia University Press.

Colebrook, C. (2002). *Gilles deleuze.* New York, NY: Routledge.

Deleuze, G. (1993). *The fold: Leibniz and the baroque.* (T. Conley, Trans.). Minneapolis, MN: University of Minnesota Press.

Deleuze, G. (2006). Immanence: a life. In D. Lapoujade (Ed.), *Two regimes of madness* (A. Hodges and M. Taormina, Trans.). (pp. 384–389). New York, NY: Semiotext(e).

Deleuze, G., & Guattari, F. (1987). *A thousand plateaus: Capitalism and schizophrenia* (B. Massumi, Trans.). Minneapolis, MN: University of Minnesota Press.

Deleuze, G., & Guattari, F. (1991). *What is philosophy?* New York, NY: Columbia University Press.

Derrida, J. (1994). *Specters of Marx: The state of debt, the work of mourning, and the new international* (P. Kamuf, Trans.). New York, NY: Routledge.

Derrida, J. (2007). *Learning to live finally Jacques Derrida: An interview with Jean Birnbaum* (P-A Brault & M. Naas). Hoboken, NJ: Melville House Publishing.

Koro-Ljungberg, M., & MacLure, M. (2013a). Data [Special issue]. *Cultural Studies ⟺ Critical Methodologies, 13*(4), pp. 219–372.

Koro-Ljungberg, M., & MacLure, M. (2013b). Provocations, re-un-visions, death, and other possibilities of "data." *Cultural Studies ⟺ Critical Methodologies, 13*(4), 219–222. doi: 10.1177/1532708613487861

Manning, E. (2013). *Always more than one: Individuation's dance.* Durham, NC: Duke University Press.

Michaels, A. (1996). *Fugitive pieces.* New York, NY: Vintage Books.

Nordstrom, S. (2010a). Learning to live with grandmother Naomie's Ghost: Longing for an impossible presence with objects. In K. Haworth, J. Hogue, L. G. Sbrocchi (Eds.), *Semiotics 2009: The semiotics of time* (pp. 616–622). New York, NY: Legas.

Nordstrom, S. (2010b). Spectral data: Speaking, writing, and acting with specters. Paper presented at the Sixth International Congress on Qualitative Inquiry. Champaign-Urbana, IL.

Nordstrom, S. N. (2013). A conversation about spectral data. *Cultural Studies ⟺ Critical Methodologies, 13*(4), 316–341. doi: 10.1177/1532708613487879

Nordstrom, S. N. (2015a). A data assemblage. *International Review of Qualitative Research, 8*(2), 166–193. doi: 10.1525/irqr.2015.8.2.166

Nordstrom, S. N. (2015b). *Spectral ruminatus.* Retrieved from https://www.youtube.com/watch?v=C8OLfW2Sovo

Palmer, H. (2014). *Deleuze and Futurism: A manifesto for nonsense.* London: Bloomsbury Academic.

St. Pierre, E. A. (2013). The appearance of data. *Cultural Studies ⟺ Critical Methodologies, 13*(4), 223–227. doi: 10.1177/1532708613487862

Truman, S. E., & Springgay, S. (2016). Propositions for walking research. In P. Burnard, E. Mackinley, & K. Powell (Eds.), *Routledge handbook of intercultural arts research.* London: Routledge.

Zawliska, Z. (2016). *Ruminatus.* Retrieved from http://zofiazaliwska.com/written-work/ruminatus/

CHAPTER TWELVE

Immanence AND Our Live Data Apology

ANNE BEATE REINERTSEN AND ANN MERETE OTTERSTAD

ABSTRACT

This is about staying with—and giving life to dead data merging research and advo-cacy; imagining creative and critical arrangements with/in data-doings. Our first example is crafted with Piketty's r>g non-distribution of capital formula (return on capital (r) being larger than our joint economic growth (g)); the tastes and smells of systemic economic inequalities in and my guts ... social contracts and what I must. Our second example is crafted with traveling pedagogies and policies; matter and mattering entangling the individual and the collective into solidarity and hope. Live data can do. Live data can become. This is our live data apology.

Keywords: Immanent critique, DataActivism, Justice

DATAWRITING

Last time, Ann Merete, we wrote about "Being data and datadream/ing pedago-gies with Pinter" (Reinertsen & Otterstad, 2013). We wrote about data erosions and infra-empiricism. We wrote about chaos-confrontations becoming with data; data killings hoping not to die. We used examples from perceptions of color and pieces of theatre and art to open up and ask questions about data, data collection and analysis. This time we have decided to write about staying with—and giv-ing life to dead data merging research and advocacy; philosophizing and creating animations and sensations of data and/as our data apologies … and action. We try this through the notion of "haptic spaces distinguished from optical space" (Deleuze & Guattari, 1987, p. 492) thus movements in bodies as physical processes as senses hopefully contributing to both the exploring of senses as well as the proliferation of multi-sensory and synesthetic regimes of communication and experience. Sensations produced in one modality when a stimulus is applied to another modality, as when the hearing of a certain sound induces the visualization of a certain color. It is a move from language-based translation to not-only-language-based transduction. Transduction here understood as a process of converting one form of energy—read also force—and/or event—into another. Data as force and an event happening in me, in you, alive, live creating momentum: *Sensation data and sensational data.* It is a Deleuze and Guattari (1987) immanent philosophy of thinking *with* data and data as event and alive to become *with:* live data doings and qualia live data becomings (more on this below).

In his treatise on capitalism and inequality in the twenty-first century Thomas Piketty (2014) notes that the numbers do not tell the full story. Rather, he notes that data focusing on how people actually live their lives with their choices and opportunities circumscribed by the ubiquitous presence of inequality are the data that reveal the true consequences of inequality, not the numbers or statistical data. He directs us to turn to descriptions of how people actually live in order to fully grasp the social significance of statistical or theoretical analyses of wealth and inequality, thus rethinking both the quantitative and qualitative in numbers. He further notes that stories and narratives are what we need in order to fully understand the consequences of pervasive inequality

> … grasp[ing] the hidden contours of wealth and its inevitable implications for the lives of men and women, including their martial strategies and personal hopes and disappointments. … Depict[ing] the effects of inequality with a verisimilitude and evocative power that no statistical or theoretical analysis can match. (p. 2)

Absolute immanence is in itself. It is not in something or in relation to something. It does not depend on an object or an-in any way connected subject. Substance therefore only perceived of as modalities in immanence. It is only when immanence is immanence in itself that we can speak of a plane of immanence. Immanence is a life, life and nothing else. It is not immanence in relation to life, but the immanent, which is nothing, which itself is a life. A life is the immanence of immanence; total power, total bliss. A life not dependent on a being or exposed for action, but in immediate consciousness. Actions and activities as constantly portrayed or sculptured in a life. A life of potentiality in every moment which is life. Such a moment is a haeccicity, not through or from a process of individualization, but from a particular and simultaneous singularity. A life in immanence beyond good or bad: Immanent data alive: A life with data knowledge.

But we do not encapsulate life—live data—in moments. Life is always and in every moment we are actualized in subjects or objects. The moments are empty, but offer an immediate and simultaneous consciousness about what has happened and what will. It is thus a notion of consciousness protesting against "bifurcation" (Whitehead, 1938), which is a tendency to separate matter from its perception, or to make a constitutive difference between "nature apprehended in awareness and the nature which is the cause of awareness" leading to a splintering of experience and dichotomous discussions about nature/culture, subject/object, body/mind, same/other and theories for/against. What emerges, are only accounts of experiences that separate the human subject from the ecologies of encounters and agency. The problem is therefore "to discuss the relations *inter se* of things known, abstracted from the bare fact that they are known" (Whitehead, 1938, p. 30).

The immanent event as life and data is actualized in matter and by the living, which makes it/something happen. Planes of immanence are virtual as long as events (read data, knowledge, life) are virtualities. The only thing that exists is relation between movement and rest, and in opposition to fixation, essence and unit (Spindler, 2013). *Sensationdata of inequalities ... urging me to act or dataproductivity because data happen in me ...*

The World Bank operates with a limit of earning one US dollar a day as the absolute poverty line. Imagine giving birth in a hospital charging money for every clean towel and bed linen. You have already five children at home.—Spending money on clean sheets? Three women giving birth in the same bed ... blood, fluids ... spreading of bacteria, viruses, diseases ... we motif each other. You are me, I am you. We are. Systemic inequality is indicative of a broken social contract. We have moved from shared accountability and responsibility to one of individual locus of control for which we are paying a high price.

ETHICAL CRITIQUES AND MORE TO COME ...

Sitting in the sun, resting and writing, feeling the warmth on the face, smelling the air, the wind whirls around and suddenly the dripping sound from the melting snow appears (Norwegian mountains-heaven). Thinking visually, sensory, transversely, livingly. Sometimes it is simple to catch "transgressive data, emotional data, dream data, sensual data, response data" (St. Pierre, 1997, p. 175), other times it is hard to get beyond the Kantian traditions of correlation proposing a world existing only insofar for humans. Correlation/ism seems still to privileging epistemology, documented for example in the newly released Norwegian Whitepaper for early childhood kindergartens (KD, St. Melding, no. 19, *Tid for lek og læring—Bedre innhold i barnehagen*, 2016–2017).[1] Such a whitepaper document co-creates emotional and response data, it creates anger, frustration, not hope but also. Responsibility. Following Barad (2007), a whitepaper document can become a relational ontology, an ontology in which individualized things and objects are no longer presupposed, simply 'given' out there. Instead Barad's theory is offering enactment of the entangled "since phenomena entail the inseparability of physical systems, which become distinguishable only as determinately bounded and propertied subsystems ... through their intra-action" (2007, p. 328). What is to be done? How to think differently of critique?

Trying to animate and becoming inseparable entangled with a Whitepaper document (Edwards, 2010), is also about mapping multiplicity searching for alternative research positions. Such ideas give hope and openings for writing critique relationally, affirmatively, unconditional and responsibly. According to Massumi[2] 'immanent critique' means that [the] critique is not an opinion or a judgment but a dynamic 'evaluation' that is lived out in situations. The early childhood political situations are embedded and intraacting with to the Whitepaper document, producing affirmative critique (Massumi, 2010, p. 338). Affirmative critique wonders and is different from criticism; there is no representation or pre-existence positions in motion, re-articulating ideas about 'learning- and learning-skills' forces professionals to think otherwise, outside the binaries of better/worse dichotomies. DataResistance is working and circulating on Facebook, in newspapers, and through academic meetings—multiplicities of thresholds are stretching the traditions of the pedagogical profession into something new. Something is happening in spacetimematterings (Barad, 2007).

Although it is hard to thinkfeel differently (Massumi, 2008)[3] explicitly in neoliberal times, where the global child/ren/hood is seen as the purveyor of economic prosperity and social stability (Moss, 2008), the necessities for alternative critical questions arise. How might it be possible to create resistance and critique beyond praxis's demanding specialists/professionals to observe, to document, to create and to test new-learners from early age? Children are encircled by professionals, which seem to achieve teach-ability in early years (Otterstad & Braathe, 2016). Preparing for schooling is becoming the new quality mantra emphasized by the preparing for international 'formal learning' rhetoric's. Additionally, language issues are increasing put weight on. Dahlberg (2016) alerts professionals to resist filling in forms, reporting writing, and going beyond preparing for inspection and auditing children. What to do?

DataWorries, DataApology and DataResistance are creating the whitepaper document. Materialized as shared opposition on Facebook, battling values that is tracking children, resisting anthropological machineries', where regimes of documenting, evaluating, disciplining, and comparing children as 'successful tools' to 'measure' children's everyday lives. The collective DataActivist movement is going on—thousands signing the national and international petition. More than 8500 signatures are materialized on Facebook (Barnehageopprør, 2016,

#Bhgopprør2016). A sensational virus is spreading and entangling children, parents, professional, history, politics, texts, and values against and within the field of early childhood. ResponsAbilities.

DataAssessingMaterials are critiqued, asking; what is measuring producing? Shifting ideas from interpreting meaning making (hermeneutics) to investigate and experiment with a vital pedagogical thinking to come. How to create critique beyond deconstructing texts, still embedded in the Kantian traditions of correlation proposing a world existing only insofar for humans. Correlation/ism seems still to privileging epistemology, producing data about children conducted by professionals, and not! New educational ontology is emerging (Barad, 2007; Braidotti, 2013), lively productive, not as anything goes, but penetrating habitual methodological research by rethinking the nature of being (Koro-Ljungberg, 2015; St. Pierre, Jackson & Mazzei, 2016). Diffractive[4] pedagogy processes (Hickey-Moody, Palmer, & Sayers, 2016, pp. 213–214), are supplying disruptive and generative potentials in educational research, by *re-thinking, re-feeling and re-making*—as doubling the loops within and against.

Here Hickey-Moody et al. (2016) allows for embodied and inventive learning processes, which are open-ended, nomadic and affirmative (Braidotti, 2006). 'Thinking together, things and/or (non)humans, demands a diverse form of scholarly accountability'. And speculation, in turn, becomes a very material process, a performative process of a world, a form of worlding itself (Åsberg, Thiele, & van der Tuin, 2015, p. 152). So how can a speculation in early childhood vocabulary connect to reality as an active verb—which might indicate to re-think *with*, to re-feel *with* and re-create *with* early childhood profession and a political whitepaper into something else … DataActivism.

TALKINGTHINKINGDOING

My method and strategic grip, my data activism is friction as sliding hesitation and questions into the materials. I am being conciously negative; thinking, doubting, hesitating thus keeping this … "Negativitetens saar aabent"/"Wound of negativity open" (Kierkegaard, 1994, p. 81). Why? To make it safer to do something unsafe and innovation. I speak of microontologies of selfmaking. The data is part of me and I must act as a writing subject releasing both concious and unconcious experiences (Reinertsen, 2016). Experiences not even necessarily accessible in a chunk of research data material, but functioning creatively giving life to notions, memories and feelings, to trigger recognitons and memories. But as events or moments only of continuous movements of endless emanating sensations made actual in the state or happening. An event is thus seen as the potential immanent within a particular confluence of forces unrelated to any material content, thus being without fixed structure, position, temporality or property, and without beginning and end. Thus as flows of empowering desire introducing mobility, resisting closure thus destabilizing the sedentary gravitational pulls of linear chronos (molar) formations. *Creativity data, data as creativity productivity.*

DATADIFFRACTION—DIFFRACTING DATA

To work within and against overgeneralizing perspectives in one way of another— resisting standards encountered and forced upon you/her/professionals, I also quest for a practical philosophy fascinated by what the 'neo-vitalist' paradigm (Deleuze, 1999) of life and politics (lifepolitics) can offer of becoming. Colebrook addresses a future of a feminist critical vitalism (2005) asserting and re-examining questions between mind and body—refusing the idea that matter requires to create meaning-making, recognition and more-of-the-same. Neo–vitalist ideas[5] might produce multiplicities of lived living processes by rejecting specific Cartesian image of thought as known products. A neo-vitalism[6] can connect to ontology as creation— immanence—not dichotomizing, and making limits, hence, in its place searching for differences. In philosophical thinking difference and becoming are supplied without ideas around reason, identity, being and the human subject. Deleuze and Guattari's (1987) multiplicities and chaos of life is generated and supported by Colebrook (2002, p. 4) saying that "the difficulty of Deleuze is tactical; his work attempt to capture (but not completely) the chaos of life. For no system or vocabulary is adequate to represent the flow of life".

Following Deleuze's empiricism, Colebrook (2002) suggests to shift the ground of the debate away from metaphysical foundations to a philosophy of immanence that stresses the need to create new concepts. The creation of concepts is itself experience or experimentation. There is a double implication here—that philosophy need not be seen as the master discourse or the unavoidable horizon of thought since artistic and scientific practices have their role to play as well. And, because ethical questions do not require metaphysics, the engagement with concepts need not be 'critical' but can be inventive, innovative and creative. A move towards a diffractive pedagogy (Hickey-Moody et al., 2016; Taguchi & Palmer, 2013; van der Tuin, 2014) might also invite data/materials to be sensed affirmatively, critiqued, arranged, rearranged and reconsidered creatively and inventive— diffracted through bodily processes where children and childhoods appear as something else.

Datadiffractions. Theorizing. Barad proposal is that theorizing can be—"… not to leave the material world behind and enter the domain of pure ideas where the lofty space of the mind makes objective reflection possible. Theorizing, like experimenting, is a material practice" (Barad, 2007, p. 55). So when data/documents rhetoric's and professional praxis's are put together, diffractively cutting-togeth-er-apart (Barad, 2014)—a vitalist movement connects early childhood values to bodily play, joyfulness, experimentation, creativeness, movements, humor, distur-bances and noise—and a Whitepaper/data cannot longer be what it was predicted to become. The Whitepaper monster is transformed and taken over by an educa-tional economic machinic orientation (Spindler, 2013), searching for pharmaceu-tical machines as a rescuer (Snaza et al., 2014), which now has been blocked. The pedagogical challenges are still many, and a re-orientation might open for other worldly scenarios that the one just mentioned. I am still data/dreaming pedagogy with Pinter, Anne (Reinertsen & Otterstad, 2013), as hope and affective flows.

DATAPRODUCTIVITY

This turns me into a "thinking territory" (Deleuze & Guattari, 1987, p. 44): data is constantly initiating deterritorializations and reterritorializations. Every piece of data is turned into events of difference and something coming towards me in being together becoming. They are flows of affects and research events and every time ... thinking begins again. I am territory. I write. Writing matters. It is important. The data is part of me working and I write. I write matter. I write things. I ultimately speak of situatedness as an immanent critique practice opening for new and clinical practices: Inner outer always eroding but creative dimensions of life only relationally super-, supra-positioned until something comes to matter. Datawritings. ...

STRETCHING DATAKNOWLEDGES ... CONTINUOUSLY

Continuing to zigzagging and to elaborate on dominating entrancing of research, qualitative inquiry is embedded in a rich variety of performances (Denzin, 2003), occurrences, meaning, styles, tastes, and symbols that historically, discursively and geographically transverses in spacetimematterings (Barad, 2007). According to Alexander (2005) various sources of data, participation, observation, interview, artefacts is used to conduct depictions of situations embedded in experiences that occurs as 'particular and natural', settings which is well documented and also is dominating my early childhood research stories, continuously. Research projects are producing data/materials, inscribed as rich data. Collected by somebody and interpreted according to several hermeneutic orientations, where a phenomeno-logical approach is giving 'voice' to how 'the insider's' 'experience', their setting and the meaning they 'attribute' to the real life, is based on the experiences 'out there'. Impossibilities to come. The ethnographer is offering social norms that govern actors in the setting—playing and conducting some form of arranging and re-arranging what is coming forward from the collected data/materials. These practices are located in a drive to access the value of the event—aspiring 'meaning-making' that might not previously been conceived. Here and now, in 'presence' is given truthfulness (Derrida), which challenge orthodox ethnography with the aim of collecting more and more data materials, reflecting real life. Hope and affective flows might change ideas of what data might be/come—how can haptic events force research in multidimensional/multisensory in different ways. Searching for an open diffractive science, not a reduction to the cultural-political-historical construction of science within humanist networks, merely a science always already broadly entangling. Such a speculation connects knowledge creation to diffracting pedagogy as intra-relating humans, more-than-humans, machines and things. This undoes knowledge production regarded as a fundamental concept to humanism, involving an embodied knower, collecting data through perception generating results. Experience and beliefs make the foundations for re/presentation.

In contrast, as you earlier have pointed out Anne, Haraway (1985, 1988) alternative knowledge production is highly local. It is what is produced in a particular situation that a body finds itself in, and simultaneously, a gaze from nowhere, a vision of what is known by a knower in that situation, as potentialities. If knowledges are plural, multiplicities within a situated locality, this idea might be in line what Braidotti (2013) suggests as a new vocabulary that invites multiplicities and the chance for change. Her idea is—emphasizing that the ways that we insert ourselves into our anthropocentric worlds and the ways that we take data into ourselves, as doings. When time is changing new techniques noticeably alter our styles of knowing. By entangling Colebrook's feminist neo-vitality (2010) entangles with Stengers (2010) might capture Massumi's creative research inventions (2008). Stenger's idea of science is that is seeks ways to let its object speak or become a subject (Snaza et al., 2014, p. 52). This encourage researchers to employ and embody intra-actions with more-than-verbal-materials by generating something unexpected to happen, become surprised, which is in line with what Manning at SenseLab[7] inspires to, searching for the active passages between research and creation.

Doing DataResistance, DataCollaboratively, through alternative social medias might include forceful bodily, stretching activist standpoints. Trying not to become against traditions as well as writing something else, might also be an ethical professional. Following Barad (2011, p. 8) writing's of her own research this research journey ends for a while

> (...) (It) is a part of that longstanding tradition of feminist science studies that focuses on the possibilities of making a better world, a livable world, a world based on values of co—flourishing and mutuality, not fighting and diminishing one another, not closing one another down, but helping to open up our ideas and ourselves to each other and new

possibilities, which with any luck will have the potential to help us see our way through to a world that is more livable, not for some, but for the entangled wellbeing of all

This quote make a short stop in the fighting against a newly published Whitepaper document which on Facebook engaged an activist group (#Bhgopprør 2016) working for children's livable world, justice, difference, ethics, and equity— not creating either/or dichotomies but over and over again searching for the shared responsibility of new possibilities for DataProductions.

POSTDATARESPONSIBILTY

I will end with a few words about responsibility, or rather my research post-responsibility and activism. Historically, and with some variations, western liberal democratic societies have understood the social contract to be an agreement of shared responsibility and accountability. This contract was a requirement for working towards creating and sustaining a fair and equitable social order. The systemic inequalities that have taken hold, and which Piketty (2014) through his r>g non distribution of capital formula has displayed for us, can be said to be indicative of—or have led to a broken contact. The prices we pay do not only include loss of human capital. But that we can be said to be both creating and sustaining immoral or even amoral social structures that are necessary for accessing opportunities.

The way I see this, post-responsibility activism allows me to use any kind of primary and secondary creative sensational data sources to provide a fuller understanding of how the lives of individuals, families, communities, and societies across the economic spectrum and in different parts of the world are impacted by the presence of endemic inequality. My aim is progressing human compassion through jolting Piketty animations.

NOTES

1. https://www.regjeringen.no/no/dokumenter/meld.-st.-19-20152016/id2479078/?ch=1&q=
2. http://www.inflexions.org/n4_t_massumihtml.html.
3. http://inflexions.org/n1_The-Thinking-Feeling-of-What-Happens-by-Brian-Massumi.pdf.
4. Karen Barad (2007, p. 72) states that diffraction attends to the relational nature of difference. Difference as a relation or, rather, as *relatings*, has nothing to do with essences (Being), but it does not shy away from 'understand[ing] diffraction patterns—as patterns of difference that make a difference—to be the fundamental constituents that make up the world' (van der Tuin, 2014, p. 235).
5. See the Journal—Theory, Culture & Society, 2005, no.1 and 2007, no. 6 for a revival of vitalist thought, on the work of Henri Bergson. Bergson offered life as inherently durational, as a creative, divergent temporal process, which Gilles Deleuze (1999) followed up.

6. Briefly a vitalist thought has been a presence in the West in one form or another since classical times and before, and has gone through a number of stages. According to Szerszynski (2005) Georges Canguilhem (1994, pp. 74–88) suggests that the history of the conceptualisation of life can be divided into four main stages: life as *animation*, as *mechanism*, as *organisation* and as *information*. And a supplement is Henri Bergson's life as *duration*, taken further by Gilles Deleuze, who provides a radical reconceptualization of life in terms of a monist temporal ontology of creative becoming.

7. www.senselab.ca/wp2/about/.

REFERENCES

Alexander, M. J. (2005). *Pedagogies of crossing: Meditations on feminism, sexual politics, memory, and the sacred*. Durham, NC: Duke University Press.

Åsberg, C., Thiele, K., & van der Tuin, I. (2015). Speculative before the turn. Reintroducing feminist materialist performativity. *Cultural Studies Review, 21*(2), pp. 145–172.

Barad, K. (2007). *Meeting the universe halfway: quantum physics and the entanglement of matter and meaning*. Durham, NC: Duke University Press.

Barad, K. (2011). Erasers and erasures: Pinch's unfortunate 'uncertainty principle'. *Social Studies of Science*, published online April 20, doi: 10.1177/0306312711406317, Retrieved from http://humweb.ucsc.edu/feministstudies/faculty/barad/barad-social-studies.pdf

Barad, K. (2014). Diffracting diffraction: Cutting together-apart. *Parallax, 20*(3), 168–187.

Braidotti, R. (2006). Affirming the affirmative: On nomadic affectivity. *Rhizome*, 11/12, http://www.rhizomes.net/issue11/braidotti.html

Braidotti, R. (2013). *The Posthuman*. Cambridge: Polity Press.

Colebrook, C. (2002). *Understanding Deleuze*. Australia: Allen & Unwin. Retrieved from https://seminario2012.files.wordpress.com/2012/02/colebrook-claire-understanding-deleuze.pdf

Colebrook, C. (2005). How well can we tell the dancer from the dance? The subject of dance and the subject of philosophy. *Topoi, 24*(1), 5–14.

Colebrook, C. (2010). *Deleuze and the meaning of life*. New York, NY: Continuum.

Canguilhem, G. (1994). *A vital rationalist: Selected writings* (A. Goldhammer, Trans.). New York, NY: Zone Books.

Dahlberg, G. (2016). An ethico-aesthetic paradigm as an alternative to the quality assurance discourse. *Contemporary Issues in Early Childhood, 17*(1), 124–133.

Deleuze, G. (1999). Bergson's conception of difference (M. McMahon, Trans.). In J. Mullarkey (Ed.), *The new Bergson* (pp. 42–66). Manchester: Manchester University Press.

Deleuze, G., & Guattari, F. (1987). *A thousand plateaus: Capitalism and schizophrenia*. London: Athlone Press.

Denzin, N. (2003). *Performance ethnography. Critical pedagogy and the politics of culture*. New York, NY: Sage Publication.

Edwards, R. (2010). The end of lifelong learning: A post-human condition? *Studies in the Education of Adults, 42*(1), 5–17.

Haraway, D. (1985/1991). A cyborg manifesto: Science, technology, and socialist-feminism in the late twentieth century. *Simians, cyborgs, and women: The reinvention of nature* (pp. 149–182). New York, NY: Routledge.

Haraway, D. (1988). Situated knowledges: The science question in feminism and the privilege of partial perspective. *Feminist Studies, 14*(3), 575–599.

Hickey-Moody, A., Palmer, H., & Sayers, E. (2016). Diffractive pedagogies: Dancing across new materialist imaginaries. *Gender and Education,* 28(2), 213–229.

Kierkegaard, S. (1966/1994). *Avsluttende uvidenskabelig efterskrift til de philosophiske smuler.* Fagernes: Pax Forlag.

Koro-Ljungberg, M. (2015). *Reconceptualizing qualitative research: Methodologies without methodology.* London: Sage.

Lenz Taguchi, H., & Palmer, A. (2013). A diffractive methodology to 'disclose' possible realities of girls' material-discursive health/'wellbeing' in school-settings. *Gender and Education, 25*(6), 671–687.

Massumi, B. (2008). *Semblance and event.* Retrieved from http://inflexions.org/n1_The-Thinking-Feeling-of-What-Happens-by-Brian-Massumi.pdf

Moss, P. (2008). What future for the relationship between early childhood education and care and compulsory schooling? *Research in Comparative and International Education, 3*(3), 224–234.

Otterstad, A. M., & Braathe, H. J. (2016). Travelling inscriptions of neo-liberalism in Nordic early childhood: Repositioning professionals for teaching and learnability. *Global Studies of Childhood, 6*(1), 80–97.

Piketty, T. (2014). *Capital in the twenty-first century* (A. Goldhammer, Trans.). Cambridge, MA and London: The Belknap Press of Harvard University Press.

Reinertsen, A. B. (2016). A phaedrus baroque art of maintenance or constant fabulating qualia becoming quality. *Contemporary Issues in Early Childhood.* Special Issue: Re-imagining quality in early childhood. doi: 10.1177/1463949115627909

Reinertsen A. B., & Otterstad, A. M. (2013 August). Being data and datadream/ing pedagogies with Pinter-a dream/dialogue/data/play about being ruthlessly honest about own motives eventually Max Stirner. *Cultural Studies ↔ Critical Methodologies, 13*(4), 233–239, first published on May 15, 2013, doi: 10.1177/1532708613487865

Snaza, N., Appelbaum, P., Baune, S., Carlson, D., Morris, M., Rotas, N., ... Weaver, J. (2014). Toward a posthumanist education. *Journal of Curriculum Theorizing, 30*(2), 39–55.

Stengers, I. (2010). *Cosmopolitics I* (R. Bononno, Trans.). Minneapolis, MN: University of Minnesota Press.

St. Pierre, E. A. (1997). Methodology in the fold and the irruption of transgressive data. *International Journal of Qualitative Studies in Education, 10*(2), 175–189.

St. Pierre, E. A., Jackson, A. Y., & Mazzei, L. A. (2016). New Empiricisms and New Materialisms. *Cultural Studies ↔ Critical Methodologies, 16*(2), 99–110. doi: 10.1177/1532708616638694

Spindler, F. (2013). *Deleuze: Tänkande och blivande.* Göteborg: Glänta produktion.

Szerszynski, B. (2005). Biopolitics and Vitalism. A paper presented at Workshop 16, 'Mapping Biopolitics', of the European Consortium for Political Research (ECPR) Joint Sessions of Workshops, Granada, 14–19 April.

van der Tuin, I. (2014). Diffraction as a methodology for feminist onto-epistemology: On encountering chantal Chawaf and Posthuman interpellation. *Parallax, 20*(3), 231–244.

Whitehead, A. N. (1938). *Modes of Thought.* New York, NY: Free Press.

CHAPTER THIRTEEN

Data, Material, Remains

ANNETTE ARLANDER

ABSTRACT

This text tries to show how in artistic research the role of research data or material and the role of research output can be interchangeable, mixed or hybridized, by using video works and blog posts created during a residency in the north of Finland as examples. The text reflects on these as data, material or remains, problematizes the use of artworks as data and asks what happens to data when the research question, the method or the material is prioritized. Finally, referring to Karen Barad's notion of agential separability, the text argues that a cut determining what is data and what is output, what is material and what is result will be enacted in each case. In conjunction with this text the reader is invited to consult an exposition with audiovisual material, titled ArsBioarctica Residency 2014, on the Research Catalogue, an online multimedia database for the exposition of artistic research https://www.research catalogue.net/view/266988/266989 and to create an exposition themselves.

Keywords: Performance, landscape, artistic research, artwork, data, material, remains, performing for camera

INTRODUCTION

The word for data in Finnish, "aineisto" is linked to the word "aine", substance or material, and could be translated as a compilation or selection of materials. This makes sense in terms of the practice in my example, since I am "picking slices of time" from a specific place by performing repeatedly for a video camera, often in a rough time-lapse manner, and editing the material into a compilation, a selection of data, if you wish. The resulting artworks could be described with another word associated to data, "jäämistö", literally the remains of the deceased, since the recorded slices of time are the "facts" that remain, a record of a time passed; they are the result or output of the endeavor of doing art, research or artistic research. In what follows, material generated in one specific case, during an ArsBioarctica residency in 2014, will serve as an example isolated in time and space, based on my earlier practice of performing landscape, which involved returning repeatedly to the same site for one year, in twelve successive years and resulted in the twelve-year project *Animal Years*.[1]

In this chapter I am going to argue or show that in artistic research the role of research data or material and the role of research output can be interchangeable, mixed or hybridized, at least in some cases. For the purposes of this text artistic research (or practice-as-research[2] or creative arts research[3]) can be understood as research where the making of art forms an important part of the process. Elsewhere I have discussed artistic research as interdisciplinary or as a speculative practice (Arlander, 2016). In artistic research the analysis, translation or interpretation of data does not always take place by linguistic means, as already Brad Haseman (2006) pointed out. Rather, as Michael Schwab (2014) has emphasized, artistic research is often best disseminated in the form of expositions, that is, artistic practice is exposed as research. Various forms of material-discursive practices can be involved, to use Karen Barad's (2007) term. Thus, in conjunction with this text I invite the reader to consult an exposition on the Research Catalogue, an online multimedia database for the exposition of artistic research, which enables publishing of an exposition in progress with a fixed reference. The exposition https://www.researchcatalogue.net/view/266988/266989 is called ArsBioarctica Residency 2014, and contains links to the video works created during that residency,[4] as well as to some blog posts both on the ArsBioarctica blog and on my private website. These materials could be considered public outcomes. The exposition also contains unedited and unpublished material, as well as such excerpts from my private digital diary, which refer to the work rather than private matters. These materials resemble traditional raw material, unedited "stuff". The status of that stuff can change in an instant, if published, and the outcomes can serve as data, too, as they are doing for me now, writing this.

ARS BIOARCTICA RESIDENCY

The residency involved two short periods in April and June 2014, which I spent at the Helsinki University Biological Station by Lake Kilpis in the far north, the thumb of Finland, near the Norwegian border and the Polar Sea, as part of the ArsBioarctica Residency organized by the Finnish Bio Art society.[5] The recordings made during these two short periods exemplify the excessive amount of material that is often created through artistic research projects. Whether it will be considered material for an artwork, data for a research report, or the remains of an experience for private archiving can rarely be decided in advance. Some of the data is created on purpose, as documentation; some will accumulate like a side effect. In performing arts all kinds of documentation is often increasing exponentially since the work involves a group of people creating it, a more or less participating audience and repeated performances, all of which tend to produce a plethora of material, as described by Yvon Bonenfant (2017). The performances for a camera on tripod during the ArsBioarctica residency are an exception to the rule in their simplicity, with no production team and no primary audience. The term data is particularly suited to describe the material since it is recorded in a semi-systematic manner to document changes in the landscape and edited with minimal manipulation to let the landscape perform. When applying for the residency, I wrote:

> My work is related to landscape rather than bio art in a strict sense. Thus I would like to explore the landscape in Kilpisjärvi and see how I could document changes taking place in the landscape during the spring or early summer. For twelve years I have performed landscape on Harakka Island, off Helsinki, by documenting the changes in the environment either once a week for the duration of a year or with two or three hour intervals during a day and night. In February 2014 this project is finished and I am curious to explore new ways of looking at the environment. Some of the techniques I have used on Harakka could probably be utilized in Kilpisjärvi as well, for instance documenting a day and night with three-hour intervals. Moreover, I am interested in looking at the details in the environment and an extreme landscape like the environment in northern Lapland would probably be suitable for that. I could come for a short visit, like one week, or for a longer period of one month, now that I am not tied to visiting Harakka regularly. Ideally I would like to come at a time when the snow is melting or almost gone and there is a lot of light.[6]

This text from the application, saved on my computer, becomes data, too, when I use it here to describe (and remember) my starting point. But by what intra-action: by my archiving it, then, or by my use of it now, or both?

MALLA IN APRIL

During my first week in the north in April ice covered Lake Kilpis and there was 150 centimetres snow on the ground. There was plenty of light, however. The blog posts "Malla—Mountain in the North" (April 5, 2014, Arlander 2014a) and "Performing Landscape in Kilpisjärvi 1–8" (April 2–9, 2014, Arlander 2014g), describe my first visit. I used the same method as before, performing for a camera on tripod in the same place repeatedly. I walked out on the ice wearing a dark blue scarf, turning my back to the camera, looking at Malla Fell in front of me, and repeated this every two- or three hours. The texts written for the ArsBioarctica blog and for my web site, like the one quoted below, were despite their personal tone written to be public from the start, as blog posts mostly are.

Malla—Mountain in the North

As part of the ArsBioarctica Residency at the Helsinki University Biological Station in Kilpisjärvi, organized by the bio art society, I am writing some working notes on their blog. In the following I summarize only some of my experiences, briefly.

When I prepared for this visit I planned to create a video work documenting a day and a night, in the same manner as I have done on Harakka Island, in connection with the series "Animal Years". While arriving here in the afternoon April 2, I realized I might have to revise my plans due to the amount of snow. I could not move freely in deep snow and would have to find a place near the house. I learned to use snowshoes and even tried skiing yesterday, but nevertheless opted for an easier solution. Why stay up all night when everything interesting happens at daytime? Documenting a day and night would be more fascinating when the sun stays up all night in the summer.

There is plenty of light already, however; the days are long. Today, for instance, the sun rose 25 minutes past 6 in the morning and sets 5 minutes to 9 in the evening. Most of the interesting changes that take place are caused by the weather, which can change in an instant, like on the Atlantic coast, where the clouds roll in and bring rain every other moment. We are only 50 kilometres from the Arctic Ocean, on the Norwegian side, and that makes the weather unpredictable. The altitude is less than 500 meters in the valley, although they call this the only mountain village in Finland, since the surrounding mountains, the fells, are high. Saana is officially 1029 meters and Malla Fell, in the North, is 942 meters or 738 meters; there are two of them. The geographical coordinates of this place, the village of Kilpisjärvi, are 20.4 degrees East and 69 degrees North. That is rather far up north, really. The amount of snow is exceptional this year, they say, at the moment 150 centimetres.

My first attempt was to video Malla Fell across the frozen lake towards north, from a spot on the shore, every two hours. I tried that on Thursday 3 April from 2 pm onwards and the changes were fascinating, so I decided to make a full day, from 8 am to 8 pm the following day, on the 4th. That day, however, the weather was more constant, and more bad, too. Grey skies, snowfall, bad visibility. The small changes in the landscape were nevertheless interesting and I made an image every two hours from the same spot, leaving my tripod by the shore in order to maintain the same framing easier. During the last session the snowfall was so heavy that I missed the framing, somewhat. In any case I have now one hour, that is, one tape (I still record on DV tapes, because of my old camera, and because I like to archive them) of material and will probably edit it into a five or ten-minute piece.

Although Malla Fell is the protagonist, I am figuring as a tiny dot on the ice as well. The first time I walked out on the ice it seemed like walking very far, so I stopped and stood there, leaving my footprints in the snow, to find the same place during next session again. Later ski tracks and the tracks of snowmobiles crossed here and there around the place, and

I realized it was very close to the shore. By that time, I could no longer change the spot, of course, but returned to my first footprints in the snow. As it turned out I had placed myself fairly centrally in the image, almost too centrally for the composition. So in the last image, where I again returned to the same spot, but where I had missed the framing slightly, my position thus moving further to the right in the image was actually more interesting, although clearly "wrong" compared to the rest of the series.

There is still time to make some more attempts, and if the weather becomes clearer I would like to try to find a spot further up on the slope, with a slightly different view of the area, and make a series from there. But how could I find another action to accompany the landscape, instead of standing still in it with my scarf? Sitting in the snow? Lying in the snow? Walking into the landscape and slowly disappearing in the snow? I can only try ...[7]

Those planned alternatives never materialized. The works I later edited of the material created in April on the lake are the single channel works *A Day with Malla (text)* (4 min 25 sec) and *Meeting Malla* (10 min). The first one was performed on April 7, 2014 between 7 am and 9 pm, with two-hour intervals. The second one combines material performed on two consecutive days, April 3 (2–8 pm) and April 4, 2014 (8 am–10 pm), again with two-hour intervals. As the title indicates the first one included a text, which I wrote and recorded during my stay at the station. Later I also edited a two-channel installation of the same material, *A Day with Malla 1–2* (8 min 10 sec), juxtaposing images of me standing on the ice, with the same images without a human figure. All works show a view of Lake Kilpis and Malla Fell, with the colors of the landscape changing with the time of day and the shifting weather.

MALLA IN JUNE

During my second week in June, the ice on the lake was almost gone, and spring was approaching fast, as described in the blog posts "Meeting Malla again" (June 5, 2014, Arlander 2014b) and "Performing Landscape in Kilpisjärvi 9–15" (June 4–13, 2014, Arlander 2014g). I chose to sit on a rock at the shore during a day and night, again with two-hour intervals and recorded a session in real time, for twenty minutes, as well. The blog post on my web site is brief:

Meeting Malla Again

Back at the ArsBioarctica Residency at the biological station of Helsinki University in Kilpisjärvi, far up in the north, close to the Norwegian border and the Arctic Sea. The exact coordinates are 69 degrees 2' 38" North and 20 degrees 48' 13" East, and only 488 meters above sea level, if my phone is to be trusted. The first time I visited this place, nearly two months ago, there was more than 150 centimetres snow, and now most of that is gone. Quite a lot still remains, though, and there is still ice on the lake. My plan is to do a sequel to the video work I recorded here in April, although this time it is not possible to walk out on the ice. And this time a colleague helps me by sending me a prompt, a poem or idea or something to use as an impulse or starting point. It is exciting to experience the light here, since it is really overwhelming, energizing and exhausting at the same time. This time I am planning to climb up to Saana Fell, too, and managed to get fairly high already on my first day. (…) I am describing my experiments and experiences, writing more or less daily, on the residency blog, which can be found here.[8]

The works later edited from the material created during my June visit, include *Looking at Malla* (9 min 20 sec), recorded on June 5 (10 am–10 pm) with two-hour intervals, showing only part of the scarf on my shoulder on the left in the image. *Day and Night with Malla 1–2* (30 min 20 sec) is a two-channel installation, recorded during a day and night, between noon on June 7 and noon June 8, which combines an image of me sitting on a rock looking at Malla (part 1) with the same view without the human figure (part 2). The real time version of sitting on the rock, performed on June 6, was edited using long crossfades into *Moment with Malla 1–2* (26 min 10 sec), a two-channel installation where I am slowly disappearing from one image while slowly appearing in the other. The view with Lake Kilpis and Malla Fell includes the shore to the right with some rocks and vegetation; the human figure is fairly large in the foreground. Besides changes in weather and light the movement of water and melting ice on the lake provide the main action.

A DAY WITH MALLA (TEXT)

One form of data, the easiest to reproduce here, is the short text, which I wrote, recorded and translated into English during my first visit to Kilpisjärvi, and added to the video *A Day with Malla (text)* (Arlander 2014c) as voice over (in Finnish) and subtitles (English):

How to be here with Malla? How do you speak to a mountain, asked the cloud? How do you greet a fell, I ask, and wonder how to express one's admiration to a giant? Malla Fell stands at the northern shore of Lake Kilpis, in the thumb of Finland, and looks elegant in its snow cover and birch hair. I see it in front of me standing on the ice. How to be here in the cold with Malla, on the ice, in the snow, under the open sky? The ice on the lake connects us and helps in approaching, but the closer I step, the greater Malla becomes. Only from afar can I even imagine seeing the whole of it. And still I see only one side. What if it is a mountain troll and conjures me into an ice statue in the middle of the lake, a stumbling block for snowmobile drivers. Or what if it is a mountain sprite, which presents me with three riddles, and crushes me with a boulder if I don't know the correct answer. Or what if it is merely sleeping and does not want to be disturbed?

　　If everything is moving, then Malla is moving, too, albeit leisurely. But in what direction? Is it slowly rising after the weight of the ice age, or rather trickling down in small pieces along its slopes? Is it able to see the polar sea in the other direction, or does the lake suffice as its mirror? Does it enjoy the snowfall and the mist around its summit, or does it prefer the clear deep blue sky and the dazzling light?

My day with Malla occurs in the light days of springtime winter. I cannot imagine what the darkness feels like, or the nightless night, or the autumn, or even when the ice on the lake melts away. Perhaps Malla is beautiful only in its winter furs and merges with the other fells and hills in summertime. What does it matter now, because now it is beautiful, right now? With Malla I learn what now really means. It means that everything can change in an instant, in an instant the clouds can fill the sky and a snowfall hides it from my sight, and I cannot see if it is still there or not. Of course I know it is there, if it disappeared it would not be a mountain, although I cannot see it in snow and mist.

How to be here with Malla, standing and watching, breathing and admiring, wondering in the wind, freezing in the darkening night? I come here for a moment and soon go away again, and do not know how to be here for the moment I am here. I return like a restless snowmobile driver, in my own traces. I remain the same, however, while Malla changes during the day, and the whole world of Malla as well. Maybe. Or perhaps rather the contrary? I am the one who leaves, and Malla is the one that stays? (Arlander 2014c)

Read separated from the spoken Finnish text, the translation feels clumsy and I feel an urge to rework it. This is how the text appears on the video, however, and if I consider it data, I should use it as it is. As material, I could rework it; as remains, I should accept and respect it.

DATA, MATERIAL, REMAINS OR ARTWORK

The data, material or remains generated during two weeks by Lake Kilpis thus consist of six video works, a voice over text and its translation into English, 17 blog posts, a series of photos of the spring brooks, photos as diary notes, some video material not included in the artworks and more. (See exposition on the RC.) My intuitive understanding of data as material would be to consider the raw footage or the unedited images to be data, and to regard the edited video works as outputs. They, too, become data in terms of research when I write about them. An artwork can be made simply by an artist's decision, like Duchamp's famous urinal, while a decision to exhibit something as art tends to be made by an institution or curator, as Boris Groys has pointed out (2013). If I am used to thinking, "this is art because I say it is art", can I also claim "this is artistic research because I say it is artistic research"? There are, however, many intermediate stages. For instance, the photos of brooks seem like a traditional form of data; they document what I saw. When compiled into slideshows for the online exposition they embody a middle position between material and work, since they are organized to be appreciated aesthetically. All of the images are included, un-manipulated, and in the order they were photographed, to emphasize their documentary character. They have a certain size and speed of change in the slide show and they are divided into two groups, with white-water images in one and water on grass in the other. These choices could be considered an expositional strategy, or a mode of organizing data.

Because my manner of conducting artistic research is somewhat unortho-dox—I tend to make art first and reflect on it in terms of research only after-wards—the artworks easily assume the position of data, when I use them as examples while writing about some theoretical issue, for instance Karen Barad's concept of intra-action (Arlander, 2014d). Her ideas on agential separability are illuminating for the relationship of data and work as well. For Barad the bound-aries and properties of a phenomenon become determinate only in the enact-ment of an agential cut that delineates the 'measured object' from the 'measuring agent' (Barad, 2007, p. 337). The framing of the image constitutes a kind of agential cut, between what is included in the image, and what remains outside. This division is produced by the apparatus, the camera, and does not pre-exist in the landscape. My preconceptions of what constitutes an interesting view are part of that apparatus, or the material-discursive practices involved. Thus the apparatus or 'measuring agent', in collaboration with the circumstances and other agents involved, including the artist, produces the 'measured object', the 'marks on bodies' or the data, in this case material for the artworks. In another instance, the same data, the same events recorded in the artworks, (and experiences noted in the blog posts) form the basis for a discussion on, for instance, performing with the weather.[9] The camera reacts through its automatic functions to changes in the environment and records them, like focusing on raindrops rather than the human being, as at the end of *Meeting Malla*. In this way data can illustrate or concretize the topic discussed.

What is thought of as output or result while working will often become data later on. The blog posts assume the role of a working journal, although written for the public, simply because they are fixed and easily accessible. The video works play the part of document and evidence, since they are public, and archived to remain. One could say that artistic practice is a way of generating data. In artistic research a situation where the art works take the role of data, something to be analyzed and complemented with writing, rather than being research results, epistemic objects in their own right, can also be criticized. In situations where artistic work is created in the beginning of the research process and the research questions have changed during the process, the artworks can be turned into research data, rather than research outcomes and qualitative methods can be applied to analyse the docu-mentation of the creative process. However, this is not really artistic research in a strict sense, since somebody else could do it. Subjectivity is not always relevant, though. The source for all the data—the material for the artworks, blog posts, research reports or other outputs—consists of events and experiences recorded in various ways. In this case the artworks are interesting as data exactly because they record events in the landscape rather than my experiences of it, as do the texts.

QUESTION, METHOD, DATA

In another context (Arlander, 2014e) I have suggested that artist researchers should hold on to at least one of the following during their research process— the question, the method or the material. Attempting to formulate and fix all of them in advance and keep them constant throughout the process is hard and often counterproductive in an artistic research process. In choosing which of these one is trying to keep constant, one at the same time also aligns with a particular research tradition. If we take these alternatives as a thought experiment we can consider what happens to data in each case:

(1) If one sticks to the question, all means for trying to answer that question are allowed. One can change the methods, the theoretical frame of reference, let the process lead; seek new data, without losing sight of what one is actually doing. This attitude is supported by Feyerabend (quoted in Hannula, Suoranta, & Vadén, 2005, pp. 38–41) and comes close to common sense. In this approach data is dispensable, any material would do.

(2) If one sticks to a chosen method, which is accepted within the tradition that one is working within, some form of research outcome will be produced even if one abandons the questions one started with. This attitude resembles a "normal science" approach, where the method is supposed to guarantee results or scientific credentials. In this approach data is produced and "chewed" by the method; the method transforms everything into specific data.

(3) If one sticks to the material, the data, one can change the questions being asked about it or the methods used to analyze it, and let the material take the lead. This attitude resembles the stress on the importance of data within much qualitative research. It is the only option if the artworks have already been made. In this mode, however, regarding the works as data, much of the possibilities of using art making as a method are lost, because it easily leads to an understanding of art as finite works rather than actions, performances, practices and events, which could be used to produce or share critical thinking, affects or alternative ways of seeing and doing things.

DATA—MATERIAL OR OUTPUT

Above I have tried to argue and to show that in artistic research the role of research data or material and the role of research output or results can be interchangeable, mixed or hybridized. Like physicists, artist researchers are entangled in the production of the phenomena they investigate, or use in their research. In most forms of research, a situation where one cannot easily distinguish research data, research method and research outcome, or where these are interchangeable, would probably be considered a problem. In artistic research it is common for the artist-researcher to mix the object, method and outcome of their research. However, as Karen Barad has claimed, what is part of the apparatus and what is part of the body being marked or measured can change from case to case and within a specific case from time to time. Moreover, for Barad "the world can never characterize itself in its entirety; it is only through different enactments of agential cuts, different differences, that it can come to know different aspects of 'itself'" (Barad, 2007, p. 432, footnote 42). We cannot see or look at everything all the time. "Only a part of the world can be made intelligible to itself at a time, because the other part of the world has to be the part that it makes a difference to" (Ibid.). For Barad there is no neat division into subjects and objects to be found in the world. Rather, this agential cut is and can be enacted each time anew. In a similar manner, a cut between what is data and what is output, what is material and what is result is enacted in each case.

And now, if my words have not convinced you, and you have not yet visited the exposition with visual and sonic data, this is the moment to do it. https://www.researchcatalogue.net/view/266988/266989

ASSIGNMENT RELATED TO THE RESEARCH CATALOGUE

1. Search for expositions on the RC https://www.researchcatalogue.net with the help of keywords. Choose one that presents its data in an interesting way. Consider whether the artworks serve as research data or research output or both, and in what way.
2. Register for a full account on the RC. Create an exposition. Try to expose or present your data in other forms than words (as images, sound files, videos, charts, maps, what else?) How can you "let the data speak for itself" in the most compelling or engaging way?

APPENDIX (WITH DATA)

ArsBioarctica Residency 2014 https://www.researchcatalogue.net/view/266988/266989

NOTES

1. For a brief description of the project, see Arlander (2014f).
2. Nelson (2013).
3. Barrett and Bolt (2014).

4. The works are distributed through the Finnish Distribution Centre for Media Art, AV-arkki and previews are available online.
5. For information on the ArsBioarctica residency see http://bioartsociety.fi.
6. Application for ArsBioarctica Residency, in the private archive of the writer.
7. "Malla—Mountain in the North" (blog post 5.4. 2014) http://annettearlander.com/2014/04/05/malla-mountain-in-the-north/
8. Post ends with link to the ArsBioarctica blog. "Meeting Malla again" (blog post 5.6. 2014) http://annettearlander.com/2014/06/05/meeting-malla-again/
9. An example is the paper "Working with the Weather" at the conference PSI #22 Performance Climates, with the following abstract:

The recent critique of the notion of environment by object-oriented thinkers like Timothy Morton (2013) prompts me to reconsider a practice I have called performing landscape. Taking into account the work of new materialists like Jane Bennett (2015), Rosi Braidotti (2013) and especially Karen Barad (2014) I will try to describe my attempts at reusing and transforming that practice. This paper discusses recording the shifting weather conditions during an ArsBioarctica residency at the biological station in Kilpisjärvi, in the 'thumb' of Finland in the Spring 2014. Performing for a video camera with Malla Fell by Lake Kilpis provides an example of working with the weather, with or without the human performer, with or without text, with regular intervals for a day and night and with real time duration. Thus problems discussed include the use of narrative, the entanglements of technology, the human figure and the rough time-lapse technique. Moreover, the melting ice that used to be a clichéd image of hope, of life returning after the long cold darkness, now resonated with the ominous overtones of dissolving glaciers and global warming.

REFERENCES

Arlander, A. (2014a). *Malla—Mountain in the North*. (blog post 5.4.) Retrieved July 20, 2016 from http://annettearlander.com/2014/04/05/malla-mountain-in-the-north/

Arlander, A. (2014b) *Meeting Malla again*. (blog post 5.6.) Retrieved July 20, 2016 from http://annettearlander.com/2014/06/05/meeting-malla-again/

Arlander, A. (2014c) *A Day with Malla (text)*. (video recording) Retrieved July 20, 2016 from http://www.av-arkki.fi/en/works/a-day-with-malla-text/

Arlander, A. (2014d). From interaction to intra-action in performing landscape. In Benavente, B. R., González Ramos, A. M., & Nardini, K. (Eds.), New feminist materialism: engendering an ethic-onto-epistemological methodology. *Artnodes, 14*, pp. 26–34. Retrieved July 20, 2016 from http://journals.uoc.edu/index.php/artnodes/issue/view/n14

Arlander, A. (2014e). Om metoder i konstnärlig forskning/On methods of artistic research. In Lind, T. (Ed.), *Metod—Process—Redovisning Konstnärlig Forksning* Årsbok *2014/Method—Process—Reporting Artistic Research Yearbook 2014* (pp. 13–25/26–39). Stockholm: Vetenskapsrådet/Swedish Research Council. Retrieved July 20, 2016 from https://publikationer.vr.se/wp-content/uploads/2014/08/--rsbok-KF-2014-pdf-hela-boken.pdf

Arlander, A. (2014f). Performing landscape for years. *Performance Research*. Special issue: On Time. 19–3 2014, pp. 27–31.

Arlander, A. (2014g). Performing Landscape in Kilpisjärvi 1–15. Published on *ArsBioarctica Residency blog*. Archived on the RC. Retrieved March 29, 2017 from https://www.researchcatalogue.net/view/266988/351018

Arlander, A. (2016). Artistic Research and/as Interdisciplinarity—Investigação em Arte e/como Interdisciplinaridade. In C. Almeida & A. Alves (Eds.), *Artistic Research Does* #1 (pp. 1–27). NEA/12ADS, Porto: Research Group in Arts Education/Research Institute in Art, Design, Society; FBAUP Faculty of Fine Arts University of Porto.

Barad, K. (2007). *Meeting the universe halfway: quantum physics and the entanglement of matter and meaning.* Durham, NC: Duke University Press.

Barad, K. (2014). Diffracting diffraction: cutting together-apart. *Parallax* 20 (3), pp. 168–187.

Barrett, E., & Bolt, B. (Eds.). (2014). Material inventions. *Applying Creative Arts Research.* London and New York, NY: I. B. Tauris.

Bennett, J. (2015). Systems and things: On vital materialism and object-oriented philosophy. In Grusin, R. (Ed.), *The nonhuman turn* (pp. 223–240). Minneapolis, MN and London: University of Minnesota Press.

Bonenfant, Y. (2017). PAR produces plethora. Extended voices are plethoric and why plethora matters. In A. Arlander, B. Barton. M. Dreyer-Lude and B. Spatz *Performance as Research—Knowledge, Method, Impact.* London and New York: Routledge (manuscript in preparation).

Braidotti, R. (2013). *The posthuman.* Malden MA and Cambridge: Polity Press.

Groys, B. (2013). *Art power.* Cambridge, MA: MIT Press.

Hannula, M., Suoranta, J., & Vadén, T. (2005). *Artistic research—Theories, methods and practices.* Helsinki: Finnish Academy of Fine Art, Gothenburg: University of Gothenburg.

Haseman, B. (2006). A manifesto for performative research. *Media International Australia incorporating Culture and Policy, theme issue Practice-led-Research* (118), pp. 98–106.

Morton, T. (2013). *Hyperobjects. Philosophy and Ecology after the End of the World.* Minneapolis, MN and London: University of Minnesota Press.

Nelson, R. (Ed.). (2013). Practice as research in the arts—Principles, protocols, pedagogies, resistances. Basingstoke: Palgrave Macmillan.

Schwab, M. (2014). Expositions in the research Catalogue. In H. Borgdorff & M. Schwab (Eds.), *The exposition of artistic research: Publishing art in academia* (pp. 92–104). Leiden: Leiden University Press.

CHAPTER FOURTEEN

"Whatever We Make Depends"

Doing-data/Data-doing with Young Children

CASEY Y. MYERS

ABSTRACT

Drawing on a new materialist relationality and post-qualitative methodology, this chapter details the ways in which "data", the author, and a group young children (re)made each other during a classroom-based inquiry. Specifically, ideas about and enactments of "data" in research with young children are shifted so that data is conceptualized as a multi-layered, multiplayer event. Vignettes demonstrate processes of *doing-data/data-doing* that disrupted traditional research methods with young children and argue for researchers in general to reconsider the role of data.

Keywords: post-qualitative, new materialism, early childhood, data, doing

INTRODUCTION

With the emergence of new materialisms as a trend within the social sciences over the past 10 years, much as already been written about how post-qualitative inquiry challenges many humanistic underpinnings of accepted methodological traditions (see St. Pierre, 2011, 2013, 2015; Lather & St. Pierre, 2013). This chapter aligns with this trend in that it moves to disrupt "settled places in our work" and allows for an exploration of "breaking methodological routine" (Lather, 2013, p. 642). Specifically, this chapter presents ways in which established ideas about and enactments of "data" in research with young children can shift so that data is not conceptualized nor performed as a static collection of artifacts, but as an a multi-layered, multiplayer event. Through several vignettes, I argue that recognizing the doings of data can reconfigure taken-for-granted research methods with young children, and also allow researchers more generally to reconsider how data figures into processes of knowing.

Taking material-discursive entanglement (Barad, 2003, 2007) as an onto-epistemological given, the vignettes presented here are drawn from a yearlong study with 16 four-and five-year old children. Through a variety of data processes, the children and I aimed to better understand and map the workings of objects, things, materials, or the otherwise non-human agents within their kindergarten classroom. What complicated this work methodologically was that common participatory methods with young children harbor hierarchical structures and essentialized understandings about data that do not align with a new materialist onto-epistemology or a corroborating post-qualitative approach to inquiry. For example, a variety of material processes, including children's photographs, drawings, videos, along with more traditional ethnographic methods of long-term participant observation and interviewing, have become accepted ways of gathering or "listening" to young children's perspectives. It is argued that these drawings, videos, and photographs enable children to explore the ways in which they perceive their own experiences and communicate their ideas in ways that are meaningful to them (see Clark, Kjørholt, & Moss, 2008). Such approaches operate under the assumption that the making and sharing of knowledge happens through a "voicing" of experience and this essentialized voice of the participant yields a certain transparency in its representation (St. Pierre, 2000). There is a focus on the ways in which children act *upon* materials in order to represent ideas symbolically, rendering data as passive, representational objects that children and researchers create.

In the following sections, I draw on data excerpts to demonstrate how the children and I reworked these more traditional methods of collecting or generating data, focusing specifically on how "data" became an action-oriented process, an event that was shaped by multiple human and non-human agents. I put the terms *data-doing* and *doing-data* to work in order to frame the ways in which the children and I were involved with/in data. Data was something we did and it also did something to us.

DATA-DOING/DOING-DATA

In representing our engagements with data in the sections that follow, I first turn to the more traditional ways in which particular methods for "listening" to children's perspectives methods might be enacted when *essentialism* is the founding premise of "data". Jackson (2013) posits that, "essentialism imposes itself on qualitative methodology by assuming that … rational, coherent truths that serve as foundation (data) for data analysis and interpretation" (p. 742), and, indeed, this is the way that I described them when I first proposed the research. I then juxtapose these essentialized methods of data collection with the messier assemblage of methods that we activated as we did things with data and as data did things with us.

Figure 14.1: Image collage.
Source: Author.

"BE(ING) WITH US"

The first method was originally conceptualized in my research proposal as a form of classroom participant observation wherein the primary role of the researcher would be to gain general familiarity and build rapport with children, families, and teachers, as well as experience firsthand the naturally occurring events of interest (Wolcott, 2008). In this case, the events of interest were the material-discursive entanglements of significance to the children in the classroom. I planned to use a camera and notebook to capture images and construct narratives to represent events and catalog them for later analysis. I intended for this participant observation to continue throughout the study as a means of constructing increasingly complex knowledge about the children and their classroom relations.

The ways in which I actually engaged in the field as a post-qualitative classroom researcher were quite different. In my second week of playing the role of "participant observer" in the classroom, the following interaction occurred during morning free play with two children, Petal and Paige:

Paige:	*Are you going to watch us or are you going to be with us?*
Casey:	*Do you* ... [I pause and think of how to get to the meaning of her question.]
Paige:	*Well, some teachers only walk around and some teachers play with you.*
Casey:	*Would you rather me watch you or be with you?*
Paige:	[She gestures to her and Petal's arrangement of plastic horses.] *You could be with us ... we need someone to hold all the babies.*
Petal:	*Yeah, the babies are crying all the time and they won't listen!*
Casey:	*Okay, what should I do?*
Paige:	*Look out! Here comes this baby and he is after you!* [Begins talking in a horsebaby voice as she walks a small zebra figure over and on to my leg.] *Mama! Mama! Take a picture of me before I fall into the cave!*
Casey:	*Nooo! My baby! My baby!* [I take a photo and as I reach for "my baby" Paige slides the figure down the side of my leg and into the "cave" between my ankles.]
Paige:	*(Laughing) Oh, brother! He's really gonna need a mama now!*

Here, Paige defined the practice of "Be(ing) with us" as engaging in the flow of people and materials at play. In this particular moment of being, I became part horse mother, while the space between my lower legs became the walls of a cave that threatened to swallow my baby. My willingness to accept her invitation to "be with us" was an important moment in the trajectory of data-doing, as it set the tone for the ways in which I would perform participant observer-as-data-doer afterward. This entangled way of "being with" as a mode of data-doing continued throughout the school year, but children's participation was not even or orderly.

Some children consistently requested that I be with them and our data-doings would span weeks. Other children would move in and out of being with me, engaging with me briefly, at seemingly random intervals.

When the conception of "participant observer" was actualized as "being with", there was no clear division between building rapport and familiarity with children and capturing "naturally" occurring events as units of data. According to the children, an appropriate way of "being with" them was often to engage in whatever events were occurring. Once I "be(came) with" them the flow of events and relationalities were always altered, so the boundary between our subjectivities and the field of relations was constantly in flux.

The ways in which we did data during these events did not result in an objective or representational record of children engaging with/being engaged by the material, but rather multiple "constructed cuts" (Barad, 2003) of the ongoing intra-actions between myself, the children and various other "things" (e.g., various objects, materials, animals, or otherwise environmental elements of the classroom) These constructed cuts were mostly photographs, but also comprised short video clips, narratives, and ink sketches depending on what the children requested (e.g., "take a picture of this", "write down what I say") and what mechanisms I felt were most appropriate or feasible for the task depending on what my own "being with" them entailed. For example, I constructed photos with the intention of making images of what the children requested or making images of events wherein the material seemed to play a surprising, disruptive, subversive or otherwise important role. Although the resulting images or videos could certainly be analyzed as representational points of data or simply visual records of the classroom context, what actually emerged was a combination of our intentions, my physical location through which to frame the image, my own knowledge and experience in operating my camera, the mechanism of my camera and lens in relation to the light available, the movement of actors within the event and their focal distances, and the availability of my arms/hands/fingers/eyes in relation to whatever "being with" the children entailed (e.g., if my dominant hand was needed to cradle a baby horse, I operated the camera with my non-dominant hand, which affected the qualities of the resulting image).

"DOING PHOTOS"

The second method was adapted from the kind semi-structured interviews/conferences used in "listening" methodologies described in the first section of this chapter, such as *the Mosiac Approach* (Clark & Moss, 2001). The first purpose of these conferences would be to allow me to ask open-ended questions regarding the emerging material relations in the classroom. The second would be to allow

children to critically engage with my initial documentation and general participant observation approach (e.g., viewing my photographs on a tablet computer,
confirming or critiquing my interpretation of events, questioning my practices as
a researcher, suggesting alternative trajectories, etc.). When conceptualizing and
proposing this research, I intended to ask the children questions, if necessary, in
order to "listen to how the children identify the agency of different organisms and
objects around them in their learning processes" (Lenz Taguchi, 2010, p. 66).
Despite my initial planning, these meetings did not resemble interviews
wherein I would pose questions and receive answers that could simply be recorded
and transcribed in order to "hear" the voice my participants. The idea(l) of the ethnographic interview, a traditional qualitative method "heavily invested in language
practices" (MacLure, 2013, p. 664) as a means through which to gain access to
what research participants know (or what they (do not) want you to know), did not
emerge when the children, myself, my notes and questions, and our constructed
images were gathered together.

Clara was the first to engage in a "conference". After leaving the classroom, we
found an empty meeting room and sat at the table with a notebook, camera, and a
tablet computer. She looked quietly at the photos for several minutes. When she
began zooming in and out on one particular photo of herself, I began to "interview" her with my predetermined, "child-friendly" question.

Casey:	*Can you tell me or show me what is happening in this photo?*
	Clara didn't respond, but began to hum a tune. She gradually added lyrics.
Clara:	[Singing] *Ho-ho, he-he. Diddily-deet-do-do. Following the leader, the leader, the leader, following the leader wherever she may go. He-he, ho-ho … [sighing heavily] I don't really to talk about anything. I just thought I would be doing photos.*
Casey:	*What does 'doing photos' mean?*
Clara:	[Making the pinching gesture on the touch screen that performs the zoom-in and—out function] *Like, wa-hoo, wa-hoo, look at that dark part of my eyeball! Yi-yi-yi-yikes!*
	She makes an animated, surprised expression as she looks closely at the image of her pupil.
Casey:	*Okay, you can do that.*
	I begin to take some notes in my notepad about her not wanting to answer questions and I spend a few minutes watching her with the tablet—scrolling, gesturing, laughing, humming, putting her face close to the screen and pulling it away.
Clara:	*Hey, where's MY notebook?*
Casey:	*Do you need one? I have paper … but I don't have a notebook just for you today, but you can use mine until I can get one.*
Clara:	*Will it be for kids?*

Casey: *I can get a notebook just for kids, sure.*
I pass my notebook to her and she takes a black marker from the table and begins to draw, zooming in and out of the photo, watching related videos, coming back to the original photo, drawing again. After several minutes, she holds up what is a re-construction of one of the images she had been intra-acting with in which she was playing "animals". I had constructed the event though an image that only showed her face. She pointed out to me the people, things, and events she included in her reconstruction of the event.

Clara: [Pointing to the figure she's drawn holding a camera] *Look how scared you are of my animal noises, Casey Myers!* [Referencing the humanoid animal with long claws] *My hands are coming into claws I'm meowing so real! Meow!*

This event with Clara quickly recast my initial, more humanist plans. Framing our conferences as "doing photos" rather than as semi-structured ethnographic interviews afforded a powerful shift in my own thinking and doing around data. For example, "doing photos" became less about me asking questions in relation to a piece of documentation (i.e., using the photo as an interview prompt) and more about what was emerging between the child, the images, and myself (i.e., what the photos were doing to us, what we were doing with/to the photos). My conception of a semi-structured interview was subverted in favor of an assemblage of more-than-human movements, doings, affects, materializations, and articulations. After engaging with Clara in this way, I stopped using the terms *conferences* or *interviews* and instead asked children if they wanted to "do photos" and told them that doing photos only meant that they could "have a notebook, markers, and photos and videos on the tablet to do what they wanted". Within these assemblages of "doing", images were not treated as simply symbolic artifacts that might aid discussion. Instead, they functioned as a site of productive entanglement (Lenz Taguchi, 2010). Children did remark on the agency of the material world of their classroom and the force of the multiple actors with which they engaged in the events that were constructed in the images. However, they did so not by simply over-coding images with meaning, but by engaging in the complex material-discursive "doing" of photos wherein both the children and the photos were active participants.

"BECOMING (WITH) CAMERAS"

As the research methods of "being with (us)" and "doing photos" continued throughout the school year, a new means of constructing images was introduced to the children. Children were asked to photograph whatever they considered to be "important things" using small cameras. The children were given time initially to explore and gain familiarity with the features and functions of the cameras in small group explorations outside of the classroom. I asked them to figure out how to use the cameras and if they had any new ideas they could either talk about them with the group or draw/write about them using large sheets of paper and pens that I provided. During these improvisational engagements with the cameras, the children took hundreds of photos and often discussed ways to solve potential problems, such as whether or not someone should delete a photo that they didn't take. When the children rendered these initial camera engagements with paper and pens, they grappled not only with the ways in which the cameras worked to "capture" images, but also with the ways in which the cameras, as an apparatus of both doing-data and data-doing, might impact classroom relationships and their being-knowing as kindergarten children.

> Irina: *I'm looking at the picture on the little screen and turning into a photographer! Those are my photographer pants, but now my whole body is turning into a camera! My arms are cameras! My whole tummy is becoming little cameras that eat my food!*
>
> She draws and arrow from her hand to a rendering of the camera's display screen. She then carefully draws her own face on the display.

After these initial engagements, all of the children in the class had access to the cameras during their school day. Some children used the cameras frequently, others only sporadically. I originally intended for the images that children constructed with the cameras to be reexamined through the "doing photos" method noted above—the children would be able to "do" their own photos instead of the photos I constructed for/of them. Although the children did engage with the images that they constructed for the purposes of "doing photos", they wanted to move freely between my photos and their own depending on our conversations and the ways in which their photo-doings unfolded.

Despite my original intentions of children using the cameras to generate documentary images, using the cameras in *real-time*, rather than engaging with the images after the fact, became the more generative event of data-doing/doing-data. Similarly, to how Irina had rendered in her initial drawing with/about the cameras, children tended to use the cameras to incite new becomings, such as stopping the action, entering into another child's play space, transgressing a classmate's limits, or otherwise working the boundaries of bodies and discourses. Children's becoming (with) cameras produced new sites of material-discursivity that were not always about constructing a particular image, but were more about making something *happen* (Kind, 2013). What the camera was capable of doing was entangled with the children in production of new events; many events of importance to the children weren't *captured* with the camera but *incited* by it.

Ginger: *Nia was supposed to be Margaret's partner but Nia was absent so I really wanted Margaret to pick me. She had to pick somebody, so I went over and got her (with the camera)! And she picked me!* [*Poking at the screen,* her finger touching the image of Margaret's] *I'm picking YOU!*

Bella: *I really needed Petal to play with me. I just thought it was not fair that she was just partners with Elizabeth … I wanted us to be three. So I got in there!* She runs her fingers over the screen where Elizabeth and Petal faces meet, then over the screen where their hands are clasped together and sighs.

Bella: *This all makes me sad.*

KNOWING DIFFERENTLY THROUGH DATA-DOING AND DOING-DATA

Working with children to undo the more traditional methods of "listening" allowed me to conceptualize data as processes that were fraught with connections, movements, and becomings, rather than orderly, predictable procedures. Recognizing data as both something that is *done* and something that *does*, afforded a shift away from understanding and enacting data as mere representational tool. Instead, my focus turned toward what we were doing in to make data, and what that data was doing to us in the process.

As the research project was coming to a close, many discussions during our "doing photos" sessions contemplated what we had done, what our data had done to us, and how it would be represented in my dissertation and beyond. Michael in particular offered many insights into how various actors and forces entailed within our post-qualitative methods folded and unfolded. The conceptual and practical impact of data-doing/doing-data is best illustrated in the vignette that follows, wherein Michael articulates the ways in which the data, and, thus, all associated agents, were bound-up in the knowledge we produced, at once bringing several constituents of "knowing" to the fore.

Michael touches the screen and then scrolls through the photos using the arrow keys. He moves his face close to the screen, furrowing his brow.

Michael: *When all the photos get on the computer … is this row (of photos) from the blue camera and this one from the gray camera?*

Casey: *No. It's not. When I put (the photos) on my computer from the little cameras, they get all mixed together. I don't know who took the photos unless someone tells me.*

Michael: *Well … I know some photos that I took, but I don't know if I took some of these ones. But it doesn't matter. It doesn't matter who took this photo. I can still do it, right?*

Casey: *You can do any photo you want to.*

Michael: *I can draw things for this. Do you think I should draw what is in this (photo)? It's an important thing ... I feel like want to.*

Casey: *You can do this photo however you want. We've been trying to figure things out ... by doing photos however we want.*

He examines a photo of Paige lying in the field just outside of The Playground fence. He runs his fingers over the outline of her face and then zooms in on the blades of grass. He moves his face closer to the screen and squints his eyes.

Michael: *I think you try to get some things from the picture and then add some that you want. A photo doesn't have ... everything for this research. It's for research because that's how we're doing this, right?*

Casey: *Yes, this part can be for research. Do you want it to go in (my dissertation)?*

Michael: *Yeah ... if you are doing a picture, you make some things first and then you can add more things that you want. But you don't have to stop ... you can make more new things in that rectangle. That picture frame ... that you make.*

Casey: *Yes, you can.*

Michael: *Well, I see one ear in this picture. She only has one ear? Paige has two ears though! You can't know that if you just traced. You have to trace, add, add some more whatever you think of. And this.*

He carefully adds a cluster of circles to his drawing of Paige's dress and examines the photo once again.

Michael: *Did you know there are little bugs everywhere in the grass and they can bite you? There are bugs everywhere under that part* [pointing to the grass in the photo] *but I can't see them. If you have a big marker, it might be hard!*

Casey: *What's hard?*

Michael: *I have a little hand, so I like a little marker.*

Casey: *Oh ... do you want my pen? It will make a thinner line for you.*

Michael: *Well, it doesn't matter now ... but the picture I'm making is going to be blurry because of this (marker). I sometimes have a big marker and sometimes a little one.*

Casey: *That's true. It depends on what markers I bring for the day.*

Michael: *Yeah. Whatever we make depends ... it depends. And then you go, "Wow! I made this even different-er. I didn't know a photo had those parts like that!" I like this ... Paige ... I like Paige so much!* [Drawing a cluster of shapes above Paige's head] *See? More of those things.*

Those are the bugs but I have to make them bigger. Bigger than Paige's head almost! That's how I have to do it for this research. Research is doing it the way you want. Except for when you have a thick marker ... then maybe you don't get to do it your way, so you can just make bugs like these. It's a little harder work for me.

Here, Michael highlights the ways in which the entanglements of matter and meaning were always in motion within our inquiry processes; data emerged out of, reciprocated, and disrupted multiple movements, desires, affordances, constraints, feelings, and more. As Michael said, when we entered into these encounters with data, we were often taken by surprise. There was no way of knowing what a photo-as-data could *do*, that it had "those parts like that" before we began; all of our knowing was continually enmeshed with/in the various doings of data and what emerged in-between couldn't be predicted. Inquiry, then, was not about uncovering what preexisted our investigations, but about producing something different and becoming different in doing of and with data.

Although established approaches for "listening" to young children are meant to access and then represent what children "know" through processes such as drawing or photographing, they do not acknowledge the ways in which both the researcher's and the children's knowings are mediated by the very materialities of doing-data and data-doing. Unlike these approaches, researching in the way the children and I did positions what children "know" as both creating *and* created by data. The material of the research process was not merely representing or accessing the lived reality of the children but was actively implicated in the creation of a new layer of active material-discursive relations.

With regard to the potential that these research doings hold for activating new orientations toward and enactments of data as "coming to know" in qualitative inquiry, Barad claims that, "we do not obtain knowledge by standing outside of the world; we know because 'we' are of the world" (2003, p. 829). Or, more simply, "whatever we make depends".

We make data and are remade by it within thoroughly dependent sets of relations. And the "we" of inquiry is inclusive of various human and non-human agents engaging in overlapping and multi-directional processes of doing. Taking Michael's statement as serious advice might allow qualitative researchers to consider the conceptual and practical implications of doing-data/data-doing, whether it be in inquiry with young children or otherwise.

REFERENCES

Barad, K. (2003). Posthumanist performativity: Towards an understanding of how matter comes to matter. *Signs, 28*(3), 801–831.

Barad, K. (2007). *Meeting the universe halfway: Quantum physics and the entanglement of matter and meaning*. Durham, NC: Duke University Press.

Clark, A., Kjørholt, A. T., & Moss, P. (Eds.). (2008). *Beyond listening: Children's perspectives on early childhood services*. Portland, OR: The Policy Press.

Clark, A., & Moss, P. (2001). *Listening to children: The mosaic approach*. London: National Children's Bureau and Joseph Rowntree Foundation.

Jackson, A. Y. (2013). Posthuman data analysis of mangling practices. *International Journal of Qualitative Studies in Education, 26*(6), 741–748. doi: 10.1080/09518398.2013.788762

Kind, S. (2013). Lively entanglements: The doings, movements and enactments of photography. *Global Studies of Childhood, 3*(4), 427–441. doi: 10.2304/gsch.2013.3.4.427

Lather, P. (2013). Methodology—21: What do we do in the afterward? *Qualitative Studies in Education, 26*(6), 634–645. doi: 10.1080/09518398.2013.788753

Lather, P., & St. Pierre, E. A. (2013). Post qualitative research. *International Journal of Qualitative Studies in Education, 26*(6), 629–633.

Lenz Taguchi, H. (2010). *Going beyond the theory/practice divide in early childhood education: Introducing an intra-active pedagogy.* New York, NY: Routledge.

MacLure, M. (2013). Classification or wonder? Coding as an analytic practice in qualitative research. In A. Coleman & J. Ringrose (Eds.), *Deleuze and research methodologies* (pp. 164–183). Edinburgh: Edinburgh University Press.

St. Pierre, E. A. (2000). Poststructural feminism in education: An overview. *Qualitative Studies in Education, 13*(5), 477–515. doi: 10.1080/09518390050156422

St. Pierre, E. A. (2011). Post qualitative research: The critique and the coming after. In N. K. Denzin & Y. S. Lincoln (Eds.), *Sage handbook of qualitative inquiry* (4th ed., pp. 611–35). Los Angeles, CA: Sage.

St. Pierre, E. A. (2013). The posts continue: Becoming. *International Journal of Qualitative Studies in Education, 26*(6), 646–657.

St. Pierre, E. A. (2015). Practices for the 'new' in the new empiricisms, the new materialisms, and post-qualitative inquiry. In N. K. Denzin & M. D. Giardina (Eds.), *Qualitative inquiry and the politics of research* (pp. 75–96). Walnut Creek, CA: Left Coast Press.

Wolcott, H. F. (2008). *Ethnography: A way of seeing.* New York, NY: Roman & Littlefield Publishers.

CHAPTER FIFTEEN

Grappling WITH Data

KAREN MALONE

ABSTRACT

What matter? What theories? Does it matter what matter? Does it matter what theories I am grappling with if I am becoming something new with my past data? When considering bodies, and phenomena as the product of assemblages, association and relations between human and non human worlds, do I need to collect data within this ontological framing? Does the onto-metho-epistemological paradigm of my collecting, limit my possibilities of encountering my data differently? Drawing on Karen Barad's diffractive ways of seeing, by reading with, not against data and allowing the data to work through me, this chapter explores the grappling of engaging with a retrospective reading of past child-dog-body data from La Paz Bolivia.

Keywords: being with data, dog-child kin, common world, posthumanism, intraspecies relations

INTRODUCTION

I am sharing my grappling with data as I seek to explore possibilities for engaging with ecological posthumanism, and new materialism approaches in my past children's environments research studies. I am doing this in order to move away from generalisations, and grand narratives that seek to universalise children's experiences. I am endeavouring to provide a glimpse of the complexity of a common world, an ecological community that includes all entities. I am seeking new ways of being 'with data' instead of wrestling with it, taming it into shape. At a time of impending crisis, I am wanting to disrupt human/nonhuman binaries that seek to undermine possibilities for considering how we, humans, can be in the world differently with our nonhuman companions. In these theoretical meanderings I take up the challenge espoused by Affrica Taylor (2011) when she writes: "... in encouraging childhood scholars to engage with geography's hybrid nature/culture analytic, I am not seeking to provide an answer to the 'nature' of childhood but to open it up to a new form of political enquiry which attends to the interconnect-edness of the human and more-than-human world" (p. 431).

ENCOUNTERS WITH DATA

Noisy. Smelly. Present. Wandering. Nails on cobble stone streets. Messy fur. Foraging. Barking. Intruders. Protectors. Guides. Dodging vehicles. Swaying. Waiting. Being with humans. Standing idle on street corners. Sleeping in gutters. Resting under trees. Sneaking into the shade of yards. Being yelled out. Running in packs. Moving alone. Digging in garbage. Finding food. Interrupting. Messing up order. Being present. Being with humans. Together. Synchronistic relations. Them following children. Children following them. Children feeding them. Children protecting. Protecting children. Intervening. Children intervening. Familial care. Mutuality. Protection. Assemblages. Bodies. Kin. Companions. Leading. Moving on. Children with researchers, with others moving through. Walking on.
     By paying attention to the act of walking, being with and becoming nature with others (human and nonhuman) I am seeking to acknowledge the encounters of human nonhuman through the experience of the other. As this data was pro-duced before I began to consider these issues of the representation of the other and its capacity to contribute to an ongoing view of human excemptionalism, I find it difficult work. Some say it is limiting to work retrospectively with data using a posthumanist/new materialist approach to my analysis. You need to be collecting data with those approaches in mind. My grappling is focused on what possibilities are available to me, to be with my old data differently. I am willing to sit with the tensions/ambiguities/uncertainty of my analysis. I encounter the data with this openness in the hope it will become something different, something new will be produced through these changing relations. As it sits before me. Photographs stacked up on the table. Transcripts of interviews. My journal. I turn to my journal. The journal provides the affective data. The walking with was met with markings and images on my page. But first I will start with how I came to be here.
     Children in three very disadvantaged communities in La Paz were asked to take a disposable camera with them throughout their journeys in and around their homes and neighbourhood, in order to reveal closely the 'everydayness' of living

in the community. This research was part of a UNICEF and La Paz city council project where they were wanting to for the first time engage with children living in the most poor communities of the city to find out directly from them their experiences of growing up. I had been invited to lead the project.

When the photographs came back I was quite taken aback by the enormity of the focus on 'dogs'. Children had taken over 200 photographs of dogs, amounting to around one quarter of the photographs. By pouring over these photographs I could begin to see that the child-dog intra-action was central to their being in, and being with the community. A community that was not merely human. At first viewing the children's photographs represented an 'intra-species' relation that was more akin to a 'friendship' than ownership where the dog was denigrated to 'pet' or belonging to human. Being a child with dogs in La Paz, illustrated the complexity of entanglements, yet unlike how Tipper (2011) who describe children embedding animals in webs of kin-pet relationships as literally 'part of the family'—the child-dog La Paz encounters revealed child-dog inhabiting intimate relations not afforded to human adults. To build on this initial data I went out on the mobile research activities, walking with and through the communities with the children. The dogs appeared from footpaths, laneways, tree's and came along with us on our journeys.

Figure 15.1: Dogs, photograph collage, La Paz, Bolivia.
Source: Author.

When I began my analysis of the data I was hoping a posthumanist/materialist reading of nonhuman encounters in La Paz will help me to unpack the political, ethical, and ontological questions about human-nonhumans relations through my deepening sensitivity to the intra-species I had experienced around me. The materialist reading in particular exposed the physicality of the relationships, an embodied reality of knowing others and what it means to live in oneness with the nonhuman. The photographs and stories spoke to me in this way, they set the scene and while I published the stories using these approaches (Malone 2016, 2017) I was at times uncertain about whether how I was presenting the data did not reflect my new theoretical ambitions.

While reflection or critical analysis enabled opportunities for me in the past to be see similarities and cohesion in my data across place and time (reflecting sameness), working with intra-action and diffraction was about opening up of data, "to diffract it, and to imagine what newness might be incited from it" (Lenz Taguchi, 2012, p. 6). "Diffraction", according to Barad (2007, p. 74) "has to do with the way waves combine when they overlap, and the apparent bending and spreading of waves that occurs when waves encounter an obstruction" (Barad, 2007, p. 74). Therefore, diffraction as an apparatus for analysis seeks to explore the effects of interference, rather than what is mirrored in data. To understand what exists before and after this inference and what difference the inference has made in creating something new. Or as Donna Haraway so aptly states, "Diffraction is an optical metaphor for the effort to make a different world" (cited Barad, 2007, p. 71). I decide it is better now to move beyond just the photographs and texts, taking them with me metaphorically into the neighbourhood in order to map where the effects of differences appear (Barad, 2007), both in a real sense to encounter child-dog relations but also in order to expose my own ontological thinking (Cole & Frost, 2010). As I know it will be exposed when I consider new materialists ways of being and knowing.

Materiality of thought, the experience of shifting the reality and therefore the opening up of new possibilities through photographing-thinking-while-walking and focusing on the other rather than my human self. I am through the research process of walking/wandering being affected by the differences in my relations with children and dogs. I embody my research potential and endeavour to move my human self out of the storylines, only as an intermediary interference. I want to understand how these unique encounters come to be; where the waves of being dog and child intersect and how they come to be in relation differently than those I have experienced in my western middle class life. Dog in bed, on lap, being child, being directed, managed, master-slave relations.

This theorizing through intra-action and diffractive analysis endeavours to de-centre the human, to take issue with human exceptionalism, by viewing interspecies encounters as 'social' where the nonhuman animals are more than simply *objects* being directed and responding to the interactions of the human but to be understood as *subjects* in their own right who exercise agency (Barad, 2007). Because "[p]osthumanism doesn't presume the separateness of any-'thing'. Let alone the alleged spatial, ontological, and epistemological distinction that sets humans apart" Barad (2007, p. 136). Therefore, by thinking through the data using a posthumanist approach and engaging with the tools of diffraction I am disrupting the Cartesian divide between human and non-human by challenging the simplistic dichotomies of animal/human, nature/culture, object/subject (Barad, 2007). These dichotomies are constructing what has come to be '*viewed as other*', what is '*valued about other*' what happens when humans are '*placed in relation with other*'. By taking up the position as other, the data of being in this place with dogs and children has the opportunity to reveal something different about what it means to be nonhuman and be in relation with human others.

To do this means shifting ontologically and methodologically. By no longer identifying entities as separate bodies but seeking to reconfigure these relations in order to view all beings as mutually implicated in an entangled co-constitutive story of bodies many different kinds of bodies (Lenz Taguchi, 2012).

Rautio provides some possibilities for researchers on how to go about research that is attentive to these outcomes. Based on Maggie Maclures baroque method she states:

> Methods that confuse scale, time and space would tap into the very grounding as if logic according to which everyday life is undergone. Follow children who write, draw, speak, jump and shout without a clear purpose. Create space for this. Join in. Interrupt yourself as a researcher, stay on your toes, change methods in the middle of your data collecting phase if that is what it takes. Seek the moments in which children produce the unfinished and the pointless and move on. Celebrate data that does not fit into categories. Replace categories and themes with tangents and rhizomes to explore ever proliferating and mutating connections that condition human existence. (2013a, p. 403)

Capturing and troubling the everydayness of children being in relation with dogs.

BEING WORLDY WITH OTHERS

As a residue of the Spanish conquest the majority of Bolivia's population are Catholic but like the coming together of human/nonhuman, subject/object the dichotomies of ancient/new world, Indigenous/Catholicism have intertwined. Through this entanglement, this rupture, something new has evolved. God is worshipped but, just as important, is Pachamama or Mother Earth.

As we are walking Yesonia explains the Panchamama to me: "We live and eat from the land. Pachamama is our mother and we have to respect her, my family we make offerings to the

Pachamama to make sure we have good luck". She then pauses to draw me an image of the Pachamama in the dirt—it is partially an image of mother Mary holding baby Jesus but she is sitting in the bowl like shape which is Mother Earth. "This is the planet', she says pointing the stick at the bowl, "we share with plants and animals".

Belonging to and being worldly with. Learning to live together. Shared co-habitation (with the more than human) helps to animate the posthuman predicament. Becoming something new, being something different through these encounters provides opportunities to imagine a world where humans aren't the only central force. Taking up and occupying all these new imaginations, I continue to walking metaphorically with my child-dog bodies.

"If we are to take the postconstructionist challenge seriously", writes Lenz Taguchi (2012) "we need also to address the question of agency of these bodies and how this agency is articulated in our data, including the agency of bodies that we do not understand as 'human', but as 'non-human' or 'more-than-human'" (pp. xx). Becoming a human/nonhuman body through the co-minging with other. To be mutually constituted is to be becoming-with nonhuman. The theory of ecological posthumanism I am wrestling with and exploring in my work, contests the arrogance of anthropocentric approaches—even those found in by enabling a shared sense of the world. A 'posthuman ethics' unlike a deep ecological ethic urges us to experience the principle of 'no-oness' in our view of subjectivity, by acknowledging the ties that bind us to multiple 'others' in a web of complex interspecies interrelations (Braidotti, 2013). This enabling of a multiplicity of ecologies/beings defines community as central—the world is, and becomes, a community of beings. I am interested in incorporating the work of Smith (2013) here, who defines an ecological posthumanist perspective as a strategy for supporting his concept of an 'ecological community'.

This posthumanist ecological community emphasises the myriad of ways that beings of all kinds, including human individuals and collectives interact to create, sustain, or dissolve community. Others have also explored these ideas, such as Jean Luc Nancy (1997) stating we are always been 'beings in common' (Smith, 2013)—bodies being sensed ecologically. Donna Haraway (2003, 2008), although not calling herself a posthumanist, has also discussed a new way to consider community. She argues subject/object nature/culture divides are linked to patriarchal, familial narratives, and calls for an enlarged sense of community based on empathy, accountability, and recognition extending to the nonhuman as subjects such as cells, plants bacteria and the Earth as a whole. Therefore, to speak of ecological communities, that we are 'beings' objects and subjects in common, means we can't, humans, be exempt from the consequences of being in this common world with others. We are no longer the master of a nonhuman and human destiny we have designed.

By adopting a post-humanistic approach and considering the value of theoretical tools of new materialism, I am in my grappling seeking to reconfigure children's relations with other 'entities' or objects by expressing their encounters with all objects and entities as being shaped through noticing and being attentive to the "… space in between children and their environments" (Rautio, 2013a, p. 4). I analyse data that does not fit into neat categories of certainty with closure (as I have done in the past). Rather I am sitting with, and being open to data in order ensure complexity and open-endedness of phenomena are not sacrificed. Drawing from Bruno Latours concept of 'learning to be affected'—that requires the researcher to develop more than cognitive modes of attention—I want to become attuned to the multifarious ways human and nonhuman bodies and entities move, affect each other.

I am spending more time now sitting in parks and streets watching human and nonhumans intra-acting. Smelling, feeling, moving between imagining and becoming.

Intra-action therefore supports the capacity for human-nonhuman encounters to co-merge (to take up an intersubjective position) where all things are 'agentic'— that is agency is not something a body (human or nonhuman) or an entity has, but that it is a relationship brought about by intra-action. Rautio (2013b) for example explains the distinction between more common ways of thinking about interaction and her use of Barad's offering of intra-action as meaning a shift between entities taking turns in affecting each other, to a co-merging of entities within, during and through the encounter.

Hultman and Taguchi (2010) term a "diffractive way of seeing" (p. 535) as involving reading with, not against data. Allowing the data to work through you. I will interrogate my struggles with diffractive analysis later, but I am aware that as a researcher engaging with my data through posthuman/new materialist approaches I am seeking to bring my being and knowing together, it is impossible to separate knowing and being, 'they are mutually implicated', Barad (2007) names this way of thinking as onto-epistemology. My onto-epistemological self.

PRECARIOUS DATA

Children are closely affected by dogs, dogs are closely affected by children. It is an ancient alliance of dogs supporting human survival by their capacity to be alerted to, and have sensitivity for, the precarious landscape. The child-dog intra-action and cohabitation provides a space for this mutual reciprocity, care and protection, to be thrown together, to be living well together. By troubling the notion of "distinct borders and clear division between humans and non-humans", both child and dog can be thought of as "*performative mutually interactive agents*" (Hultman & Lenz Taguchi, 2010, p. 528, italics in original). The child-dog accounts of intra-species companionship and survival in urban spaces challenge the sanitized boundaries and binaries maintained by western middle class sensibilities. The 'unromantic' child-dog relations experienced by impoverished urban dwelling child-dog bodies of La Paz contradicts western centric views of humanized urban environments where nonhuman 'animals' are wild, unwelcome and marginalized.

Unlike a western centric theorising of human-dog relations which often sees the dog presented as a substitute dependent child—humans findings solace in the seemingly unconditional love from their dogs, the child-dog relations and 'being together' in La Paz is more likened to Donna Haraway (2015) notion of 'making kin'. The purpose of, or to make 'kin' according to Haraway is to recognize the coming together of different entities who may not be tied purely by ancestry or genealogy. She argues the stretch and re-composition of kin represents the under-standing that earthlings are all kin in the deepest sense—kin becomes the purest of entities in assemblages of the human, more than human, other than human. And by the fact that "all earthlings are kin in the deepest sense, and it is past time to practice better care of kin-as-assemblages" (2015, p. 162). Kin relationships emerge in this study as a deep sensitivity by the children when describing the sim-ilarities of the child-dog experiences.

Figure 15.2: Dog-child kin relations, photograph, La Paz, Bolivia.
Source: Author.

Nothing epitomizes the precarity of the planet for more, then the view from the high mountain plateaus of the Alti-plano as the plane flies towards the El Alto airport. Spread out in front is the immense sprawling valley where the city of La Paz is perilously situated. The vastness of the crowded slum communities perched on the high reaches of the escarpment and spilling down into the steep, treeless, ravines and gorges of the valley. A shared vulnerability, human and non-human worlds in a dance for daily survival. Hanging on. A human imprint at a global-scale, urbanisations spreads across the land like a parasite. The *Anthropocene*, the name we are coming to call this spread of humanity. Humans with the power to heat the planet, cool it eliminate species or engineer entirely new ones, to re-sculpt the earths' surface and to determine its biology. No part of this planet is untouched. The rate of destruction is alarming. Every year over four million hectares of forests and eight million hectares of soil erosion lost. Thirty-one billion tons of CO_2 emissions and eight million tons of toxic chemicals released into the environment. By 2020, seventy-five percent of wildlife extinct. Sixty million humans every year moving into cities.

This crisis presents enormous challenges and research has a significant role to play. Although the Anthropocene has been contested it is being utilized to do useful work, to galvanize already emergent forms of thinking and acting within the humanities and sciences. Responding to this call of the Anthropocene has compelled me to move away from a business as usual approach to the analysis of my data. Through the introduction of new theories, namely posthumanist and new materialist approaches, I am grappling with the complexities of considering what might happen if I viewed my research data differently? If I *did* data differently? Part of this is to consider what happens if humans as the 'subject' did not occupy central stage in the stories and narratives of my data. What could happen if that which was designated as peripheral, those phenomena (nonhuman entities, earthings, other) that exist in the background of my data moved to a central position?

Kay Anderson (2014, p. 3) states this focus on "challenging the idea that humans occupy a separate and privileged place among other beings has been the central goal of post-humanist agenda", with critical posthumanists taking on the task of challenging well established humanist discourses that "separates and elevates humans from the natural world". Its contests a 'human/nature dualism'. This dualism not only strips humans of all of their own 'natural' dimensions—that we are an animal and part of nature, but also installs the idea that other nonhuman animals and things are not comparable to humans—they don't have emotions, attachments, comparable to humans. Humans are politicized as earthly master, superior being.

This reimagining of data incorporates a new ontological focus a shift from conceptions of objects and bodies as occupying distinct and delimited spaces, and instead sees human bodies and all other material, social and abstract entities as relational and that these "… assemblages of relations develop in unpredictable ways". By using Barad's work I am supporting the idea of a 'flat ontology.' A flat ontology emerges from an understanding that all entities (humans, dogs, rocks, mountains, trees) have ontological significance, and are always in relation to one another in non-hierarchical ways. Barad for instances writes:

> Neither discursive practices nor material phenomena are ontologically or epistemologically prior. Neither can be explained in terms of the other. Neither is reducible to the other. Neither has privileged status in determining the other. Neither is articulated or articulable in the absence of the other; matter and meaning are mutually articulated. (2007, p. 152)

Diffractive analysis therefore makes us aware of our embodied involvement in the materiality of the event of analysing data.

The complexity of the child-dog relations of La Paz challenged me to consider what 'living well together' with a host of species and histories might contribute to a common world. Living well with animals means inhabiting their/our stories to try to reveal the complexity of those relationships. The work of theorizing interspecies encounters through an ecological posthumanist lens has drawn me to consider a co-habitation of child-dog-bodies as an active history of body connectedness. The story of child-dog relations in La Paz is a cobbling together of 'cross species' conversations that take their inherited histories seriously. They are tied together by genealogy, a history of child-dog as bodies entangled on this land since Spanish colonisation, a time when dogs were brought to this land by settlers. I am reminded here of the studies of Pacini-Ketchabaw and Nxumalo (2015) with raccoons and children, when they argue also of this inherited settler history. "We have to learn how to stay with these awkward multispecies relations, that continuously make us ambivalent and throw us into grappling with the trouble of mutual flourishing in messy colonialist spaces" they write (2015, p. 165). Staying with the trouble.

Being with the world and understanding these encounters as messy, troubling encounters of past and present kin according to Rautio (2013a)

> [I]t is about realising that the relation is always already there, and as much influenced by behavior and existence of other co-existing species as it is by our actions. (p. 448)

In recalling this ecological narrative of child-dog encounters, to consider the importance of applying "messy methodologies" (Rautio, 2013a, p. 403) in my reading of the data. That is, to recount data that does not fit categories of certainty with closure; rather to explore possibilities where the "complexity and open-endedness of phenomena" are not sacrificed (Rautio, 2013a, p. 403). Like Taylor and Pacini-Ketchabaw (2015, p. 512) I am reiterating that we are implicated in our existence on the planet through our multi-species relations and "despite the human predilection to reiterate human exceptionalism, including within many epic and heroic narrations of the Anthropocene, the fact is that our human lives are totally dependent on the lives of other".

I struggle with what this means for me. I am trying to represent the data in my writing. What should it look like? Does representing this complexity through linear text contradict the act of being different with the data? As Haraway (2015) insists "we need stories (and theories) that are just big enough to gather up the complexities and keep the edges open and greedy for surprising new and old connections", if we are to imagine or embrace "flourishing rich multi-species assemblages" (p. 160). What are these stories? And how can I present them without always become the central narrator?

By reimagining in a materialist manner I am seeking to acknowledge 'the intricate web of interrelations of the many subjects/objects and their' relations to their multiple ecologies, the natural, the social, the technological—this is an entangled messy soup of assemblages interfering and diffracting each other's own subject positions—I am performing on and performing with multiple understandings of data and through this diffractive turn I am implicated as existing in relation to all phenomena in this place. I continue to struggle.

CONCLUSIONS

In this difficult research work I am hoping to notice the subtle ways 'other entities' in my research have been in the past disregarded as little more than aesthetics, background context for the stories of children in their communities. Working with an ecological posthumanist/new materialist approach for exploring human-nonhuman encounters in the urbanized seemingly denatured world of humans living with others in slum communities of La Paz I am foregrounding the more-than-human world to bring into view the multiple storylines of everyday encounters of all other entities with children's bodies, researchers' bodies and how they are entwined. A landscape that seems devoid of nonhuman entities and yet they are constantly shaping humans in often hidden, indiscernible and undetectable ways. By re-storying human-other relations I am interfering with, and disrupting romanticised images of children living in an utopian world of nature relations that are restorative, indulgent and human generated. I have sought to capture the complexities of these 'ecologies', layers of which I have captured just a glimpse. And by doing that I am moving away from methodologies that reduce data to discreet representational categories and themes as I have done in the past through critical theoretical analysis. I am using open conceptual frames to allow porosity and fluidity between ways of being and knowing. And by drawing on feminist theorists such as the work of Karen Barad, and Maggie Maclure, I am seeking to consider the difficulties of engaging with data outside of a reflexive self aware body and looking beyond and beneath my business as usual critical stance where I am a single separate subject outside of my data:

The materialist critique of representation would also confound interpretation, to the extent that this implies a critical, intentional subject standing separate and outside of 'the data', digging behind or beyond or beneath it, to identify higher order meanings, themes or categories. This again is the logic of representational thought, operating under the 'logic of instead': instead of multiple instances, interpretation substitutes patterns or meanings. (Maclure, 2013, p. 660)

Throughout my grappling with new theories to retrospectively explore past data I have been employing new materialism and posthumanistic approaches, in order to open up the possibilities when agency is no longer the property of humans alone (Barad, 2007). This new materialist ontology "supplies a conception of agency not tied to human action, shifting the focus for social inquiry from an approach predicated upon humans and their bodies, examining instead how relational networks or assemblages of animate and inanimate affect and are affected" (Fox & Alldred, 2014, p. 1). Therefore, I am now considering if the bodies, and phenomena are a product of the assemblages, associations and relationships through which humans are connected to the more-than-human world in diverse and complex ways. I am then exploring ways in order to present my research in such a way to illustrate this.

In this chapter I have considered ways of being with my data differently as a means for encapsulating the complexity of human and more-than-human worldly relations. My work is not just to promote ways of including the materiality of other entities into the storylines of my research, but I have come to the data from a different place. I seek to notice and to be attentive to what has for the most part in my research data been hidden or extinct.

Bolivia contains forty percent of all animal and plant life in the world. As I move around La Paz I am seeking to notice now what animals, besides the dogs, co-exist here in relation with humans. My search is unproductive, mostly animals have abandoned this place or are extinct. Rock pigeon's adorn statues, forage in bins, follow humans who feed them crumbs. I see no other birds. Cats also can be seen occasionally sleeping in hollows, playing within yards and sometimes living in houses. Like dogs, these two companion species have both travelled to this place as human kin, taking up and learning to be with human settlers in these harsh urban landscapes. One day while walking in the city I see bee's buzzing at a lemonade stand on the streets corner. I have never encountered another insect in my travels. Mostly the nonhuman animals who live here are synanthropic, ecologically associated with humans. These non-humans who dance on the valley floor with humans are members of a select species of animals that live near, and benefit from, an association with humans. Learning to adapt to the somewhat co-constructed habitats that humans create around them.

I finish with a quote from Donna Haraway as her influence on my thinking about data to explore the notion of human-nonhuman companions as kin has interrupted and disrupted my usual ways of being with data. I am now different through this experience. I have developed a noticing of the nonhuman in my landscapes of my cities and my data, that never existed before.

> … all earthlings are kin in the deepest sense, and it is past time to practice better care of kinds-assemblages (not species one at a time). Kin is an assembling sort of word. All critters share a common "flesh," laterally, semiotically, and genealogically. Ancestors turn out to be very interesting strangers; kin are unfamiliar (outside what we thought was family or gens), uncanny, haunting, active. (Haraway, 2015, p. 162)

REFERENCES

Anderson, K. (2014). Mind over matter? On decentring the human in human geography. *Cultural Geographies, 21*(1), 3–18.

Barad, K. (2007). *Meeting the universe halfway. Quantum physics and the entanglement of matter and meaning.* Durham, NC: Duke University Press.

Braidotti, R. (2013). *The Posthuman.* Cambridge: Polity Press.

Cole, D., & Frost, S. (Ed.) (2010). *New materialisms. Ontology, agency, and politics.* Durham, NC: Duke University Press.

Fox, N., & Alldred, P. (2014). New materialist social inquiry: Designs, methods and research assemblage. *International Journal of Social Research Methodology, 18*(4), 399–414. doi: 10.1080/13645579.2014.921458.

Haraway, D. (2003). *The companion species manifesto: Dogs, people and significant otherness.* Chicago: Prickly Paradigm Press.

Haraway, D. (2008). *When species meet.* Minneapolis, MN and London: University of Minnesota Press.

Haraway, D. (2015). Anthropocene, capitalocene, plantationocene, chthulucene: Making Kin, *Environmental Humanities, 6,* 159–165.

Hultman, K., & Lenz Taguchi, H. (2010). Challenging anthropocentric analysis of visual data: A relational materialist methodological approach to educational research. *International Journal of Qualitative Studies in Education, 23*(5), 525–542.

Lenz Taguchi, H. (2012). A diffractive and Deleuzian approach to analysing interview data, *Feminist Theory, 13*(3), 265–281.

MacLure, M. (2013). Researching without representation? Language and materiality in post-qualitative methodology. *International Journal of Qualitative Studies in Education, 26*(6), 658–667.

Malone, K. (2016). Theorizing a child-dog encounter in the slums of La Paz using posthumanistic approaches in order to disrupt universalisms in current 'child in nature' debates. *Children's Geographies. 14*(4), pp. 390–407. DOI: 10.1080/14733285.2015.1077369

Malone, K. (2017). Ecological Posthumanist theorising: Grappling with Child-Dog-Bodies, in Malone, K., Truong, S,. and Gray, T (eds) *Reimagining Sustainability in Precarious Times,* Singapore: Springer.

Nancy, J.-L. (1997). *The sense of the world.* Minneapolis, MN: University of Minnesota Press.

Pacini-Ketchabaw, V., & Nxumalo, F. (2015). Unruly raccoons and troubled educators: Nature/culture divides in a Childcare centre. *Environmental Humanities, 7,* 151–168.

Rautio, P. (2013a). Children who carry stones in their pockets: On autotelic material practices in everyday life. *Children's Geographies, 11*(4), 394–408.

Rautio, P. (2013b). Mingling and imitating in producing spaces for knowing and being: Insights from a Finnish study of child-matter intra-action, *Childhood, 21*(4), 461–474.

Smith, M. (2013). Ecological community, the sense of the world, and senseless extinction. *Environmental Humanities, 2*, 21–41.

Taylor, A. (2011). Reconceptualizing the 'nature' of childhood. *Childhood, 18*(4), 420–433. doi: 10.1177/0907568211404951.

Taylor, A., & Pacini-Ketchabaw, V. (2015). Learning with children, ants, and worms in the Anthropocene: Towards a common world pedagogy of multispecies vulnerability. *Pedagogy, Culture & Society, 23*(4), 507–529.

Tipper, B. (2011). 'A dog who I know quite well' everyday relationships between children and animals. *Children's Geographies, 9*(2), 145–165.

CHAPTER SIXTEEN

New Empiricisms
AND THE Moving Image

Rethinking Video Data in Education Research[1]

ELIZABETH DEFREITAS

ABSTRACT

This chapter explores how experimental film tactics can be used in developing alternative video research methods. By considering a more experimental paradigm that plays with the digital nature of video data, the paper explores alternative ways of attending to questions about body, milieu and learning. Drawing from the work of Gilles Deleuze on the moving image, and the history of film and film studies, the chapter shows how to work with video data in innovative ways.

Keywords: new empiricism, video data, moving image, Deleuze

INTRODUCTION

Video data is one of the most common forms of data for educational researchers studying classrooms and teaching experiments (de Freitas, Lerman, & Noelle-Parks, 2016; Erikson, 2006; Goldman, Pea, Barron, & Derry, 2007). Software protocols for analyzing vast video archives are deployed regularly, allowing researchers to annotate, code and sort images (Derry et al., 2010; O'Halloran, 2013). But many of these software packages "mold" the data and reconfigure it, sorting and chunking it even before human eyes have seen it (Van nes & Doorman, 2010, p. 6). The use of video analytic software without adequate attention to how such software is structuring the data becomes increasingly problematic as we begin to rely more and more on findings based on this data.[2] We need to examine how this technology shapes what we are able to see. Like any other technical apparatus, video technology brings with it a particular way of producing subjects. The danger is that we are all too likely to treat the video image as a recording of "raw data", indexical of a given time-space relationship, as though it were a transparent realist representation of an event.

In this chapter, I situate education video research within the history of "scientific cinema", and I suggest alternative ways of doing video research based on experimental film tactics. By looking at how the *moving image* has been used in the physical and social sciences since its introduction in the late 1890s, we can better appreciate how our video practices are part of a particular socio-technical production of data. And by considering a more experimental paradigm that plays with the technical apparatus and the presumed nature of viewing, we can open up to new insights about our research. Thus my aim is to bring into conversation three groups: education researchers, historians of film, and experimental video artists. My hope is that this conversation can open up the field to new kinds of empiricism.

This chapter focuses on the question of the body, and how the body is reconfigured in video data. This chapter is part of a larger project, studying the way the human body is both produced and recruited through different kinds of empirical research in the social and physical sciences. My work draws on the philosophy of Gilles Deleuze to rethink the nature of bodies and the nature of learning, and to study the non-human dimensions of human life. The challenge, as I see it, is how to develop methods of inquiry that can do this. In the first section, I introduce the ideas of Henri Bergson, and explain how Deleuze draws extensively on Bergson in his analysis of scientific cinema and the moving image. I then discuss a software experiment that allows for new ways of thinking about video data, bodies, and classroom intra-action.

BERGSON AND NEW EMPIRICISMS

Although Bergson influenced Merleau-Ponty and phenomenology, his approach to the human body was quite at odds with their more Humanist leanings. In addition, Bergson was critical of psychological explanations of thought and activity, which made him an unlikely source for the burgeoning schools of psychology that would come to dominate much of education research. On the other hand, there were important enthusiasts for Bergson's work, like Norbert Wiener, the originator of cybernetics in the 1940s, who saw in Bergson a stochastic approach to time and movement suitable to the study of bodies in a post-information society. Recent interest in new materialist philosophies has brought Bergson back into the spotlight, in particular through the work of Gilles Deleuze (1986, 1989, 1991), Elizabeth Grosz (2004), Brian Massumi (2015) and Claire Colebrook (2014). In this chapter I build on this work to show how we might begin to explore new experiments with digital technologies as we continue to rely on the moving image in our research.

Bergson critiqued the kind of science that tried to "shut up motion in space" (Bergson, 1896/1988, p. 218), a science that was drawn to fixity and invariance, and to reducing motion to a sequence of still images. He noticed that scientists tend to focus on the states of rest, and then demote motion as a secondary linkage between states or positions. In contrast, Bergson argues that movement is primary and that movement "deposits space beneath itself." (p. 217). In this approach, everything is mobile, and everything is always already moving, even if certain things are freer to move than others. The *most* freedom of movement belongs to *thought*, the least to that which is visibly individuated as an object (all objects, however, are still modulations of thought *as duration*). Bergson argues that our scientific apparatus for measure *and* our perceptual organs may be calibrated to sense one rhythm of movement but not another, and we wrongly assume that movement can only be sensed through that one calibration. For Bergson, time is not an absolute frame of reference, as it was for Newton, nor is it an *a priori* cognitive condition for all experience, as it was for Kant. Bergson was interested in generating a metaphysics that matched new developments in physics (Bergson, 1989, 1903, 1907) especially relativity theory. *Duration* was the term he used to describe how time was the flexible—almost muscular—vitality or virtuality of the world. It was through this metaphysical concept of duration that Bergson could claim memory and matter commingled. His aim was to present a theory of that commingling that helped us understand how all of the past impregnates the *moving* present, and indeed how duration is the virtual or the potential in the apparent fixity of matter.

For Bergson, duration is the crucial force that mobilizes and sustains all bodies as spatio-temporal folds rather than as sensory-motor responses to stimuli. There is indeed sensory-motor movement, typically in response to stimuli, but this is only one of *two* kinds of movement. The second kind of movement refers to how bodies are always folding and vibrating with the indeterminacy of intensive duration. This second kind of movement—a kind of rumbling typically beyond our perception—is a movement of constant alteration characterizing the open whole of duration. This second kind of movement is not a spatial alteration that occurs across extension, but an alteration that enfolds in the flow of duration. These latter movements are genuine mobile sections of duration, and they are to some extent beyond conventional conceptions of movement (de Freitas & Ferrara, 2014).

Bergson offers a 'robust' alternative to the dominant phenomenological approach we see today in studies of embodiment. Rather than focus on the sensory-motor and organic image of the body, Bergson's method has us plug into the heterogeneous temporalities and rhythms of duration. Drawing on Bergson's ideas on movement, we might study the body less as a phenomenological organism with built-in "I can" cognitive and motor capacities (which is the convention of phenomenology), and more as an indeterminate crystalline contraction and expansion of duration. This becomes a highly impersonal and non-human body, but perhaps for that very reason it offers new insights into the desire of research to comprehend embodiment—the desire to study the body as an enclosed organism with internal will or autopoetic capacity.

SCIENTIFIC CINEMA

Bergson was writing at the dawn of cinema, in the 1890s, when film recordings of moving bodies dominated the genre. He was not a huge fan of the new cinema, because he said it achieved the trick of false-movement whereby we 'see' movement based on a sequence of discrete immobile images. Cinema simply taps into our perceptual tendencies, given our current sensory capacities and bodily arrangements, but it doesn't plug into continuous movement or duration. In her book, *Screening the body* (1995), Lisa Cartwright uses the term "scientific cinema" to describe the early cinema that Bergson was referencing. The early film makers, like Lumière, were experimental physiologists who were interested in recording the movements of the human body. Indeed, many of Lumière's contemporaries regarded his invention of the cinematographe as a key contribution to physiology. The Lumière laboratories manufactured film stock and equipment for science—hundreds of films in the Lumière's catalogues cover a vast array of different studies of bodily movement. This genre dominated the first decade of film. Many of these early films were devoted to the study of the ephemeral movements of bodies—movements that occur so fast we are often limited in our grasp of them. For instance, the famous Edison/Dickson 1894 film entitled: *Kinetoscopic Record of a Sneeze* was hugely popular amongst both scientists and laypeople (see figure 16.1). These and other similar films of the time were spectacles of corporeality, viewed in laboratories or at professional meetings, while frame analyses were published in professional journals. Forty-five frames of the film were reproduced for Harper's Weekly in 1894.

This fascination for capturing sensory-motor movement fueled interests in mass industrialization and standardization. Doane (2002) shows how the early cinema was part of the restructuring of time and contingency in capitalist modernity. Early cinema promised to capture the immediacy of a fleeting moment, the "duration of an ephemeral smile or glance", and also the potential for capitalizing on such knowledge (p. 3). In 1914 Frank B. Gilbreth, a disciple of Taylor (of Taylorism), created cyclographs and chronocyclographs in which the movements of someone were recorded with the aim of creating an archive of efficient motion (see image 9). In one case, an expert surgeon is tying a knot, in another a woman is folding a handkerchief, another a man is working a drill press. In each case, the body's movement was recorded by attaching a small electric light to the limb and using time exposure to generate a representation of the movement as a continuous line in space (see figure 16.2). He then translated the lines into wire models of what he called "perfect movement". The link between this use of the moving image and the desire for efficient factory workers points to how often research technologies serve an archival habit. Foster (2004) and Sekula (1986) make a similar point about photography, showing how the "archival impulse" often serves attempts to regulate and govern the unruly body within a "society of control" (21–22).

Figure 16.1: Frames from Edison/Dickson 1894 film entitled: *Kinetoscopic Record of a Sneeze* (public domain image).

Figure 16.2: Frank B. Gilbraith motion efficiency study (public domain image).

According to Doane (2002), these studies of movement were related to the massive standardization of time in the West during industrialization, structuring the way bodies were meant to participate in industrial labour. By the early twentieth century, the standardization of factory labour used such films for improving productivity. Today, we use video in a similar fashion in teacher education and teacher accreditation. The moving image is a way to entrain the body to perform in particular ways.

Drawing on Bergson's theses on movement, Deleuze (1989) will propose two kinds of moving image—the first is the movement-image and the second the time-image. The time-image will be Deleuze's term for Bergson's second kind of movement. He characterizes early scientific cinema in terms of the *movement-image*, an image that answers our desire to capture motor-activity in terms of mechanical cause and effect. He also points to a new kind of post war cinema that breaks with the conventions of this movement-image. This new cinema operates through the *time-image* and connects with bodies in radically different ways. In the time-image, says Deleuze, the body is not only the sensory-motor body, the body that lends itself to control, but a body that is a contraction of forces, a body that taps into 'extensity' (a Bergsonian *port-manteau* word that combines intensity with extension). This body is in a direct relation to time, rather than an indirect representation of time. The movement of the time-image operates in the intersticial segments that are not captured in the frame-by-frame analysis of film and video. For Deleuze, the time-image can be found in certain post-war experimental and avant-garde film makers, such as Godard and Resnais.

Within the history of scientific cinema, the time-image breaks with the phenomenological image of the body, and its desire for presence, and directly links to the force and shock of time itself. In education video practices, this would entail studying video as a structuring of light or pure optic image, a means of dis-assembling the human body, and opening up our analysis to the fundamental difference (duration) that re-assembles and sustains bodies. This is no longer a body that is the source of its will and action, but instead a Bergsonian body—a zone of indiscernability. This proposal points to the undecidability of the body, "the non-choice of the body", the body without organs. This is a body that is constantly assembling, dissembling and re-assembling. In the next section, I explore one possible technique for exploring video data in these alternative terms.

AFFECTIVE STATES AND SCRAMBLING

Deleuze shows how we might rethink the body as a Bergsonian "zone of indeterminacy" through the time-image or the crystal-image of post-war film. He also points to the need for a new experimental method that takes up the time-image using advanced digital methods (Deleuze, 1989). As an example, I offer here the Solass experiment. As in the Galilean tradition, this experiment taps duration and number in unusual ways, re-assembling and recruiting bodies, and opening up science to the study of new kinds of relationships.

In this section, I discuss a digital experiment with classroom video data, and I argue that my experiment taps Bergson's second kind of movement—a movement that refers to the modulation (expansion and contraction) that characterizes the open whole of duration, by which bodies are actualized and endure. Affect plays an interesting role in Bergson's theory of duration and embodiment. He suggests that there are states of becoming that are between mind and body, and that these "affective states" are "a series of intermediate states, more or less vaguely localized" (Bergson, 1896/1988, p. 52). Looking at video for how affect flows along lines of tension between bodies is challenging, and my aim here is to track the changing tension in a learning event. In reality there is no one rhythm of duration; it is possible to imagine many different rhythms which, slower or faster, measure the degree of tension or relaxation of different kinds of consciousness and thereby fix their respective places in the scale of being. (Bergson, 1896/1988, p. 207)

How might we plug into this heterogeneous duration of an event? What can we do—as researchers—that might allow one to study video data for the crystalline structure that sustains the provisional individuation of a body or an action? How can we provoke or shock our 'audience' into thinking the time-image? If we aim to escape from the phenomenological movement-image that always seems to serve state-sanctioned control, then we need to be more radical in the way we work with these digital images.

The method of video analysis discussed here is inspired by the Argentinian video artist Leonardo Solaas, who creates social web applications and generative experiments using various computer algorithms. I have used one of his applications, available at solaas.ar.com, called Doodl, which is a tool that interacts with video images. Doodl is an online drawing tool that programs a series of robots to interact with digital images. The robots act like a swarm of "autonomous computational agents that drift endlessly over the surface of the screen, leaving a trace" or stream (Solaas, solaas.ar.com). The algorithm decodes colours in the source image in terms of differentials (differences between colors in pixels) and quantifies the colour intensity in adjacent cells and translates that data into "a force field" that influences the speed and direction of the flowing lines that are drawn. In other words, the tiny drawing bots roam randomly (and endlessly) across the image, continuously calculating a relational difference in intensity that is then translated into the speed and direction of the drawn graphic (see figure 16.3).

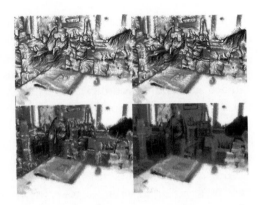

Figure 16.3: Doodl video images of early childhood classroom (see color version in de Freitas (2016) *Deleuze Studies*).

This is not a representational tool in the strict sense of resemblance, in that the bots are generative of slightly altered and unscripted new videos "documenting" the event, due to the randomness of the roaming across various parameters (# of robots, speed, thickness, angle). The result is always a new video that records this randomly roaming incorporation of the video data.

The video is endless because the doodling can never end (the bots roam and bounce off each other indefinitely), and so the video is never finished and resists closure. The video is then a sort of dynamic diagram of the event under study. These videos are excellent examples of how to shock the viewer into considering how bodies are slowly and vaguely individuated, provisionally abled, and open to future reconfigurations. Thus this kind of video helps us think about the actualization and individualization of bodies in ways that regular video analysis cannot. As the video plays, we are folded into the event, slowly building a very layered temporal crystal for each source image that we use. This method seems to offer us a way to tap into a new dimension for each 'frame' in the video, a dimension of intensity that both cuts away and dis-invests in the usual temporal unfolding of the sensory-motor movement-image. This video experiment seems to conjure a new aspect of time and memory that subverts any easy reading of the video in terms of narrative emplotment.

The eerie scrambling and smudging of the Solass experiment, evocative of a Francis Bacon painting, gets to the heart of the time-image and demonstrates Bergson's thesis that it is "we who are internal to time, not the other way round" (Deleuze, 1989, p. 82). I am particularly interested in how Doodl uses *color differentials* to study the process of individuation, because in so doing it problematizes the line as that which separates an inside from an outside. Deleuze (2003) suggests that Bacon's skill at "coloring sensation" is what allows us to get at the post-human body without organs. He says "The formula for the colorists is: if you push color to its pure internal relations (hot-cold, expansion-contraction), then you have everything" (p. 112). Colorism aims to show how colour itself is the variable relation or differential relation on which individuation depends. The technique of the colorist is "the production of light and even time through the unlimited activity of color" (p. 112). In pushing colour to function in this onto-generative way, Bacon and other colorists, and perhaps thus Doodl too, force us to rethink the nature of bodies and movement.

These videos also underscore how "any moment whatsoever" is rich with diverse temporal dimensions, and that the present has an infinitely contracted past and an indefinite future. Indeed, according to Deleuze (1989), it is this radical contraction that allows for the present to pass on. Such a form of video analysis explores the empty time of the event, the intersticial time, a different time revealed inside the event, made from the simultaneity of three implicated presents (will happen, is happening, has happened), a threesome that forms the paradox of action.

Rather than a phenomenology that would invoke the "lived body", this method attends to the "profound and almost unlivable power" or "vital power" of dispersed affect (Deleuze, 2003, p. 39). These are videos that generate the lines of force or intensity that track the flow of affect, undulating lines that show how we are *always becoming nonhuman* just as they show us how we are also actualized as a human figure. Such a method of video analysis supports efforts to study the asymmetrical entanglements in classrooms, where assemblages are formed between human and non-human agents (de Freitas, 2013; de Freitas & Sinclair, 2014).

RITUALS AND PROVOCATIONS

Classrooms are often places of ritual; indeed, socio-cultural studies have often critiqued school for how it disciplines bodies through such ritual. This is undoubtedly true. On the other hand, within anthropology, research has focused on ritual as a way of *communing with an impersonal time*, a way of plugging into Bergson's duration. Visual ethnographers record ritual actions in an attempt to understand this aspect of impersonal dispossession. For this very reason, taking on the notion of the experiment became important in visual anthropology in the 1970s (Glowczewski, 2014; Pasqualino & Schneider, 2014). For instance, Rundstrom created a film (*The path*) about the ritual of Japanese tea ceremony that deploys all sorts of avant-garde devices that disrupt the realist narrative, including superpositioning of images and jarring montage.

In the context of education research, video research might better attend to the study of classroom ritual through the use of experimental film practices. An entire history of avant-garde experiments with the moving image could be used as a resource for the making of new cinematic conventions in scientific cinema in our field. A vast array of experimental filmmakers could be tapped for inspiration, from Dziga Vertov or Maya Deren, Michael Snow or Stan Brakhage, Bill Viola or Dan Graham. Maya Deren's work in particular is interesting for those interested in ritual, because of her focus on the induced trance that often accompanies ritual. Researchers might turn to her methods as they consider how to convey the ritual-like experience of school learning. Ritual performances reveal a kind of "possession" by which people are put into a trance-like condition. In education research, we've used the term "ritual" to indicate the lack of significant meaning in school mathematics, but perhaps looking at ritual through Deren's eyes might shed more light on how ritual *compels one to participate, as a form of impersonal dispossession*. Deren's interest in performance developed during the surrealist period, and she considered viewers as participants in a kind of ritual trance. "For Deren the purpose of a film was to plunge spectators into a second state and reveal to them an unfamiliar world" (Pasqualino & Schneider, 2014, p. 6). The anthropologist Jean Rouch (*Les Maitres fous*) spoke of a "ciné-transe" that used the camera and editing to bring the spectator into the highly ritual activity under study, enticing them to see the event through the eyes of the possessed. More recently filmmaker Ben Russell has been making a series of films since 2005 (*Trypps*), exploring trance induced by music, ritual, dance or drug. All of these examples from the history of film might inform the way we study ritual in classrooms.

Experimental film makers have also developed methods for exploring the complexity of memory and the archiving of the image, in some cases actually physically scoring or burning the film, an act that makes coding into literal destruction and alteration (Peter Delpeut's *Lyrical Nitrate*). Stop-motion animation, in which non-animate objects appear to move, could prove to be an incredible cinematic experiment for studying the strange dispersal of agency in classrooms, where non-human agents as well as concepts partake in the distributed agency of a learning event. Finally, like the Solass experiment discussed above, techniques that tap the digital nature of video offer up all sorts of new techniques, attending to the materiality of video (the pixel) rather than film (the grain). Wanono (2014) describes how her work in anthropology has taken up new aesthetic-political perspectives that reflect the digital technology she is using. She uses programming as a creative language to re-assemble the pixels in her documentary video, using particular tactics that reflect her theoretical and political concerns. As she realized how reliant social scientists were on video, she also realized "the embarrassment of social sciences regarding the technical apparatus of our research" (Wanono, 2014, p. 186).

As a knowledge-production device, the software for video processing has to be taken up and played with experimentally. Attention to technique and machinic processes can help us better communicate the political and social concerns and questions that fuel our research: "digital code is, in fact, both a physical input into a system and a symbolic expression needing interpretation" (Wanono, 2014, p. 188). The work of the new media theorist Lev Manovich, with twitter data and video archives, uses algorithms to reclaim digital data for alternative purposes. As computational culture saturates life, and we become increasingly immersed in screen culture, a new political-aesthetic emerges:

> Now, from 2012, many digital artists are engaged in this challenging reconstruction of the real. They are inspired by different aesthetic languages, political analysis, social backgrounds, but are also convinced of the necessity to introduce queer objects into the field, to challenge its boundaries and limitations. (Wanono, 2014, p. 194)

Inspired by these anthropologists and artists, and informed by the Bergson-Deleuze notion of the time-image, this chapter advocates for a new experimental paradigm in video research. Such experimentation seems urgent as we rely increasingly on software to mold our video data, and as the human body is increasingly tapped for biometric data in education research. Studies of the movement of bodies in classrooms are an important site for such experimentation precisely for this reason. The problem as I see it is a lack of attention to the techniques of research, in this case video techniques. The very same technologies that serve the control society, and thereby archive and conscript bodies for human capital, can and must be appropriated and mutated in an attempt to break with confining conventions of embodiment.

NOTES

1. This chapter includes some revised material from de Freitas (2015) and de Freitas (2016) published articles in *The International Journal of Qualitative Studies in Education* and *Deleuze Studies*.
2. There have been attempts within the learning sciences to address these issues, such as Hall (2000) and Tobin and Hseuh (2007), who argue that classroom video data are "blurred genres that are simultaneously social scientific documents and works of art" (p. 79); while Hayes (2007) explores the power of aesthetics in school video ethnographies, attempting to direct viewer attention to the logic and technique of video production.

REFERENCES

Bergson, H. (1889/1910). *Essai sur les données immédiates de la conscience*. (F. L. Pogson, Trans. *Time and Free Will*). Whitefish, MT: Kessinger Publishing, 1910.

Bergson, H. (1896/1988). *Matière et mémoire*. (N. M. Paul & W. S. Palmer, Trans., *Matter and Memory*). New York, NY: Zone Books, 1988.

Bergson, H. (1903/1999). *Introduction à la métaphysique* (T. E. Hulme, Trans. *An Introduction to Metaphysics*). Indianapolis, IN: Hackett Publishing, 1999.

Bergson, H. (1907/2005). *L'Evolution créatrice*. (A. Mitchell, Trans. *Creative Evolution*). New York, NY: Cosimo Books, 2005.

Cartwright, L. (1995). *Screening the body: Tracing medicines visual culture*. Minneapolis, MN: University of Minnesota Press.

Colebrook, C. (2014). *Sex after life: Essays on extinction, vol. 2*. Open Humanities Press. DOI: http://dx.doi.org/10.3998/ohp.12329363.0001.001

de Freitas, E. (2013). The mathematical event: Mapping the axiomatic and the problematic in school mathematics. *Studies in Philosophy and Education, 32*, 581–599.

de Freitas, E. (2015). Classroom video data and the time-image; An-archiving the student body. *Deleuze Studies, 9*(3), 318–336.

de Freitas, E. (2016). Re-assembling the student body in classroom video data. *International Journal of Qualitative Studies in Education, 29*(4), 553–572.

de Freitas, E., & Ferrara, F. (2014). Movement, memory and mathematics: Henri Bergson and the ontology of learning. *Studies in Philosophy and Education, 33*(6), online now: http://link.springer.com/article/10.1007/s11217-014-9455-y

de Freitas, E., Lerman, S., & Noelle-Parks, A. (2016). Qualitative methods. In J. Cai (Ed.), *Handbook for research in mathematics education*. NCTM Publishing.

de Freitas, E., & Sinclair, N. (2014). *Mathematics and the body: Material entanglements in the classroom*. Cambridge: Cambridge University Press.

Deleuze, G. (1986). *Cinema 1, The movement image* (H. Tomlinson & B. Habberjam, Trans.). Minneapolis, MN: The Athlone Press.

Deleuze, G. (1989). *Cinema 2, The time image* (H. Tomlinson & R. Galeta, Trans.). Minneapolis, MN: The Athlone Press.

Deleuze, G. (1991). *Bergsonism* (H. Tomlinson & B. Habberjam, Trans.). Brooklyn: Zone Books.

Deleuze, G. (2003). *Francis Bacon: The logic of sensation*. Minneapolis, MN: University of Minnesota Press.

Derry, S. J., Pea, R. D., Barron, B., Engle, R. A., Erikson, F., Goldman, R., … Sherin, B. L. (2010). Conducting video research in the learning sciences: Guidance on selection, analysis, technology and ethics. *The Journal of the Learning Sciences, 19*(1), 3–53.

Doane, M.-A. (2002). *The emergence of cinematic time: Modernity, contingency, the archive*. Cambridge: Harvard University Press.

Erikson, F. (2006). Definition and analysis of data from videotape: Some research procedures and their rationales. In J. L. Green, G. Camilli, & P. Elmore (Eds.), *Handbook of complementary methods in education research* (pp. 177–192). Mahwah, NJ: Erlbaum.

Foster, H. (2004). An archival impulse. *October, 110*(Fall), 3–22.

Glowczewski, B. (2014). Beyond the frames of film and aboriginal fieldwork. In A. Schneider & C. Pasqualino (Eds.), *Experimental film and anthropology* (pp. 147–164). London: Bloomsbury Academic.

Goldman, R., Pea, R., Barron, B., & Derry S. J. (Eds.). (2007). *Video research in the learning sciences*. Mahwah, NJ: Erlbaum.

Grosz, E. (2004). *The nick of time: Politics, evolution and the untimely*. Durham, NC: Duke University Press.

Hall, R. (2000). Videorecording as theory. In A. E. Kelly & R. A. Lesh (Eds.), *Handbook of research design in mathematics and science education* (pp. 647–664). Mahwah, NJ: Lawrence Erlbaum Associates, Publishers.

Hayes, M. T. (2007). Overwhelmed by the image: The role of aesthetics in ethnographic filmmaking. In R. Goldman, R. Pea, B. Barron, & S. J. Derry (Eds.), Video research in the learning sciences (pp. 67–76). Mahwah, NJ: Lawrence Erlbaum Associates.

Massumi, B. (2015). The supernormal animal. In R. Grsuin (Ed.), *The nonhuman turn.* Minneapolis, MN: University of Minnesota Press.

O'Halloran, K., (2013). *Multimodal Analysis Video.* Singapore: Multimodal Analysis Company.

Pasqualino, C., & Schneider, A. (2014). Experimental film and anthropology. In A. Schneider & C. Pasqualino (Eds.). *Experimental film and anthropology* (pp. 1–24). London: Bloomsbury Press.

Sekula, A. (1986). The body and the archive. *October,* Winter, 3–64.

Tobin, J., & Hseuh, Y. (2007). The poetics and pleasures of video ethnography of education. In R. Goldman, R. Pea, B. Barron, & S. J. Derry (Eds.), Video research in the learning sciences (pp. 77–92). Mahwah, NJ: Lawrence Erlbaum Associates.

Van nes, F., & Doorman, M. (2010). The interaction between multimedia data analysis and theory development in design research. *Mathematics Education Research Journal, 22*(1), 6–30.

Wanono, N. (2014). From the grain to the pixel, aesthetic and political choices. In A. Schneider & C. Pasqualino (Eds.), *Experimental film and anthropology* (pp. 183–198). London: Bloomsbury Press.

Irruptions

DataHoles

MIRKA KORO-LJUNGBERG, TEIJA LÖYTÖNEN,
AND MAREK TESAR

We would like to continue, again, by experimenting with methodologies of h o l e s, DataHoles: data-by-courtesy, data-memory-h o l e s, data-pass-through-h o l e s, data-purifying-gesture-h o l e s especially in relation to ... cuts ... A. ... We offer some potential methodological connections with DataHoles, and what these have prompted in our thinking and inquiry practices. Similar to the impossibility of introducing DataHoles and LiteratureHoles, these ... L ... also cannot be potentially 'captured', described or legitimized in existing methodological, scholarly discourses, or existing ideologies. Livant (1998) referred to a whole without a hole as a "part in drag trying to pass itself off as everything, which. ... isn't a bad definition of ideology" (p. 446). However, DataHoles and LiteratureHoles may form more or less imaginary presences for more describable and discussable (past, future, and endlessly becoming) methodologies, ideologies, texts, and readings.

DATA-BY-COURTESY

Wake, Spencer, and Fowler (2007) proposed that holes are regions of spacetime. "Holes are (roughly) regions of spacetime that are located at certain discontinuities in the surfaces of material objects" (p. 373). As such dataholes produce discontinuities at the surface of the 'visible' and lived data. At the same time dataholes unite these discontinuities through a shared space (of nothingness or emptiness). For example, work on silence (Mazzei, 2007) (absence in talk) and vibrations (Gershon, 2013) (absence in 'hearable' sound) in the classroom could function as data-by-courtesy forming dataholes that produce and generate in by-passing and through discontinuances.

Ontological pluralism refers to the existential difference; some things existing in a different way than others. McDaniel (2010) argues that holes as well as their host "enjoy the same kind of reality" (p. 628). From this perspective being or nonbeing is not linked with the host or the hole. "Holes are ontologically dependent on some host or other but it is not the case that each particular hole is ontologically dependent on some particular host or other. ... if you destroy most of the fabric except for a small amount that surrounds the hole" (p. 633) you have destroyed the host but the hole can be left. Holes could be seen as 'being-by-courtesy' (p. 643).

'Data-by-courtesy'?
Where?
In a h o l e.
Silent, invisible dark h o l e.
Mysterious.

Lingering (Bresler, 2008, 2014) with/in 'data-by-courtesy'
to sense data more,
to sense data differently.

Data-by-courtesy offers a secondary status to data and serves as one way to decenter data. Data-by-courtesy might enable scholars not only to sense more and differently but also to acknowledge data a minor gesture of the major (see Manning, 2016). Data could be experienced as a moving force, lingering rock in a shoe, or becoming hiccup in the somewhere between the stomach and tongue. This way data would be felt and dealt with without worrying too much about their origins or host status.

"In moments of recognition, our seeing stops short and we lose our chance to experience the uniqueness and complexity, the 'thinginess' and 'thereness' of the object. In seeing as, we fail to see more." (Higgins, 2007, p. 390)

Lingering with(in) h o l e s.
Becoming (in) h o l e s.
Becoming a h o l e, a stain, a blind spot, in inquiry practices.
Maybe becoming data-by-courtesy.

MEMORY H O L E S

From Wikipedia: The Memory Hole was a website edited by Russ Kick; first launched on July 10, 2002, last post on May 11, 2009. Before being hacked in June 2009, the site was devoted to preserving and publishing material that is in danger of being lost, is hard to find, or is not widely known. Topics include government files, corporate memos, court documents, police reports and eyewitness statements, Congressional testimony, reports from various sources, maps, patents, web pages, photographs, video, sound recordings, news articles, and books. The name is a tribute to the "memory hole" from George Orwell's novel Nineteen Eighty-Four, a slot into which government officials deposit politically inconvenient documents and records for destruction.

A

L Can we include it? Would be great if we could.

It is a hole. Data hole. Z

H Let's throw in a traditional quote.

That may be great. E

I Get those lost readers back on track.

Guide them back from holes. M

E R'S

[A L Z H E I M E R'S]

Fontana introduced the principle of immateriality into the materiality of the surface, into the concreteness of its concretion (even its material concretion), by creating a free constellation of holes in it, by breaking its finite surface, by inserting the allusively emblematic, through physically explicit and tangible presence of a spatial *elsewhere*. (Fontana, 2006, p. 71)

Perforation or hole that Fontana later called Attase (expectations) are
cuts
both expressive and narrative.
The absence of something; absence of rhythm and temporality.
For Fontana cuts are infinite dimensions of space that highlight waiting
and simultaneous nullifying and building.

H o l e s are timeless void spaces.

Purifying-gesture-hole

The Cut is a decisive breach, that furrows and penetrates the symbolic purity of the monochrome, a kind of purifying gesture, and at the same time unambiguous symbol less of a romantic, instinctive or reckless gesture than of a conceptual, configured mental space … My cuts are above all a philosophical statement, an act of faith in the infinite, an affirmation of spirituality. (Fontana, 2006, p. 23)

Can cuts perform through their variation and multiplicity? Manning (2016) proposed that to activate artfulness objects "must continue to vary and its variation must be serial, in the sense that each object-variation must remain lively with the incipient memory and the imperceptible traces of its passage from one site to another" (p. 72).

Unintelligible cuts provoke different kinds of dataholes. Sensemaking can no longer lay its foundation in language even if language might be known (for some). Unintelligibility might be sensed through nonsensical and absurd—which also engages and attracts data. "Ruskeat juuret kiipeilivät ja ryömivat, niitä oli kaikkialla, ne harppoivat makuupussin yli. Puut seisoivat nyt liikkumatta, mutta pimeässä ne olivat kulkeneet suoraan hänen ylitseen. Koko metsä oli riuhtaissut juurensa maasta ja vaeltanut hänen ylitseen aivan kuin hän olisi kivi" (Jansson, 1965, p. 144) ... "musta lampi ryömi syvemmälle peruskallioon. Se vetäytyi koristen alaspäin ja sisäänpäin, ja aallot syöksyivät merestä yli kannaksen kiiltävänä, vihreänä vesiputouksena. Mutta lampi ei täyttynyt. Se vetäytyi pakkoon ... hiekka valui pois niiden [myyrien ja metsähiirien] tassujen alta ... Aamun sarastaessa saari nukahti" (p. 165). Saari ja vesi (aineisto, materiaali, data, tieto) nukahti ja imeytyi itseensä, omaan aukkoonsa ja sisäiseen aukeamaansa (sekä symbolisesti että materiaalisesti).

"Cuts, stones, holes, tears compete in the making of 'pictures' at once sensual and symbolic, tormented and alive." (Fontana, 2006, p. 28)

Fontana gave us great quotes. Great data. Great h o l e s.

Fontana introduced the trans-objectiveness of the painting <—?—> physicality of the painted surface and the h o l e that passes through it.
The real behind the canvas is brought into the painting.

Pass-through-data-h o l e s ...

"We can pass our fingers through whatever holes we want without thereby passing our fingers through material objects" (Wake et al., 2007, pp. 373–374). Are these passings research-creations?

For Manning (2016) research-creations "open the field of experience to the more-than of objects and subjects preformed" (p. 12). Research-creations are pragmatically speculative practices and immanent activities always producing an immanent critique. Furthermore, "the differential, the active hyphen that brings making to thinking and thinking to making, ensures that research-creation remain an ecology of practices" (p. 13). Research-creations are concerned with artful and artistic practices. Data as such are (products of) research-creations and practices that think. Data thinks and dataholes express potentially generating new forms of experience, collective expressions, and extralinguistic forms of knowledge.

ESCAPES FROM DATAHOLES

Potentially illusive and impossible access points to or toward data are being created through the cut; an entryway, or opening between two emerging planes of emergence or data plateaus. Doubling, multiplying or absent text/image/sound/sensation/vibration/movement might also generate other illusions. For example, these reproductions might provoke illusions of depth, multidimensionality of hole-ness, and maybe a type of abyss. Depth-data, hole-ness-less-data, and abyss data or data abyss. Where have 'data' gone in their (in)visible absence? How long does it take for data to return? Or have data disappeared beyond their possible return and the absence of data produces a vacuum for future data or an escape route for coded and ordered 'data lines'? It is possible that a produced data 'hole' cannot be filled in, fixed, or glued together once the 'original' has been removed or reproduced. Separated data no longer match the 'hole' and thus they cannot fill the 'hole'. Separated data are too small, big, flat, round, clean, and clear all at once. Existing and generated data dimensionality escapes the material (data, text, paper, ink, and scissors, and hand movements) that produced it. According to Livant (1998) "the etymology of the word 'hole' refers not to an empty place, but to a place where something is hidden" (p. 446)

MTM: *How many holes do you have in your data?*
MMT: *If I count them I assume that holes exist and thus holes are material objects.*
TMM: *It cannot be—holes are perforations. Or maybe they are matter in the wrong place. Or the matter surrounds the hole creating a lining and material connection to the host.*
MTM: *Can a single datahole have many linings some including more data and some less data?*
DATAHOLE: *Impossible—not.*
MMT: *Are two dataholes the same hole once they are united by a common part— the hole?*
          Do two perforations in the same (empty) space make one or two dataholes?
TMM: *Does the number of dataholes matter or do various act of perforations generate the hole? What is the datahole; the absent matter or act of 'holing' or neither or both?*
DATAHOLE: *one hole, two holes; the same thing?*[1]

WHERE DO HOLES AND DATA GO NEXT—IF THEY MOVE—TRAVEL?

We don't know. Do they travel for pleasure? For business? Escaping and removed data, that are always already absent yet present at the same time (e.g., through traces, hosts, and ghosts), change research processes and ways in which scholars approach data and inquiry. Maybe generate a resisting move. Manning (2016) asked "How does the rhythm, the cadence, the intensity of the text compose with its words? Where does thought-feeling escape or resist existing forms of knowledge?" (p. 39).

Throughout this book our irruptions have focused on diverse possible functions of 'data holes'; literal, material, figurative, interactive, and metaphorical holes that have potential for various differing textual, affective, and material appearances and disappearances.

> Sometimes it is necessary to restore the lost parts, to rediscover everything that cannot be seen in the image, everything that has been removed to make it 'interesting'. But sometimes, on the contrary, it is necessary to make holes, to introduce voids and white spaces, to rarity the image, by suppressing many things that have been added to make us believe that we were seeing everything. It is necessary to make a division or make emptiness in order to find the whole again. (Deleuze, 2003, p. 21)

A 'hole-thing' might serve as a production which interrogates differences in holes and sensations that absent holes can generate. A 'hole-thing' and datahole might not work but they could operate as broken machines, disjointed ideas, and limping and stuttering scholarly and creative practices. 'Dataholes' might also operate as voids that are always attached to some kind of unknown, befriend, and maybe also hostile hosts. Dataholes infiltrate and diffuse existing 'data', processes, materials, affects, and (un)recognizable knowledges. Sometimes dataholes may produce 'copies of the original' and illusions of data's accidental connections and present content. When studying dataholes more carefully qualitative researchers may also encounter depth-data, hole-ness-less-data, abyss-data, and/or data-abyss and and and. We wonder where 'data' have gone in the void and their absence and what might fill or take over the dataholes and their hosts if anything were to happen.

NOTE

1. This dialogue has been inspired by Lewis and Lewis (1970) and Casati and Varzi (2004).

REFERENCES

Bresler, L. (2008). Research as experience and the experience of research: Mutual shaping in the arts and in qualitative inquiry. *LEARNing Landscapes, 2*(1), 267–279.

Bresler, L. (2014). "Seeing as" versus "seeing more": Cultivating connections in arts-based research. In C. Smilan & K. Miraglia (Eds.), *Inquiry in action: Paradigms, methodologies and perspectives in art education research* (pp. 218–226). Reston, VA: NAEA.

Casati, R., & Varzi, A. (2004). Counting the holes. *Australasian Journal of Philosophy, 82*(1), 23–27.

Deleuze, G. (2003). *Cinema 2: The time-image* (H. Tomlinson & R. Galeta, Trans.). Minneapolis, MN: University of Minnesota Press.

Fontana, L. (2006). *Lucio Fontana: Venice/New York.* New York, NY: The Solomon R. Guggenheim Foundation.

Gershon, W. S. (2013). Vibrational affect: Sound theory and practice in qualitative research. *Cultural Studies/Critical Methodologies, 13*(4), 257–262. doi: 10.1177/1532708613488067

Higgins, C. (2007). Interlude: Reflections on a line from Dewey. In Bresler, L. (Ed.), *International handbook of research in arts education* (pp. 389–394). Dordrecht, The Netherlands: Springer.

Jansson, T. (1965). *Muumipappa ja meri.* Helsinki: WSOY.

Lewis, D., & Lewis, S. (1970). Holes. *Australasian Journal of Philosophy, 48*(2), 206–212.

Livant, B. (1998). The hole in Hegel's bagel. *Science & Society, 62*(3), 446.

Manning, E. (2016). *The minor gesture.* Durham, NC: Duke University Press.

Mazzei, L. A. (2007). *Inhabited Silence in Qualitative Research: Putting poststructural theory to work.* New York, NY: Peter Lang.

McDaniel, K. (2010). Being and almost nothingness. *Nous, 44*(4), 628–649.

Wake, A., Spencer, J., & Fowler, G. (2007). Holes as Regions of Spacetime. *The Monist, 90*(3), 372–378. Retrieved from http://www.jstor.org/stable/27904042

POST-anthropocentric INQUIRY

Gaile S. Cannella, General Editor

The goal of *Post-Anthropocentric Inquiry* is to provide scholars and readers with critical opportunities to contest anthropocentrism, (1) by creating a *textual* field of *Post-Anthropocentric Inquiry* that generates critical spaces for (re)thinking ways of being/living and performing, as well as methodologies and inquiries, that decenter the human, (2) while at the same time attempting always/already to *actively* transform inequities and injustices performed by human privilege on nonhuman others, traditionally disqualified human others, and the natural world more broadly. This *Post-Anthropocentric Inquiry* can represent difference and the multiple, while at the same time exploring and welcoming notions of indistinction. Work that further develops and expands current notions of becoming (animal, earth), new feminist materialisms, and critical posthuman sensibilities are example locations from which an intersectional, non-anthropocentric politics may emerge.

Single or multiple authored manuscripts are encouraged that facilitate the development of *Post-Anthropocentric Inquiry* by addressing conceptualizations and/or becomings of the construct, multiple issues within, research purposes, reconceptualized methodologies, and/or the potential for multiple forms of posthuman inquiry broadly. Over a wide range of volumes that cross disciplines, the series addresses broad issues and questions like the following: What is post-anthropocentric inquiry? What is made possible, enabled by post-anthropocentric approaches and research methodologies? How is post-anthropocentric research conducted without (re)privileging the human? How does the work in fields that would decenter the human, like critical animal studies, intersect with professional content and practices in fields like education or medicine? How can coalitions be formed (and actions taken) that decenter the human and increase possibilities for all forms of justice, while countering capitalist and technological orders that devalue all forms of life?

For additional information about this series or for the submission of manuscripts, please contact:

Gaile S. Cannella, gaile.cannella@gmail.com

To order other books in this series, please contact our Customer Service Department:

(800) 770-LANG (within the U.S.)
(212) 647-7706 (outside the U.S.)
(212) 647-7707 FAX

Or browse online by series: www.peterlang.com